*To my mother – for her optimism, humour,
love and eclectic library of books*

WATER WAYS

A thousand miles along Britain's canals

JASPER WINN

PROFILE BOOKS

This paperback edition published in 2020

First published in Great Britain in 2018 by
Profile Books
29 Cloth Fair
London EC1A 7JQ
www.profilebooks.com

1 3 5 7 9 10 8 6 4 2

Typeset in Minion, Brandon Grotesque and Buket
to a design by Henry Iles.

A CIP catalogue record for this book is available from the British Library.

384pp
ISBN 978-1781257968
e-ISBN 978-1782833345

Printed and bound in Great Britain by
CPI Group (UK) Ltd, Croydon, CR0 4YY
on Forest Stewardship Council (mixed sources) certified paper

CONTENTS

Preface

The Narrowboat Pub

REGENT'S CANAL

SUNLIGHT REFLECTED off the Regent's Park Canal as I made my way to the Narrowboat pub to meet a man called Ed. We were meeting to discuss a job – well, a job of a kind. Ed worked for the Canal & River Trust and they had an idea they might appoint a writer-in-residence. Someone prepared to spend the next year or two travelling the length of Britain's canal network, getting a sense of life on the modern waterways, and fashioning a book at the end of it. My name had been put forward by a publisher friend on the strength of having written a book called *Paddle*, about a kayak trip around Ireland. (Actually, not just any kayak trip around Ireland – but possibly the *slowest ever* – having chosen what turned out to be Ireland's stormiest summer in living memory.) The only trouble, I reflected, walking along the towpath, was my complete inexperience of canals. I'd never been on so much as a narrowboat holiday.

On the other hand, I knew how to travel slowly (canals operate at a horse's walking pace), and over the years I had picked up odd bits of knowledge of canals. After all, most of us in Britain live within five miles of a stretch of canal, so they are hard to avoid. As a nineteen-year-old, I'd paddled a heavy, yellow fibreglass kayak along the Kennet and Avon Canal across the southwest of England. Back then, restoration was still in progress and I'd had to pull the kayak up the flight of twenty-nine locks at Caen Hill on a pair of pram wheels I'd found in a skip. Then, a couple of decades later, I'd walked the eighty miles of Ireland's Grand Canal – one of the earliest built in the British Isles – from Dublin to Shannon Harbour. Why I chose to do that in the depths of a cold winter, with the waters iced over, I no longer entirely recall.

At other times I'd followed lengths of rural canals in the Midlands to seek out kingfishers or spot Daubenton's bats wheeling through the dusk. And once I'd walked for a few days along a summer-warmed Oxford Canal, guitar on shoulder, as the happiest way to get to a gig in Banbury. On many an occasion, too, there'd been canalside pubs, and escapes from London traffic by cycling along towpaths.

Perhaps boating wasn't the whole point of the waterways?

I reflected on all these claims as I followed the Regent's Canal towpath past Camley Street Natural Park, and then over and around the Islington Tunnel. I felt a growing excitement at the prospect of spending time with canals as I passed intriguing remnants of boatmen's wharfs and stopped to watch a pair of coots head-bobbing across the water. The boats moored along the bank – with their wafts of chimney smoke from the salvaged pallets and foraged branches piled up on their roofs – were invitingly the homes of steampunk eccentrics, some of them doggedly preserving the traditional livery of 'roses and castles' painted panels. Then there was the bewitching cleverness of the locks – at Kentish Town and again at St Pancras – with their simple stone chambers and heavy gates, able to lift huge boats uphill with the soft power of water alone.

There was a thrill, too, at the realisation that these water roads and towpaths could carry me – or anyone – out of the city and into the countryside and on to the distant coastal ports of Liverpool, Hull or Bristol. Britain's 2,000-odd miles of waterways can transport one through (and at times under) the Pennines, along river navigations and into mill towns, on to tiny villages or across corners of the countryside, even less busy now than they would have been in the canals' nineteenth-century golden age.

I arrived at the Narrowboat in a flurry of enthusiasm and met Ed sitting on a balcony overhanging the canal, watching boats go by. We got our pints in and it began to snow, which felt magically odd on an April morning. We ordered venison sausages and mash – suitably hearty fare for the weather – and I listened as Ed told me how the canals had almost been lost in the 1940s, before being rescued and renovated by activists, enthusiasts, volunteers and government agencies. He had been at it himself for the past twenty years, first at British Waterways and latterly at the Canal & River Trust (CRT), the charity set up in 2012 to continue steering the canals' journey from industrial carriers into a sustainable haven for boaters, walkers, cyclists and anglers, and as wildlife habitats and corridors.

Ed talked of 'wellness' as a key aim of the charity, maintaining the canals as a resource that benefited the nation's health – both physical and psychological. He enthused even more about canal nature, about the growing populations of water voles, otters and kingfishers, and reeled off bird species that had found sanctuary in the linear wilderness. And there was art, too, he told me – the Trust has commissioned site-specific works for the centenary of the Leeds and Liverpool Canal, but wherever I went I would find canal-themed art and sculpture, plays and poetry.

I listened to all Ed had to say, occasionally chipping in ideas for the book. My enthusiasm, I told him, was for spending a year or so roaming the towpaths and waters on foot, by bicycle and kayak, as well as by narrowboat. 'We're quite keen on stand-up paddleboarding, too, if you want to give that a go,' added Ed. Meeting people and finding stories was the brief: slow adventures on the 'cut' (as boat people call it). Nothing more specific. I was, it seemed, their first writer-in-residence. Or, as Ed suggested, their 'writer-in-motion.'

There was just one thing that was worrying me, I confessed. As the whole reason for the canals' existence was their boating history, and as some of the most committed canal enthusiasts were boaters, it seemed perhaps a gap in my CV that I hadn't been on a canal boat ... nor did I know very much about the history and workings of barges, narrowboats, locks, wharfs, navvies and the rest.

Not to worry, said Ed, it wouldn't be a problem for long. The waterways are full of people who know *everything* about *everything* to do with canals ('far more than me,' he confided). And the great thing about them is they like nothing better than to explain and demonstrate things. It is a welcoming community, he assured me, entirely free of the exclusiveness of yachties and sea dogs. My ignorance of puddling, bow-hauling, inclined planes and the like might well serve in my favour.

But it did seem a good idea to find someone to take me off on the canals on a boat sooner rather than later. Someone, Ed suggested, who knew what they were doing and could show me the proper way to handle a boat and work locks.

1

'Have you ever been on a boat before?'

'HAVE YOU EVER BEEN ON A BOAT BEFORE?' Kate Saffin was framed in the square opening that formed the side hatch of *Morning Mist*, as if leaning out of a tiny proscenium stage. Her face was lower than mine as I stood on the towpath of the Oxford Canal and I crouched down to introduce myself properly, seeing only fringed hair, hard-worked jeans and a practical blue wool sailor's jersey.

Kate was to be my host for the next three days and she wanted to know my credentials. 'Well, I've done a bit of sailing ... crewing, mostly ... quite a bit of sea kayaking ... but no, it's actually my first time on a barge.'

Kate recoiled theatrically. As well she might, given that she was amongst many other things, an actor. As well as a theatre director, playwright and historian of the canals.

'First thing,' she admonished, 'this is not a barge, it's a narrow-boat. They are not the same. A barge is a particular boat, found on tidal waterways, estuaries, maybe on navigations, or on a few wider waterways. You won't find a barge on most British canals.

11

It wouldn't fit. This—', she gestured out of the hatch and along the long, midnight blue and burgundy hull, 'is a narrowboat. It's designed to fit a canal. Which is, as you can see, narrow.'

I looked across the ribbon of water that ran eastwards across the Midlands into Rugby. This particular stretch was wide enough to have room to moor narrowboats against both banks and still allow other narrowboats to navigate between them. But I took her point.

'Of course,' she continued, 'there are canal boats which aren't narrowboats, even though they look like them. So unless you know what you're talking about it's best just to call everything a boat. Oh, and it's always *boating*, never barging.'

Boats, I reflected, must be a bit like horses, which I do know about, having grown up with them in Ireland. Horsey people might say 'horse' about some non-specific animal but normally use something more precise – pony, cob, hunter, warm-blood, vanner, Hackney, Arab. However, you can only use that kind of vocabulary if you know what you're about. Saying 'horse' for 'pony' was like mixing up barges and narrowboats.

Kate turned back into the boat's interior. 'Now we've got that straight ... coffee? Bacon sandwich?' A thought struck her. 'You're not a vegetarian, are you?' I shook my head. 'Okay, then, get your bag inside – make sure it's well out of the way. We'll eat on the move.' She got busy in the galley (or is it just a kitchen?), sizzling and boiling, and smells wafted up of bacon and Colombian roast.

I looked around for a place to put my rucksack that was out of the way. It wasn't easy. *Morning Mist* might have been nearly the length of a tennis court, but I could almost touch both sides of the cabin if I stretched my arms. A window onto the water gave a ducks' eye view of a flotilla of ducks swimming past, while to my left was a burrow-like corridor, with doors leading off to what I assumed were cabins and perhaps a bathroom, and beyond the galley a boat's width of livingroom, jam-packed with things.

I found an alcove to one side of the ladder I'd just come down and squeezed the bag into it. I was glad that when I had called

Kate Saffin, my canal mentor, at the tiller on *Morning Mist*.

Kate and asked if I could join her for a few days of boating along the Oxford Canal, I'd told her that I'd have my sleeping bag and bivvy bag with me and would sleep on the towpath. Though big for a boat, *Morning Mist* was small for a house, and that's what she was: a floating home, cargoed with all the things that made up Kate's life. It would be all too easy to intrude.

Kate had taken me on, rather kindly, as crew on *Morning Mist*, to give me a taste of canal life, and to instruct me along the way in its mysteries and etiquette. Along with the land-based Heather Wastie, Kate forms one half of Alarum Theatre, a

13

company that put on canal-themed plays, travelling between shows by narrowboat. Their current production was inspired by the 'Idle Women' – the canal equivalent of the Land Girls, who as 'Trainees' had learnt to take narrowboats laden with coal and other essential cargoes between London and the Midlands during the Second World War. Their next show was at the Folly pub at Napton-on-the-Hill, two days' boating away.

Kate had lived and travelled on *Morning Mist* for the past seventeen years, and knew the waterways as well as the working boat people had a generation before. Before moving onto the canals she had worked as a nurse and public health researcher in the NHS, which perhaps explained the breezy practicality and efficiency. She had adopted canal life with a spirited enthusiasm, making a point of getting to know some of the last working boat families on the Oxford, Grand Union and London canals.

As we munched on bacon sarnies, Kate gave me a quick résumé of *Morning Mist*'s life. She was a steel sixty-footer, built in 1988 by Dave Thomas of Braunston, a town that generations of boat families thought of as 'home' and which still has one of the busiest narrowboat marinas. Kate was the boat's second owner. There were better narrowboats around, she told me, but 'never one I liked more – though I would like to fit a Rayburn'. Rayburns are only slighter smaller versions of Agas and incredibly heavy. But, as Kate explained, weight doesn't much matter on a canal boat; carrying is what they're designed for. You can have a quarter-ton cast iron and fire-cement cooker on board a boat and it'll sit just a tiny bit deeper in the water. Weight isn't any issue.

Space, however, is crucial. A narrowboat is the horizontal equivalent of living in one of those thin, three-storey houses where you're always leaving things upstairs and having to run up and down. Boaters need a system to avoid finding that what they want is at the other end of the boat just when they need it. Kate's method seemed to be having everything useful gathered round her chair in the long living room. Papers, a library of books on canal history, well-worn computer, music, coffee mugs spread across the sofa, or in tottering piles on shelves, or heaped on the floor. Likewise in the kitchen, where most things were kept handy on the draining board, or on the floor. It underlined how on the still waters of a canal there were none of the sea-going concerns of having to tie everything down or corral it in boxes to stop it all sliding into the bilges. Boating on the canals wasn't at all like sailing, it seemed.

We carried our mugs of coffee back along the gunwale, the narrow ledge between the hull and the sides of the cabin, and set them on the roof. Kate reached through the door into the back cabin and turned a key in a control panel on the side wall. There was a deep rumbling down in the bowels of the boat. 'Can you undo the front rope, coil it up and put it on the deck and then come back and get on here at the back,' she told me.

I set off along the towpath, jogging the sixty foot to *Morning Mist*'s bow and unhitched the rope from the ring.

'Push out,' Kate hollered. I put both hands against the top of the cabin and pushed. Slowly but easily the front of the boat pivoted out towards open water. I straightened up before I found myself with feet on land and hands on boat and the distance between too far for recovery, and walked back to where Kate had unfastened the stern rope but kept it looped around a mooring ring. I stepped onto the thin ledge of gunwale even as Kate pushed on the two small levers that increased the engine's revs and put it into gear. There was a bubbling of water at the back as the propeller turned and we began moving forward and out into the water road.

'Sometimes I think I might like a traditional boat,' Kate mused as we – well, she – cast off, slipped the engine into forward and steered us off between the moored boats. 'But she handles so well, she's solid, and I like the wide gunwales. We've got used to each other.'

The tone had changed. Kate was soft about her boat. And, with that, she set about teaching me to drive. 'First, then, the tiller ... You stand in front of it, not to the side. If you stand to the side of it and you need to pull it right across, where are you going to go? Into the water!' She shook her head, theatrically miming her disbelief: 'You won't believe the idiocy of some boat people – hirers or newbies or people who never learn.' There may not be a single right way to do things but there is at least a proper way to do them. And there is certainly a stupid way.

I was steering the boat now, standing in the companionway, my hand at the small of my back grasping the worn, warm, wooden handle. There was a gentle vibration from the boat's engine, ticking away slowly and powerfully underfoot. And the long stretch of *Morning Mist* ahead of me receding into the distance. It was enjoyable. And really, it seemed, rather easy. The boat moved gently along, following the shiny rail of water without much help from me. I took a gulp of coffee and looked around appreciatively.

Kate's voice cut into my complacency. 'Look out! Slow down. There's someone mooring up, ahead ... see them ... between those boats. Put her into neutral and just drift past ... they haven't finished tying up ... you should have seen him standing there with a rope in his hand.' There were laws and lore on the canal. All based on the courtesy of a shared space, and on the traditions that boat folk had worked out as the most efficient and safest way of doing things, and not being in a rush. Kate's courtesy towards others was ingrained – and indeed was a norm for the waterways. There are few Mr Toads 'poop poop-ing' along the canals.

Kate's teaching was calm and assured. She knew just what *Morning Mist* would do and stayed ahead of my ineptitude. 'There's a fairly sharp bend coming up. Now, steer the centre of the boat, not the front.' It seems counter-intuitive if you are used to driving cars, but on a heavy, long and narrow craft with a rudder at the back, when the tiller's pushed over, the boat pivots on the water at a point roughly halfway along its length. 'Okay, push the helm over ... a bit more ... right.' The front began moving around whilst the back swung out alarmingly in the opposite direction. 'You always need to leave enough room between the back and the bank when you're turning, to allow for that. You're always best in the centre of the water.'

We were travelling at walking pace – the plodding horse's three miles an hour for which the canals were designed – but another corner, obscured by a curtain of willow drapery and a screening of reeds, seemed to be sliding towards us at an alarming rate. Throttling back produced little effect. The boat, feeling as unwieldy as a liner, had its own weighty momentum. I was sweating as I pushed the tiller right over the side of the boat (Kate was right – where would I have gone if I'd been standing to the side of the handle?) *Morning Mist* swivelled, her bow almost touching the bank, and turned down into the clear water opening up ahead. But her stern flounced out, towards the bank, and I winced in anticipation. Kate seemed relaxed: 'Give her a quick burst of throttle to push her around, and then drop it back again'. The engine's beat increased slightly as I nudged forward the small lever inside the hatch. There was a burbling and bubbling under the counter and, although it was the boat that moved forward and followed the curve of the canal's waters, it seemed as if the actual bank was bending round to accommodate us. It was like a stately dance, guiding a partner across a crowded floor.

But, oh, the responsibility. I wasn't just steering Kate's boat along this absurdly narrow water road, but her home. A crash, or (best not think about it) a sinking, would be a disaster squared. Narrowboats make such good houses because of all that they can carry – hundreds of books, pots and cast-iron pans, wardrobes of clothes, workshops of tools that would take a shed on land to store. Boats encourage hoarding things, anything that 'might come in handy one day.' And Kate had this aspect of canal culture to a T.

The one place that there wasn't much clutter was the roof. Cruising boats need to have their tops kept reasonably clear to get under low bridges and to allow unrestricted vision. Nonetheless small things do pile up. Within an arm's reach were two mugs of coffee and a box of ginger cake, the cranked handle of a windlass for opening locks and a well-used *Nicholson's Guide – No 1: Oxford, Grand Union and the South East* – which detailed all the canals between London and Birmingham, and had been made all the more valuable by Kate's pencilled notes on bus stops near the canals, shop opening hours and the best places to moor for the night. In the middle distance of my rooftop view was the centre rope and its fixing eye, a couple of rope-work fenders, the solar panel, a car tyre ('might come in handy') and a folded canvas tarpaulin. Further along were Kate's bicycle, buckets and a mop, a ladder, and a box affair that was some obscure part of the dry toilet recycling process.

'I'll take the tiller now,' Kate said. "We've got Hillmorton Flight coming up ... three locks in a row ... and you're going to be busy.' Hillmorton had always had been one of the busiest flights on the whole canal system and so there were two separate lock chambers side by side to double capacity. 'I'll drop you off,' instructed Kate, 'then I'll use the right-hand lock – take that windlass and don't drop it in the water.'

I hopped ashore, the heavy cranked metal windlass in my hand, and clambered up a slope to the height of the next pound of water. Looking down from the edge of the chamber, I could see Kate nosing the boat into the dank depths. My bird's-eye view showed that there were mere inches between the boat's hull and the stone sides of the chamber. I was learning that the canals were a precisely made water machine with all the pieces, including the boats, finely measured. It seemed a ridiculously tight fit, though it did show just what was meant by a 'narrow' canal.

Kate had already shinned up the ladder from the depths and was on the other side of the chamber. 'Close the gate,' she called across, already pushing on the big balance beam that pivoted her gate shut. I did the same and the two massive 'doors' came together in a shallow 'V'-shape. The boat was now enclosed at the bottom of a deep, dark box. We walked up to the single gate at the other – 'uphill' – end of the lock. The water road on this far side was the new, higher level, and *Morning Mist* was still far below it. The miracle of the lock was to lift tons of boat merely by filling the box with water and floating her up.

'Raise the paddle – slowly ... we don't want her thrown all over the place,' Kate told me, as she fitted her windlass onto the spindle of the rack and pinion to raise the paddle and let water into the lock chamber. 'You're winding the wrong way ... that's it ... right, just about halfway ...' There was a rattling sound of the pawl on the gear as I swung the windlass round a few times, and a bubbling in the depths under the boat. The water and *Morning Mist* rose ... and kept rising until the boat's cabin roof was up by my shoulder.

'Open the gate.' Kate was already aboard. I pushed on the beam of the single uphill gate. It opened easily with the weight of the water in the lock and the level on this higher stretch of canal now equalised. The boat thrubbled its way slowly out of the chamber, eight or nine feet higher up than it had been. Back on the boat, Kate told me not to get too comfortable – there were two more locks coming up, and more after those. I was going to get plenty of practice 'lock wheeling', she promised. Seeing my puzzled expression, she explained that the phrase came from when boaters had first got bicycles – 'wheels' – in the early-twentieth century and a crew member would pedal on ahead to set locks and speed up the process of getting through them.

We, though, were in no such hurry, and I could ride on the boat to the next lock. A couple of dozen – maybe a hundred - more locks and I imagined I'd have lock wheeling cracked.

As we chugged on, I noticed the number of boats moored to the bank – grown into the ban, in some cases. There were boats that hadn't troubled a lock in decades and were more house than boat, and quite often near-derelict house at that. With the absence of cellars or attics, their roofs were nearly always piled high with findings: salvaged branches, logs and other burnables; colourful plastic kayaks, buckets and tanks, planters and grow-bags, wheelbarrows, old car roofboxes and rusty bicycles. I was reminded of the caddisfly larvae you see in streams, which pull up bits of gravel and twigs or plant stalks to make a camouflaged and protective casing.

We passed a narrowboat shop, the *Hype Hardware*, which could clearly supply any missing items. Moored on a remote stretch of towpath, waiting for passing custom, it had the familiar look of those 'we-sell-everything from a needle to an anchor' shops of my childhood in West Cork. Hand-painted boards hung along the boat's hull advertising its wares. Fire rope, glue,

Hype Hardware ... the Amazon of canal living.

brushes, kindling, oils, WD-40. There were perennials and herbs, compost at two quid a bag, and hats, gloves, socks, brollies and antifreeze against the approaching winter chills. More placards listed string lights, dog food, dog toys, duck food, brooms and mops, fuses and Rizla papers. The litany of canal goods was like a Gilbert and Sullivan patter song.

Standing to steer, I had a gangly heron's-eye view of passing farmland. Indeed my hand on the tiller felt agricultural, as if I was guiding the wooden handle of a medieval plough, pulled by a couple of plodding oxen. 'Tiller', I thought to myself, wondering if there was a connection with 'tilling'. The fields were shaved short after harvest. Sheep moved across pastures. There was a peppery-sweet cumin and honey smell off the water. And the fragrance of grass juice where canal maintenance men had mown a stretch of towpath.

We passed the Braunston Turn where the Grand Union and the Oxford canals became a single waterway for a few miles, mingling and exchanging waters and boats before taking their separate but almost parallel routes to London – one through Coventry and Oxford and on to the Thames, the other a dedicated canal from Birmingham. In the late afternoon we passed a pair of cast-iron bridges – Grand Union numbers 94 and 93, neatly picked out in black and white.

Whilst it was light we moored up, beside an 'accommodation bridge'. These bridges were essential structures when the canals were dug, arcing from field to field or village lane to village lane, to avoid forming a moat between rural communities, or dividing farms. Different bridges were needed, too, for canal business – 'roving', 'changeline' and 'turnover' bridges – so that horses could cross over when towpaths changed sides. Canal bridges tend to have specific forms, decreed by whatever local materials were abundant – stone, cast iron, wood. Here it was red brick.

As Kate brought *Morning Mist* into the bank I stepped ashore from the midpoint, with the centre rope to pull on. As instructed. Like steering, mooring was all about controlling the middle of the boat and letting the ends follow. It was, I thought, like some kind of yoga: all *Morning Mist*'s movement turned around her central chakra, powered by her chi. Though I didn't say this out loud, as Kate was giving me a practical lesson in how to hammer in the 'pins' and tie up the front and rear ropes 'properly'. 'You wouldn't believe the number of people who take their ropes right across the towpath – ridiculous. I mean, what are walkers and cyclists meant to do? Jump them? Fly?' It was another of the waterways' laws of courtesy.

Kate disappeared below to cook supper whilst I took her bicycle down from the roof and mended a slow but persistent puncture that she had complained of. Then I strolled down the high, south-facing hedge and plucked a tub of blackberries. It was a perfect September evening, with a tractor mumbling across a distant hillside before shuffling out of sight and earshot, leaving a freshly tilled silence behind. Kate brought out folding chairs and a feast of sausages, baked potatoes and roasted vegetables. We snapped the tops off a couple of bottles of beer and settled back into the dusk, treating the empty and remote towpath like a patio.

I was beginning to see the attraction of life on the canals, which plays on so many characteristics of the English psyche. Boating, of course ('Believe me, my young friend, there is nothing – absolutely nothing – half so much worth doing as simply messing about in boats,' as Ratty tells the landlubberly Mole in *The Wind in the Willows*), and DIY-ing and fixing up homes. A love of gadgetry, too – composting loos, solar-powered LED lights, and folding bicycles – and of history and rural life and industrial nostalgia. But, above all, two life-enhancing qualities: the peace of slow travel on water or along towpaths away from roads, and the sociability of the canals – inclusive without being tribal, supportive without being regimented.

There was a sense of community in canal life and a place for everyone that accommodated extrovert flourishes – joke boat names, flags, themed decorations, loud, good-natured groups in the canalside pubs – as well the loners who chose to moor up on remote pounds, and keep their towpath-side curtains closed.

Over the beers, I told Kate my plan to travel, during the course of the next year, a good spread of Britain's hundred-odd canals, and to do so using just about every possible form of slow transport. I would travel by narrowboat and barge (once I had got to know the difference between them), kayak, bike, perhaps even the odd stretch by paddleboard. And a lot of walking. I hoped to crew on some of the canals' remaining working boats; to find out what drives anglers to sit through freezing nights in the hope of catching a tiny perch or a tiddly rudd; to stroll with dog walkers, run with towpath warriors and marathoners; and to join the volunteers rebuilding the waterways' heritage infrastructure of locks, tunnels and pounds.

Kate listened indulgently, then stood up to pack away plates and chairs. The process was quick, ordered and practised, like everything she did. 'Early start tomorrow. Coffee first thing ... or do you have tea?' Coffee, I requested, and slipped off to set up camp on the towpath.

There, installed in my bivvy bag, I was lulled to sleep by a hootenanny of tawny owls, calling keenly from the woods now there were colder, darker, longer nights. I woke – was it around six? – to a thick, muffling autumn mist, hiding detail whilst making the air luminous. The outside of my bivvy bag was soaked in dew and the grass was sponge-wet. In shorts and T-shirt, and barefoot, I walked down the towpath. Ahead was a heron, indistinct in the damp, pearly atmosphere, as watchful as a pickpocket until it made its sudden rapier move – an uncoiling dart and strike of its head into the folds of the passing water before snapping its neck back with a small bronze fish held between its bill. The heron froze back into immobility against the stilled bank's reed-grass. Then another sudden strike and, this time a beak-pinched

eel, wriggling and shining like a silver watch-chain, before being
gulped out of sight.

As I walked back to *Morning Mist* there was the slow, muffled
whump-whump-whump of a ghostly boat, coming through the
red-brick half-circle of bridge number 100. It passed with barely
a ripple as I rolled up my sleeping kit. Kate had opened the side
hatch and she passed out a mug of coffee. I could smell bacon
frying. 'We'll eat on the move. Get your stuff on board, and you
can start the engine ... Remember how?' I made my way to the
back of the boat whilst Kate unshackled us from the shore. The
engine caught with a slow grunt, like a horse being led out of a
stable and harnessed up to plough, and then ticked over with
easy power.

We warmed our hands on the mugs of coffee. I'd hoped there'd
be sun behind the grey as the mist evaporated, but instead there
was the zinc, silver and lead shades of low clouds. We could
at least see the landscape now, and along the waters ahead.
Kate let go of the tiller: 'Take over, I've got work to do down
below.' With the grace of familiarity she tightroped back to the
centre hatch along the shoe-narrow gunwale running outside
the superstructure. Before she climbed down she called back:
'Remember! Slow right down for moored boats, into neutral if
anyone is actually mooring. Oh, and there's some tight bends
coming up, so don't cut them close – hold a middle line – or we'll
be aground.' She disappeared and then Jill-in-the-boxed out of
the hatch again: 'Blow the horn if you're unsure about anything,
and I'll be straight out, okay?

Being alone on the tiller felt like a huge responsibility. I throttled
back, just to reassure myself that the engine would respond. Its
thudding beat, which had been keeping time as I hummed 'The
Green, Green Grass of Home', dropped down till it became the
slow DUM-DUM-DUM-DUM of the *Jaws* theme. By inching up
on the throttle I could make the engine beat faster just like in the
film. So I did. There was a sharp shout from deep inside *Morning
Mist*: 'What's happening up there? Everything alright?'

A ghostboat in the morning mist.

I stopped messing around, just in time for a tight corner. I pushed the helm over. Far ahead of me I could see the bow turning slowly – too slowly? – whilst under me the stern pivoted around and swung towards the bank. I pushed the tiller over more, right over now, and, remembering Kate's tuition from the day before, gave a little kick to the throttle – DUM-DUM-DUM – then quickly turned it back down to a slow THRUM-THRUM-THRUM again. There was a bubbling at the stern, and a churning up of dirty muddy water. The canal was low after the long hot summer. Sixty foot ahead of me I could see the bow gliding into an already thin strip of water just as a narrowboat came the other way around the corner. The coming boat looked far from narrow as it drove on into the gap between the overhanging willow branches and the immaculate paintwork of Kate's boat.

Our combined speed was around five miles an hour. The pace of an energetic toddler. But it wasn't the speed, but the relentlessness of the two boats' momentum, that was heart-stopping. A crash in slow motion between two huge objects – between two houses, lest I forgot – is a longer, bigger crash.

There was no crash. The two boats slid past each other. I remembered something else Kate had warned me about. As one passes another moving boat, especially in narrow canals, the limited amount of water has to move around a lot to let both boats push through it, and as it rushes back in behind the passing boat you feel your own boat being sucked in towards the other craft. 'Be ready ... steer the front away early,' she'd said. I pushed the tiller hard over and, counter-intuitively, *Morning Mist* slid on in a perfectly straight line. There was less than a foot between the two hulls. I feigned ease, hand nonchalantly draped along the helm. 'How do!' I said, as the other helmsman and I passed almost shoulder to shoulder. That was the accepted 'one of us' greeting that Kate had taught as proper boating form. Terse but able was the note to be aimed for.

'How do!' came back. I felt I'd got away with something.

The coming miles had more sharp turns. At one almost hairpin bend, where steering the boat round was like trying to manoeuvre a sofa through a narrow corridor, Kate's head popped out of the hatch. 'I'd forgotten how tight this one was ... I would have ... oh, well, you seem to have managed. You might be quite useful one day. Anyway, coffee? Ginger cake?' She disappeared again.

A while later she came back with mugs, the cake box and talk. She pointed out Braunston church, the 'cathedral of the waterways', in the distance, and talked about how many of the ancestors of the Grand Union boating families she had known had once had houses in the town, and thought of it as 'home'. In times past, wherever they might die on the waterways, their wish was to be brought back to be buried in Braunston cemetery. Their coffin would be loaded on their boat, and a crew of family and friends would work it back along the canals, the other working boats pulling aside to give the funeral barge the right of way through locks and along the pounds.

Kate was talking about the Skinners, the last family to work the Oxford Canal, who had still used a mule rather than an engine into the 1950s, when she interrupted herself. 'See all that weed we've just been through ... Just throw her into reverse for a few seconds to unwind any that's got caught in the propeller. You don't want to have to clear the prop – horrible job.' And then some further canal lore: 'Do you know what to do if someone goes overboard?' she asked. 'You shout "STAND UP!" Kate grinned, imparting what was probably the oldest canal joke in the book to a first-timer who hadn't heard it before, and headed back to her office, down below.

I was left at the helm, making slow but steady headway, and gradually relaxed, measuring off time in units of darting kingfishers, their needle-sharp calls announcing their taking to the wing, and calibrating progress by our circling around the 390-foot windmill-topped hill at Napton. I was used to being at sea, where tides and currents push one around, but here it was the land's contours that determined our course, taking us on a disorientating 180-degrees arc around the hill's bulk, so that it lay first to the south west, then due south and then seemed to move around to the northeast. At which point we'd arrived at the Folly, below Napton-on-the-Hill.

We found a gap between other boats, I stepped ashore with the centre rope, and within minutes we were moored. Heather, the other half of Alarum, was waiting with her accordion case, and the three of us carried the theatre – the show's props and costumes fitted into a tea chest – up to the pub. The Folly at Napton was the very essence of a canal hostelry. Before the canal it had been a 'farm pub', the Bull and Butcher; then, after the canal opened, had quenched the thirsts of working boatmen anticipating the uphill flight of nine locks to reach the eleven-mile pound across remote high country beyond Marston Doles.

Mark Roden, our host, had an Edwardian moustache and a ready grin. 'We're the last chance of a drink for five hours if you're going south,' he greeted me, 'What are you having?' I wasn't 'going south' until the following day and it was early afternoon and there was a show to put up, but what the heck. I asked for a recommendation. 'Don't laugh, but have a "Shagweaver". It's from the North Cotswold Brewery, and they're in sheep country, historically anyway, and shag was a kind of rough woollen cloth, so it's really "wool weaver". The main thing, though, it's good. In fact, you know, I might have one myself.'

Mark pumped out the beers at a bar set up in a marquee on the lawn. There was a low stage, strings of bunting, and tables and chairs set up for the evening's show. There was the aroma of grass heating up under canvas, as well as the hoppy smell off my pint. It all added up to create a nostalgic essence of village fete. But there was work to be done. Alarum needed lighting and Mark pulled out bulb holders and extension cables. 'They'd be better if we had shades on them – more like stagelights,' mused Kate. I owned up to having worked backstage in theatre once and offered to create something Heath-Robinson-esque out of silver foil, tape, cardboard and string. 'Well, do your best,' Kate encouraged me. So between sips of beer I fashioned shades around each bulb holder and then, balanced on a chair atop a table, stretched up to string them across the front of the stage. That done and feeling the need to walk off the Shagweaver, I offered to head up the flight of locks and give out the show's flyers to any boat crews who'd moored higher up.

It was a pleasant stroll, stopping off to talk to boaters working their way down through the locks, or chatting to dog walkers on the towpath. At one point a gap in the hawthorn hedge revealed the startling sight of a large field full of water buffalo. Perhaps a hundred of them, grazing. At the top of the flight of locks a perfectly polished boat had moored up and a couple of boaters and

Heather and Kate on their 'Idle Women' tour

their dog had set up folding table and chairs. It was a location chosen from experience, I guessed. And I was right. Elaine and John were retired teachers, very much at the 'organised' end of the boating fraternity's spectrum, their cruising time-table and their boat's layout carefully planned. They seemed aware of this contrast with the more free and easy boat crews. Ever so slightly disapproving, too. 'Hire boats are a bit of a problem, I feel,' John said. As a teacher he didn't think that people could take in all they needed to know in a short instructional talk, before being let loose at the helm. He reckoned accidents were on the rise: collisions, running aground, sinkings even. 'A lot of it's phones,' Elaine joined in. 'People are always distracted and their attention is fragmented. You've got to be alert on the canals, and know what you're doing.'

The conversation suggested one of the paradoxes of the canals. Everyone on them is a proud and sometimes prickly individual – it's almost the defining characteristic. They are a place to be yourself. But boaters still fall into identifiable communities. And unlike a village, where houses stay static and neighbours often know each other for years and even over generations, canal craft – houses as much as boats – are constantly being reshuffled. One's always got new neighbours to get on with – or not.

Back at the Folly the marquee was filling fast. There was also a faint but acrid smell of something burning. 'I think it's those stage lights,' someone pointed out helpfully. They were right. The heat reflected from the silver foil was slowly melting the plastic bulb sockets. I climbed up to alter my design a bit, hoping that Kate hadn't noticed. But she was too busy preparing for her entrance from the 'wings', backstage being the lawn, now lit by the last colours of an Indian summer sunset. She delved into the tea-chest and pulled out an ancient woollen jumper, a windlass and a tattered notebook journal, and within minutes had taken us seventy-five years back in time to the Second World War and into the lives of the women who'd signed up as trainees on the 'idle' canal boats that needed crews to keep them moving and transporting essential supplies.

Kate's character, Isobel, joined this hard but exciting new world, learning from the more experienced volunteer boat women and even more from the working boat families, before finally graduating to taking her own engined boat and its towed butty with other new recruit 'Idle Women' up and down the Grand Union and Oxford canals. It was a tough life. Isobel laments the difficulty of steering a straight course, the complexity of the locks, the cramped living quarters, basic provisions and harsh weather. But she stays on, proud to wear trousers, earn acceptance from the professional boat families, smoke and assert herself when her patronising husband visits. She discovers that she can do 'men's work', and rather well, too.

Apprehension. Concentration. Tranquillity. Exhilaration. Working the tiller, chugging through the countryside on the misty waters of the Oxford and Grand Union canals, I'd felt very much what the trainee had experienced, though I only realised this as Kate evoked her character on stage. My instruction the previous day had begun as if I too was a trainee, tasked with absorbing the huge amount of boating and canal lore that had been worked out and passed down through the generations. It all seemed a bit confusing and with the intermission coming up I joined the queue for another pint of Shagweaver.

Many of the audience were off boats and knew each other. Others were land-based locals. Everyone was friendly. I volunteered to sell raffle tickets, though found myself chatting as much as tearing of strips of numbers and counting out coins. Someone had a long story about the (indeed shaggy) dog sitting patiently at his feet.

At another table Peter and Maureen told me that they lived aboard a narrowboat. 'I've had major surgery,' Maureen said matter-of-factly, 'and people ask how I recovered on the boat ... but it's our home, and it's all on the flat on a boat ... it's the perfect recovery place, with all that peace and quiet. Practical, too. I had to go in and out of the Queen Elizabeth in Birmingham and the canal's right by the hospital, so we just moored up and I could be in and out in minutes.' I tore off a strip of tickets and handed them over. Peter pulled out money. Maureen was looking serious: 'It's the people on the canals that make it special ... we've all got the same concerns – water, electricity, moorings. It's that level of sharing I remember from my childhood in Leeds. People talk to each other.'

They certainly did. The hubbub of chatter only quietened when the stage lights – I was watching them anxiously – went up for Heather's one-woman show, 'Women of the Waterways'. In period costume, accordion to hand, she recited and sang her way through a wider history of the women who worked on the waterways. One song recounted the adventures of Molly Traill on her run from Ellesmere Port to Birmingham in the narrowboats *Willow* and *Ash*. Lubricated voices sang the choruses and were still humming them at the show's end, after the bar closed and they filed back to the canal banks.

Kate, Heather and I headed back to *Morning Mist* in the dark for a cup of tea and a slice of cake and a post-mortem. The show, we agreed, had been made by the venue and the warmth of the audience. On the towpath, I rolled out my sleeping bag in the dark and wondered whether to bother with the bivvy bag; there was a hot, heavy feel to the air. Luckily, I did bother, for I was woken in the small hours by a downpour that went on into the grey dawn, water being sopped up by the grass under me to make a muddy waterbed. Secure and watertight, head down inside the bag, the drops were so heavy and continuous it was like someone bashing on a snare drum. But with perfect synchronicity the rain stopped, quite suddenly, just as Kate threw open the side hatch to tell me there was coffee and bacon sandwiches ready.

As strolling – or cruising – players, Kate and Heather were moving on in *Morning Mist* to reach their next show venue. I helped them up through the flight of nine locks, and, with two of us lock wheeling – Heather experienced, and I the beneficiary of two days of Kate's instruction – the climb uphill went easily. Kate could stay aboard at the helm, and we made good time.

With an early afternoon train to catch, I jumped ship above the top lock before the eleven miles of pound across country where few roads touch or cross the canal. It seemed strange that there could be anywhere so remote in central England but I'm learning that the canals have a different geography and time to the rest of the world. The waterways were set to the speed of a walking horse or a slow-turning diesel engine. As a water machine they had carried the nineteenth-century industrial world out from the towns and cities and into the farmlands and across hills and moors, and they'd brought the countryside, and its mountains of coal, into the heart of the metropolis.

Today the canals are a world of retro technology that had developed as if our modern world of cars and rush never existed. Perhaps they were a form of escapism from the modern world. But I couldn't see much wrong with that. In fact, I was enchanted to find that something as authentic and historic and alive and as fun as the canal system lay so close to hand.

Kate had known and learnt from some of the last working boat people, and in turn had used her plays and writing to pass on that knowledge. She'd also spent two days patiently and generously teaching me the basics of boat handling. In a small way I'd become a link in a chain of knowledge and skills that stretched back over centuries through the whole history of the canals.

2

Locks Ancient and Modern

A FEW DAYS WITH KATE had been a perfect introduction to canal life and lore. I now knew my narrowboats from my barges. But something I hadn't grasped, it seemed, was what exactly a canal was? Spend any length of time with a bunch of boaters – experts or bluffers alike –and you will soon find this is a source of great and enduring dispute. You'll get your ears dinned with words like 'locks', 'cuts', 'pounds', 'navigations' and the like, as if each word, like a higher trump, settles the matter. Yet it rarely does. A river with a few locks and some dredging is a canal to some, but is more correctly a 'navigation'. Many of Britain's best-loved canals are stretches of river interspersed by lengths of purpose-dug channel – so, are they partial canals, or not canals at all?

Locks seem to be crucial, but some canals – like the Ashby-de-la-Zouch, known to all as a canal – have scarcely any, whilst the first length of the Bridgewater Canal, opened in 1761 and feted by many as England's first canal, had no locks at all. Then there are canals that are really just 'cuts', joining one waterway to another, like Britain's shortest canal, the 154-foot-long Wardle.

I put the problem to Jim McKeown, a manager at the National Waterways Museum at Ellesmere Port. Neatly positioned where the Shropshire Union Canal meets the Manchester Ship Canal and the River Mersey, the museum is one of Britain's repositories of canal history. Jim thought a bit. 'Well, a true canal', he pronounced, 'is a completely man-made waterway, devoid of connection with any rivers'. That ruled out a fair number of canals, including some that contrarians might lay claim to being Britain's earliest, but which by that definition are really just parts of rivers that have been straightened or deepened – *canalised* – so they could function more reliably. A 'true canal' seemingly had be 'cut' into the landscape, be independent of natural navigable waterways, instead taking its water supply from local sources, and most pundits would say that locks would be the defining characteristic.

I asked Jim which was Britain's earliest true canal and he pondered a bit more. The Exeter, he reckoned. It was an independent channel cut to bypass a river weir, and though it did take waters from the River Exe, it used locks to raise and lower boats along its course. Locks trumped everything else it seemed. And all this in the 1560s.

It was clearly a canal I needed to explore.

'The impulse to harness the power of water', I mused aloud to my friend Isobel, who had gallantly agreed to walk the Exeter Canal with me on a cold February afternoon, 'must be one of the defining acts that have made us humans what we are.'

'And beavers?' she muttered, head buried in the folds of her scarf. 'Does it make beavers what they are, too?'

I ignored the quibble and waved an arm to take in the scene of advanced civilisation – the farmland, the houses across the canal, people on the towpath pushing prams and crouched over fishing rods. 'And I bet it all started with playful curiosity,' I continued. 'I mean, what kid can resist damming a stream or stamping through a puddle to see how the waves roll to the edges and overflow, or throwing a stick into a river current to see how it's carried downstream, or digging channels on a beach to divert the incoming tide?' Inconveniently, we had to sidestep a father and his two children all peering into their phone screens. 'It's all part of understanding the potential and putting to work this elemental power. And we've done it for centuries – used water to fill moats, float boats, turn mill wheels or irrigate arid land.'

We had reached a point called Matford Brook, and just beyond it Isobel and I could look from the towpath across the canal and down onto the river's course. The difference in levels showed rather neatly the difference between a river and a canal. There was the river pulled by gravity on its twisting falling course to the sea, with its marshy banks, prone to flooding and droughts, and its depths broken by rapids and shallows. And beside us lay the canal – a road of calm, placid water, held aloft by its neat and regular banks. By containing and controlling the water with lock gates and weirs and sluices, its currents and hazards had been banished, allowing it to be navigated in all seasons.

The odd thing, though, was that Exeter was not a place that would seem to have needed a canal. The city had been settled in pre-Roman times and thrived well into the Middle Ages precisely because it could be reached by a navigable river from the sea. The city stands on a sandstone outcrop, nicely positioned above rich farming land, and with a hinterland of ancient mines, nine miles inland from the coast at Exmouth. This was the lowest point of the River Exe that was fordable or bridgeable and so an ideal location for a trading post. Smaller seagoing vessels could, depending on the tide, be sailed, or drifted, or poled or hauled by ropes to reach the city. Under the Romans, it was trading across the Mediterranean, and by medieval times it was a fully-fledged city, packed with wool merchants and boasting three market days a week.

However, in the 1270s the Countess of Devon, Isabella de Fortibus, began making problems. One of England's wealthiest

The Double Locks pub on the Exeter Canal –the 'double locks' were added in 1701 to replace a trio of locks with guillotine gates.

landowners (she owned swathes of Devon and Hampshire and the entire Isle of Wight), the Countess was an indefatigable 'improver' of her properties and a strong litigator. She began taking more of the water from the tidal stretch of river to create a head of power for her mills on the banks of the river at Topsham, then building the 'Countess Weir' across the Exe, which made the passage of any substantial ships impossible. Smaller boats intent on reaching Exeter could still get through but had to negotiate a 'flash' lock.

Flash locks were ropey inventions of medieval river transport. They were essentially just a gap in a dam across the river, usually blocked by planks to hold back the waters above a weir. The gap could be opened up, creating a stream of rushing water, through which a boat could be pulled or winched up against the current (at great effort and expense in water), or shot downstream with the outward rush (at great danger to boats, crew and cargo). Whilst open, a flash lock let through torrents of water, often draining the whole upstream stretch, which might then take days to replenish. Still, it was the best technology had to offer and was used on numbers of waterways across England and the continent. Here, towards the top of the tidal reach of the Exe, it seems possible that the flash lock could have been opened at high tide when the water levels above and below the weir were a similar height, making passage easier and safer.

Water was money, then as now. It was also a limited resource, being needed for irrigation, fish traps, transport and for the medieval age's 'heavy industry' of milling. The construction of a weir to power Isabella's mills was hugely disruptive. Initially, it seems, it was more of a breakwater, stretching out from one bank to divert water down into the mill's flume and power the mill wheels. But this wasn't enough for Isabella. She opted to build a full weir across the whole river to raise the water level, effectively bringing water traffic to a halt. Unsurprisingly, the weir triggered intense conflict with the merchants and guilds of Exeter, who found their city all but cut off from the sea. Goods that had once floated easily up to the city walls had to be transferred to pack animals downstream or to smaller boats that could be pulled through the flash lock, or reloaded above it. The once thriving salmon fisheries were also rendered useless.

A brief respite came with Isabella's death in 1293, when the river route to the sea was reopened. But in 1317 Isabella's cousin Hugh de Courtenay not only rebuilt the weir but, rather than providing a flash lock, barred river traffic altogether. He then extended the quays at Topsham, where all goods to and from Exeter had to unload and load, extracting tolls for the privilege. Despite numerous attempts to petition monarchs and launch judicial suits and appeals, this abuse of landowning privilege continued for the next 250 years until, finally, Edward VI granted permission to reopen the river in 1550. But by then it was too late. The river had silted up to such an extent that it was barely navigable by any craft.

Rather than dredging the tidal river, a confederation of Exeter city guildsmen and traders decided in 1563 to build a canal to link the city to the navigable waters downstream. It was a brave decision, made at a time when the technology of canals, let alone locks, was basic. And was it even a canal they wanted to build? Earlier in the century, plans had been laid to clear the river and install a 'floodde hatche', a tidal lock gate allowing ships to enter through a gate on the high tide, the gate then being closed to hold water back in the river as the tide below drained. Which is a nice engineering concept, but not a canal.

So Exeter built Britain's first canal, finding a remarkable man called John Trew of Glamorgan as its engineer.

How Exeter's canal pioneers found John Trew – and how Trew came to know about canals – began to fascinate me, after walking along the Exeter's locks and bank. There was little about him in canal histories. But then I came upon a letter published in 1838, written by Philip Chilwell de la Garde to Sir Henry Ellis, a Fellow of the Royal Society. De la Garde was an obsessive on the subject of the Exeter Canal. He had fossicked out medieval court cases, statutes, royal correspondence, petitions and – the benefits of a classical education – read through documents in Latin and medieval English to piece together the story.

Trew had, seemingly, some civil and military engineering, and also mining, experience. He was engaged by the City of Exeter for the sum of two hundred pounds, with twenty-five pounds' expenses. It was a good commission – about a million pounds in today's money. He was also given the position of overseeing transport, landing and loading of goods – 'shillingstones, lyme, wood, cole, fyshe, corne, or grayne' – after the canal was built, taking rates for these services based on a scale of charges covering weight and distance. It was an arrangement that made him very much a stakeholder in the canal's success.

John Trew must have been a confident and charismatic character, and able as well. How did he convince the powers that be in Exeter that it was possible to build a canal, and that he could raise the water by use of locks? Nobody had built or seen such a thing in Exeter – or possibly in England – before. Perhaps he had a way with words. I'd like to think that he nailed some wood together and made a working model of a lock and then with buckets of water and toy boats demonstrated how he could do the impossible and raise ships uphill on water.

Where did Trew learn about locks and canals? He might have worked on watermills – the big industry of his day – which threw up hydrological challenges in powering their grinding stones. Maybe his military engineering experience had included designing and making harbours and dry docks and channels. He could have worked in the fenlands of East Anglia, which had been dredged and dyked for drainage, and used early flash locks for moving agricultural produce and peat and reeds and building materials and people around.

Or perhaps Trew read Herodotus, whose *Histories* recount Xerxes ordering the cutting of a canal wide enough to take two triremes, with oars out, across the Halkidiki peninsula above Mount Athos, to avoid the treacherous waters around its tip which had claimed 300 of Darius of Persia's fleet. Herodotus recounts how various nationalities of troops cut a section each. Whilst most dug a 'U'-shaped channel, whose sides soon caved in, the Phoenicians dug theirs in a 'V'-shape, wider at the top than specified, which proved more stable. Although a sophisticated piece of engineering, with breakwaters across both ends where the channel ran into the sea, the Xerxes commission wasn't a true canal, but more of a channel.

Trew wasn't working in a total vacuum, however. On the continent, 150 years before he began work at Exeter, someone had built the first pound lock – a chamber with gates at either end, between two different levels of water, that could be filled and emptied through sluices. This allowed a boat to go 'uphill' by floating it in from the lower section, closing the gate behind it and letting water in through a second gate to raise the water level to the upper height; the gate could then be opened and the boat set free on the next higher stretch or 'pound' of water. Boats could go downhill by reversing the process. Though the water itself was always moving downwards – and therefore was dependent on a source of water at the canal's highest point – the waterway was able to raise boats up and down over high ground.

It was the technological breakthrough that Kate and I had used to raise *Morning Mist* up the Hillmorton Locks some 450 years after Trew's time.

How and where had this canal technology begun? The chief suspect is China in the fifth century BCE when, almost contemporary with Xerxes, King Fuchai of the State of Wu ordered the Grand Canal to be built between Beijing and Hangzhou, linking rivers, marshes and lakes to carry traders and troop supplies. But the innovation which must have had the greatest influence on European and British canals came in the tenth century with the upgrading of the junction at the Yellow River. The flash locks used for hauling boats up or floating them down were unusable whenever the flow of water was too strong, and that was often. At those times the laden boats were winched up and down a slope between the different heights of water. That wasn't easy, and ships would often break up and scatter tons of precious cargo to the mercy of local bandits. Then in 984 a canal official and engineer called Qiao Weiyue invented the pound lock.

Like all the best inventions, the workings of a lock are simple and obvious. Simple and obvious enough that today's casual boat hirers – well, most of them – learn how to use the immense, quiet power of a lock after only the most basic of instruction. It was simple enough to grasp, and its benefits so great, that Italian travellers – in the footsteps of Marco Polo – took note of the magic 'lock' that could lift boats up and down hills, and brought a description of the technology used back to Europe.

It seems probable that John Trew had travelled – and by the 1500s he didn't need to go as far as China, as sophisticated canal systems had been developed and improved and put in place in Europe. He might have seen pound locks and their gate systems in the Low Countries, where there had been crude attempts to raise ships between different levels of water since the late 1300s. A rough example at Vreeswijk has been dated to 1373, though historians consider the one built in 1396 at Damme near Bruges the first real pound lock. These pound locks, employed in China and then the Low Countries, and introduced to England by John Trew, used heavy portcullis gates, raised and lowered from a frame like a guillotine to cut off the water at each end of a lock.

If Trew had travelled in Italy, however, he might have seen the Navaglio, one of the Milanese canals, with its eighteen pound locks engineered by Bertola da Novate in the 1450s. And he would have been introduced to a truly revolutionary technology. For it was here that the world's greatest designer, Leonardo da Vinci, taking a break from dreaming up helicopters, scuba-diving suits and three-barrelled cannons, dashed off a design for the miter lock. The blueprint for this is in his *Codex Atlanticus* and its brilliant concept is a pair of hinged gates that meet at an angle, holding them closed against the weight of water and making them easy to open when the water level on both sides is equalised. The design also introduced built-in sluice hatches ('paddles', as they are known today) that are raised or lowered to empty or fill the lock chamber. Employed for the first time in

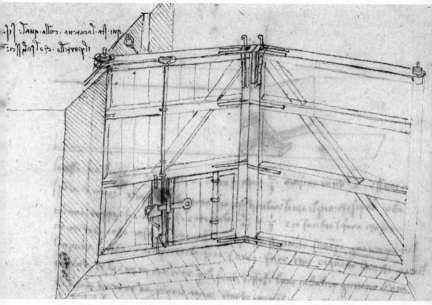

Leonardo invents the miter lock – complete with 'paddles' – still in use, five centuries later, on almost every canal in the world.

1497 on the San Marco lock on the Navaglio, Leonardo's design was, amazingly, the last word in lock technology. More than 500 years on, it remains in near universal use, familiar to all leisure boaters on the British canal system.

The new-fangled miter lock was described for the first time in Britain, twenty years after Trew built the Exeter Canal, on the River Lea. William Vallans in his *A Tale of Two Swannes*, published in 1590, describes the 'newly made' lock near to Waltham Abbey:

> *Downe all along through Waltham street they passe,*
> *And wonder at the ruines of the Abbay,*
> *Late supprest, the walles, the walkes, the monumentes,*
> *And everie thing that there is to be seene:*
> *Among them all a rare devise they see,*
> *But newly made, a waterworke: the locke*

Through which the boates of Ware doe passe with malt,
This locke containes two double doores of wood,
Within the same a Cesterne all of Plancke,
Which onely fils when boates come there to passe
By opening anie of these mightie dores with sleight,
And strange devise, but now decayed sore.

Trew's work in the 1560s was, however, rather more laboured. He'd initially set his workers to digging a channel parallel to the east bank of the Exe, possibly because there was already a sizable leet (as they call a flume in Devon) to the mill. But they hit rock. The Exeter folk must have had their confidence shaken, but Trew, undaunted, transferred the workings to the west bank of the river. A ribbon of land, between seventy and a hundred feet wide, was bought along its route and the digging of a channel begun anew.

It was this channel, the course of the canal, that Isobel and I were walking alongside now. Bigger and longer from subsequent improvements, but still Trew's canal in essence. Along the canal and river were suburbs, roads and streets whose names litanised the history of the endeavour: Countess Wear Road, Topsham, Weirside Place, Old Mill Close, The Quay. And the Double Lock pub at the Double Lock.

It was Trew's use on the Exeter Canal of a substantial pound lock – with its 'double' gates (one at either end) making a chamber that could be filled or emptied to raise or lower a small amount of water and a boat – that was the innovation in British canal design. And the engineering need was substantial: seven sluices along its course to take off excess water and tame floods, and three locks in total. Trew completed the nearly two miles of his original canal here, making it possible for large boats to move from below the obstructive Countess Wear to the port-basin of Exeter, bringing their loads of 'shillingstones, cole, fyshe' and the other goods that the citizenry were eager for.

The story should have ended there and happily with the visionary entrepreneur, Trew, sitting back and taking his substantial dues on the cargoes being floated in and out the city to everyone's increased prosperity. However, de la Garde's research presents a gloomier outcome. He records that Trew 'like most projectors of improvements and benefactors of mankind, seems to have realized no money by his work'. The engineer and the city chamber fell into protracted litigation. It seems that vessels of ten tons were unable to access the canal at all states of the tide, as required in their contract. That boats of fifteen tons and more were getting up to the city at most tidal levels wasn't good enough.

Exeter's revived porte – with packhorses complementing the canal craft.

A letter from Trew to Lord Burleigh states his position thus: 'The varyablenes of men, and the great injury done unto me, brought me in such case that I wyshed my credetours sattisfyd and I away from earth.' Perhaps it was this appeal that led to him being awarded an annuity of thirty pounds and a sum of two hundred and twenty-four pounds. The last heard of John Trew was that he had been engaged to work on Dover Haven at ten shillings a day, but dismissed for having protracted the work.

Trew's achievement at Exeter, however, was monumental and enduring. Exeter became a 'coastal' city once more and a 1579 document, a decade or so after the canal's creation, refers to its 'porte' and a 'faire and open keye.' A Mr Rawlyns, a tailor, had been appointed porter and keeper of the water-gate, and a Mr Smyth was given permission to build a crane. Things were going well in Exeter at the end of the 1500s.

It was nearly dusk by the time Isobel and I arrived at the 'porte'. We had made our way along the stretch of the canal into Exeter past anglers hunched over their rods, dressed in combat gear and surrounded by arsenals of keepnets, rods and bait boxes. 'There's big pike in there,' one told us, 'could be up to thirty pound. And there's catfish, too – don't know how they got there, but they must love it, they get really big.' Rather than extending his arms outwards in the traditional fisherman's 'one that got away' gesture, he lifted a hand a small child's height off the ground, whilst staring into the dark slab of water: 'They can hit fifty pounds.' Was that what he hoped to catch, we wondered. But, no, they were 'tackle breakers' and he wanted a pike.

The 'porte', like so much of Britain's canal heritage, had moved from commerce to leisure. Although inland, it had a sea-side feel, and it was no surprise to be find that the BBC had used it as a location for harbour scenes in *The Onedin Line*. Nor that, for decades, 'Onion Johnnies', travelling back and forth between

Devon and France, had stored their onions and bicycles in a dedicated warehouse before setting off to pedal their strings from village to village.

These days, the 'cellar' lock-ups with their big rounded double doors had been turned into businesses and craft shops, while restaurants and bars and pubs occupied the old warehouses. There were many to choose from, most with watery names: the Bridge Inn, Drakes Bar, Mill on the Exe, Port Royal, the Ship and Pelican. We were finally tempted into the Prospect Inn, beside a cobbled alley, which had the look of a Cornish harbourside snug. Hot whiskies, after a cold canal walk, were in order.

3

The Coal Duke 'Dunce' and the Home-School Engineer

THE EXETER WAS A LOCAL TRIUMPH: a fully realised canal, with tame still waters whatever the weather, and ships raised up and down by locks. It was a creation forged by imagination and confidence, community, finance and cutting-edge technology. But it was far ahead of its time. Sixteenth-century England didn't have enough high-value, bulky cargoes to move around; there was no reason to build anything national – no call, nor thought, for a whole network of canals. It was if John Trew had come up with all the hardware of an airport – the runways, control tower and baggage carousels – but there were no planes.

Trains of packhorses, and coastal and river shipping, were adequate for shifting goods in a medieval economy, when the luxuries and comforts that both rich and poor aspired to were reliable sources of food, simple utensils and better clothes. The medieval industrial revolution lay in improved sheep breeding, higher-quality wool and a growing efficiency in spinning, weaving and finishing cloth. These spawned the luxury of fine wool fabrics for the general population, as well as silks and linens for the wealthy.

All very welcome. But it wasn't worth building canals just to move a few fleeces and some bolts of tweed around. That would require a commodity of far greater value, with multiple uses and a far greater ability to change everyone's lives. A commodity like coal.

For the 200 years after the Exeter Canal was built, the majority of the goods and materials people used, consumed and aspired to were produced locally. In Norfolk roofs were thatched with reed. In the southwest, walls were built from cob; in the Cotswolds, from sandstone; in the north, from granite; in the east, from bricks. Rich and poor alike were most likely to heat their houses with wood – unless they lived right next to a coal mine. Coal was a wonder fuel but it was too expensive and bulky to move around, and its value as a heating fuel wasn't great enough to innovate major change. It was only when it began driving the commerce and profits of the Industrial Revolution, when it begun to be mined in large quantities, that more efficient transport was needed and canal cutting made sense.

That and thwarted love. In 1748, on the unexpected and early death of his elder brother, the twelve-year-old Francis Egerton, described as sickly and a bit of a dunce, became the 3rd Duke of Bridgewater. He inherited a considerable fortune, extensive lands and, crucially, a large mountain of coal under his estate at Worsley, to the west of Manchester. As a young man he made the obligatory Grand Tour of Europe, returning with the usual marble busts, Italian paintings and memories of grand balls. But what had most impressed him was a visit to the Canal du Midi, the first great French canal, completed in 1681, which extended the River Garonne to link the Mediterranean with the Atlantic, servicing the European wheat trade and transporting other commodities. The Duke noted with enthusiasm its locks and aqueducts, allowing cargoes of heavy materials to be moved around efficiently and cheaply from coast to coast.

But back to thwarted love. Having returned home, the Duke fell in love with and became engaged to the dowager Duchess Hamilton, an Anglo-Irish beauty with a racy past. Her sister

Francis Egerton, 3rd Duke of Bridgewater, depicted in front of his eponymous canal – and the famous Barton Aqueduct over the Irwell.

was even racier and became the subject of a society scandal, and the Duke, damning by association, broke off the engagement. It seems a priggish thing to have done, and perhaps he had regrets, especially when the Duchess moved up in society to become the Countess of Argyll. But the episode turned Bridgewater into a card-carrying misogynist; he lived his long life unmarried and refused even to have female staff in his house.

Instead, the Duke focused his life's energies on coal, industry and canals, in the exploitation of which he found a formidable ally in the steward of his lands, John Gilbert. A decade older than his employer, Gilbert had ambitious and original ideas for the estate's development. In an era when rural and aristocratic innovation was mostly taken up by breeding heavier cattle, faster horses and larger mangelwurzels, neither man seemed to have been interested in agriculture. Instead they focused on that mountain of coal at Worsley, and puzzled over how to most efficiently mine it and transport it to the nascent but growing nearby industrial towns. Moving coal by horse and cart or with pack ponies, as they had been doing, was slow and expensive, and ever larger amounts were needed to smelt metals and to make lime both for agriculture and cement.

Clearly, cheaper, high-volume transport would be the key to wealth in all commodities, and especially in the case of coal. So, taking inspiration from the continental canals – and from 'navigations' such as the 1757 Sankey Brook, which 'improved' a river to link the Haydock Collieries to the Mersey – Bridgewater and Gilbert plotted to build a canal from the Worsley mines to the nearest navigable river, the Irwell, from where coal could be shipped on to Manchester and other industrial areas.

It was time for me to head north – and back through two and a half centuries – to see the Duke's canal for myself. Time to imagine an era when roads were a slow, dangerous and expensive way to move cargoes, when railroads hadn't been dreamt of, and when canals were the bright shining future. I hoped that the Bridgewater Canal would show how a country-wide web of waterways had spread across thousands of miles in just a few decades, and what forces had driven their rapid construction. For the Bridgewater arrived as an apparently fully formed length of canal technology, becoming a blueprint for much of the 3,000 miles of British waterways built over the following century. It was also the springboard to success for the first and arguably most influential of the new breed of canal engineers.

I arrived early in the morning at King's Cross station with a new – well, secondhand – folding bike I'd bought for my canal explorations. I planned to cover around half the 2,000 miles of the canal network and if I did them all at three miles an hour, walking or boating, that would be very slow travel. A collapsible bike, I figured, would be just the thing. I clicked its clickable parts, flipped the pedals, collapsed the seatpost and dropped and turned the handlebars. The bike fought back by pinching my fingers, battering my shins and staining me with oil. But it finally succumbed to become a compact package of tubes and wheels – it was a process part origami, part Meccano, part judo.

I was inordinately pleased with the bike. It was small enough to carry on any form of public transport, comfortable enough to do a fifty-mile trip in a day, could carry a couple of packs, and was sturdy enough to survive the roughest of towpaths. I had acquired it the previous day from Harley Street. The bike's owner was a trichologist – a scalp specialist with a confidence-boosting full head of hair – and had wheeled the bike out from his consulting room. 'I'm only selling because I'm commuting on a road bike now,' he said, regretfully patting the seat. It felt like buying someone's beloved horse.

As the train headed northwards, I noticed just how often the railway line crossed canals, or ran parallel to a waterway for mile after mile. Naturally enough, both forms of transport exploited the levels of valley floors, followed contours around hills and took the same passes to cross over high ground. Sometimes the silver rails and the pewter waters would be shadowed by a stretch of motorway, again using the flattest way from point to point. Bit by bit I was beginning to understand how canals fitted into the landscape. Occasionally I could even see some combination of topography, industrial town and open country and predict where the canal would run close to the railway again. It gave a gentle satisfaction, like being able to identify birds or periods of architecture.

In Manchester I hopped onto a bus heading to Worsley. 'Bridgewater? Delph Mines? No—', the bus driver was happy-glum. 'There's a canal alright, but this bus isn't going near it.' I retained my trust in Google Maps as we circled out from the city centre, through bustling down-at-heel streets, and then into the smarter suburb of Worsley. The passengers had thinned out to just a couple of matronly grannies with shopping bags and a pair of teenage girls in Goth make-up that seemed extravagant for mid-morning. I got off the bus by a bridge that spanned the start of the Bridgewater Canal at Delph and thanked the driver, who remained adamant that this wasn't where I wanted to be.

It was. I was standing at the geographical and chronological start of the 'canal age'. There were discreet information boards with archive photographs and maps and box-outs and bullet points and captions. Diagrams of the mines. Descriptions of the pulleys and trolleys used. A sketch of a gravity-driven coal wagon that ran on tramlines downhill to the canal, a brakeman on a platform with a lever to slow it down, and behind him on another platform a free-riding pony that would pull the empty truck back up the hill. There was a bleak quote from an 1843 *Northern Star* newspaper article: 'Who would be a collier to be exposed hourly to death: to have his head split in two and his brains dashed out: all for four pence a day?'

From the road bridge I looked down into an old quarry working – two cliff walls of grey rock above a lush, reedy expanse of mud and shallow water stained with russet iron sediment. There were nettles and marsh marigolds. Glitzy blue dragonflies helicoptered across the water's surface or touched down on dead branches poking out of the swamp. The sweet rootsy, fruity smell that comes off still water and earth and wilted marsh plants baked in hot sun rose up on the air. It was a primal smell, hinting at the layers of vegetation that were laid down 300 million years ago in the Carboniferous era, and then compressed over time into coal.

In the 1750s this hill, now fringed with beech trees and creepers, was being mined in the traditional way, with picks and shovels and barrows and trolleys trundling underground. Almost the hardest work was moving the tons of coal from the cutting faces to the mine's entrance for onward transport. That and pumping and bailing out the groundwater that seeped through the hillside and flooded the workings. As the Duke and John Gilbert were planning their waterway to take coal to industry, one or other must have come up with the idea of cutting canals into the hillside to carry the coal by boat from where it was mined. These underground canals would also channel away the floodwater. It was an inspired idea that would end up over the coming century as nearly fifty miles of underground canals, on four different levels, interlinked by hoists and inclined planes. Strings of narrow, long boats like floating pit ponies would carry up to two tons of coal to the main canal to be loaded into larger 'M' or 'Mine' boats that could transport thirty or so tons onwards along the surface canal to Manchester.

With this plan in mind, Gilbert brought in James Brindley as engineer – a decision that turned out to be inspired. Born into a family of comfortably off yeoman farmers and craftsmen in the Derbyshire village of Tunstead, Brindley had been schooled by his mother because of the remoteness of their Peak District home. She must have nurtured a talent for invention and practical problem-solving, for at a young age he became a millwright, one of the most technically demanding branches of civil engineering at the time. Next, young Brindley turned his inventive mind to mining problems, coming up with an innovative way to use the flow of underground water to power pumps to keep the workings of the aptly named Wet Earth Colliery from flooding.

Brindley's growing status as a tunnel engineer was presumably the reason that Gilbert and the Duke hired him to work on their underground channels. Brindley, though, quickly came up with a further, bigger idea for the surface canal. He suggested that, rather than building a canal to the River Irwell, where the boats would join a competing waterway and pay cargo charges to another company, the Duke should build a totally independent canal directly to Manchester.

It was this total artificiality – 'an independence of rivers', as Jim McKeown at the Ellesmere Port Museum had explained when giving his opinion on whether the Exeter Canal was the earliest canal in England – that defined a canal. The Bridgewater met this criterion. But as a contour canal it would end up without any locks. Nonetheless, it is celebrated by most historians as the first canal of the modern age.

Canal building is like a very expensive and very slow game of Monopoly mixed with snakes and ladders. Landscape is rarely flat and the ability to lift water up and down hills with locks is another definition of a canal. But there is a lot of gambling on decisions. Take the most direct course and you're letting yourself in for building costly locks, tunnels and reservoirs; follow the contours of a landscape and you might double, treble or quadruple the distance covered. A genius canal engineer like Brindley was able to juggle the competing forces of expenditure and reward, using a sixth sense to read the geology and lie of the land and intuit where water to fill the channel could most easily be obtained. He would also learn how best to factor in the commercial points served along the route, and how to weigh up the competing finances of digging and finishing off locks

Bridgewater 'M' or 'Mine' boats – 'starvationers' – designed for the Bridgewater canal in the 1750s. They were the blueprint of the canal narrowboat.

and tunnels against cutting a longer route. But that's all normal canal-builder genius. What Brindley had was genius squared; the ability to come up with a completely unexpected solution to a problem.

The problem in question was that Brindley's new route for the Duke's waterway would have to keep to the same level whilst it crossed a valley and the River Irwell. Brindley proposed an aqueduct carrying the canal thirty-eight feet above the river, leaving enough room for large boats to use the navigation below. The Romans built aqueducts to carry water high above valleys, and the Duke may have seen aqueducts for shipping on the Continent, but it was a dizzyingly audacious idea in England, where nothing of its scale had been tried before. Brindley's idea was scathingly dismissed as a 'castle in the air' by critics and faced a tough test to get official sanction from the committee set up to advise Parliament, who needed to pass an act to authorise the canal's construction.

Undaunted, Brindley met the committee and won them over by making a model of his aqueduct in cheese. It is tempting to imagine him taking his pocket knife to a substantial block of Cheddar and carving out arches, buttresses and, along the top, the channel that would carry the canal. Perhaps even a few crumbled biscuits to represent the valley sides and rocky river course below – a blueprint in comestibles for the first 'navigation' of the canal age. Or, as Brindley would have said, 'novogation'. The home-schooled engineer approached writing with the same logic he applied to cutting canals through baffling contours. He took the line of least resistance, peppering his journal entries and official reports with words like 'novogations', 'ochilor servey' and 'ricconitoring' or, indeed, in another of his papers, 'a raconitering.' Read his written words aloud and you can hear his practical northern voice.

Perhaps as persuasive as the cheese modelling was the support of town councils and businesses in Manchester and other urban areas for the building of surface canal. In applying for his Act of Parliament, the Duke promised that the cost of coal would drop from seven pennies a hundredweight (112lb) to four pence. This was an attractive proposition for everyone.

Things moved fast after the cheese course and subsequent granting of the Act. Surveying was finished. Tunnelling and digging began. Brindley had barges constructed to carry forges and metalwork shops and carpenters' sheds that could then be floated along the canal as it was cut and flooded, the water held back from the actual work by temporary dams. To cut the canal the Duke employed his own estate workers and local labourers and perhaps fenmen from East Anglia and others used to digging ditches. Work began early in 1760, and by July 1761 the canal was open to Stretford – a distance of more than six miles. Even more impressive, Barton Aqueduct was carrying boats through the sky only eleven months after work was commenced. By 1764, the canal had reached Castlefield Wharf, right in the heart of Manchester.

Such speed and innovation cost money. The Duke closed his London house and cut back on all personal expenses to concentrate his resources on the canal. But the huge workforce needed paying and, as he extended his waterways and their infrastructure, he went deep into debt, in 1764 borrowing £25,000 from Child's Bank on the security of his canal, and further significant sums the following year. In today's money, it is estimated that he was in hock by as much as £2 million. But over the following decades, with the extended waterways complete and operational, with coal being hauled out of the ground in ever greater volumes and shipped onwards to industrial areas, profits flowed. The Duke would eventually become one of the richest men in England, acquiring more estates, extending his waterways empire, and building the opulent Bridgewater House in London's St James's. 'The dunce' had done good.

Standing on the bridge at the start of the Bridgewater Canal, I imagined how it would have been at the height of the Duke's success. I would have been looking down on boats piled high with coal coming out of the mountainside. Brindley – or perhaps Gilbert, for its hard to know how many of the land agent's own ideas were attributed to the 'father of English canals' – had come up with a simple 'barge' design. The 'Mine' boats were little more than oblong boxes, with heavy planking fixed to exposed ribs, inviting the nickname of 'starvationers'. At first they were 'bow-hauled' by teams of men plodding along the bank, like tug-of-war teams caught in Sisyphean toil, but once a proper towpath was built horses were drafted in as engines to take the boats down to Manchester and the Duke's warehouses, wharfs and businesses.

I had been intrigued by the name given to the hollow holding the mine entrance – Delph. Romantically, I'd imagined it perhaps as a romantic Grand Tour memory of the Duke – from Delphi, perhaps. But local research showed me that it was common to use the phrase 'coal delphs' about coal diggings in the 1700s, a corruption of a 'delved' place – as in the entrance to the Duke's mines. The sandstone quarried out was used to build the Bridgewater Canal's banks, wharfs and bridges.

An American traveller, Samuel Curwen, wrote in 1777 that he was shown around the mine workings by Gilbert. The underground canals had already grown by then to some six miles in extent. A hundred men were employed daily, Curwen

Brindley's pioneering Barton Aqueduct (top) with sail-barges, assisted by horses. The River Irwell runs below it.

reported, each turning out a ton of coal a day. The miners were paid two shillings and the labourers around a shilling. The coal, he summarised, cost two pence a hundredweight at the pit, three pence halfpenny when shipped to an urban 'key' and fourpence-halfpenny delivered to a house or factory. The Duke's promise of a steep fall in the price of energy had been fulfilled.

I would have liked to follow in Curwen's path, exploring the underground canals. Up until the 1960s it was possible, as the mines were still worked – albeit by a much reduced workforce and using a simplified infrastructure. The waterways historian Charles Hadfield described going in with local guides for a visit. The original eight-foot headroom over the water had in places halved through subsidence, he wrote, and he and his guides were reduced to lying flat out in the boats to clear some particularly low stretches. Black-and-white photographs show them in tweed suits (that medieval wool economy struggling on), crouched down in boats that were still built along the lines of the practical 'starvationers' of two centuries before. The tunnels and their waters looked calm and still.

What I would have seen just over two centuries before, when the canal had been in operation for a few decades and the Duke's businesses lined the canal banks, would have been all bustle and business. Josiah Wedgwood, a friend of Brindley, visited in 1773 and reckoned that Worsley had the 'appearance of a considerable seaport town'. The canal waters split under the bridge, creating a small island where a nail-makers' workshop was established in the 1760s and was kept busy for a century or more, turning out nails to fasten together starvationers, wheelbarrows and carts. More workshops, crafts and industries started up in Worsley. Lime kilns, brickmakers, cotton spinning, boatbuilding and ironworking. Warehousing, of course, for goods being trans-shipped on the canals and cranes powered by a horse turning a windlass, a 'horse-gin' as it was called (predating the 'en-gine') to lower and raise cargoes between road and water level. There would have been a massive level of industrial noise. Shipwrights

The entrance to the Worsley mines and underground canals – and (below) today, blocked off and barred.

hammering and nailing. The thud of mallets on caulking irons. Sawing and axing and adzing. Shouting and banging. The rumblings of iron-tyred carts on cobblestones.

The noise was so immense that workers claimed they often couldn't hear the clock striking one for their return to work after lunch, and so were late. The Duke commissioned a clock that would strike thirteen times at one o'clock, allowing no excuse for lateness. He was a famously hard-nosed employer. When miners complained about the hardness of the rock in one seam, how little coal it contained and their labours producing little for a lot of effort, the Duke listened, then took out his snuffbox, and told his workers that they'd keep digging as long as there was – and he held up a pinch of snuff – that much coal to win.

As well as industrial pursuits, the Duke set up passenger boats (a penny a mile) to ply the canal, pulled by a pair of cantering horses, one ridden by a postillion. Below the bridge he built a packet house for passengers to wait in, with his canal offices above. 'The Packet House' still exists, though it is a nineteenth-century mock Tudor replacement, and there is still a boat service navigating the canal here. Bridgewater Cruises ran Sunday lunch and cream tea cruises on board the *Francis Egerton*, complete with crystal glasses, silverware and white linen. Bridgewater might well have approved. He used a boat to travel in comfort and at speed down what had become known as the 'Duke's Cut' to reach his own expanding businesses in Salford and Manchester. The prow of the boat was equipped with a blade, shaped like a scimitar, to cut through the tow ropes on any boats that didn't clear the way fast enough. The craft's name, oddly, was the *Duchess-Countess* – a rare display of sentimentality, presumably, in reference to his one-time fiancée, Elizabeth, Duchess of Hamilton and Countess of Argyll.

I pedalled off down the towpath. It was a weekday morning and I had the track largely to myself. A few dog walkers. A young mother rocking a buggy. A gaggle of Canadian geese who waddled off the paved way with truculent looks, leaving a cobbling of greenish shit pellets behind them. The surface – goose faeces aside – was smooth, tempting me to push on a bit. But the folding bike was not just a convenience but a deliberate way of going slowly, though a bit faster than walking, and forcing me to look around. Across the water I gazed on to Worsley Boatyards, and I could just see the span roof over England's oldest canal dry dock, dating back to the Duke's time. A heritage vessel, the 'fly boat' *Dee*, poked out of the entrance channel. There were several houseboats, moored along the bank opposite – one of them called the *Onion Barge G* (canal boaters like their puns).

I passed The Granary, which had started off as a water-driven forge, then used to store grain and was now repurposed as offices. There was the faint trace of a lime kiln on a branch off the canal, where local limestone was brought in on boats and crushed and burned to make waterproof mortar. Metropolitan

It's hard to resist a pun on a narrowboat.

expansion was insatiable for materials. And coal was driving more and more of the Industrial Revolution. Firstly through the making of iron from ore and limestone. And then turning that iron – and later steel – into things in forges and foundries. There was glassmaking, too, as well as chemical extraction to be used in processes from tanning leather and dying cloth to creating lime for enriching farmland and making mortar.

The real game changer in the Industrial Revolution was lagging behind the development of the canals. In the early 1700s Thomas Newcomen had invented his atmospheric engine – the first true commercially viable, piston-driving steam engine – to pump out water from mines. Hundreds of them were soon in use. But James Watt's engine, which used steam to create a continuous rotary power that could be used to drive machinery, wouldn't be invented till 1781, and another twenty years would pass before a Cornishman called Richard Trevithick had the idea of putting an engine on a track. So for half a century or so the canals would rule supreme. Bridgewater, Gilbert and Brindley had realised not just canals' technology but their changing potential, as coal, canal and steam engine became an unstoppable trinity of power.

I cycled on past street names and landmarks that told the canal history: Old Boatyard Lane and Chandlers Row. Further away from Delph more modern businesses had sprung up and withered, with derelict industrial sites razed back to bare earth. I swooped under a railway line, sending pigeons perched on its girders clattering off, and then through another underpass where the water and towpath went below the Liverpool Road.

There was no sentimentality in canal building. I knew that the Barton Aqueduct had been demolished a century before, when the Manchester Ship Canal had been built. But in its place was an equally ambitious piece of waterways architecture, the Barton Swing Aqueduct. An inspired piece of Victorian can-do engineering, Edward Leader Williams' gizmo solved the problem of carrying the Bridgewater Canal across the massive ship canal at the same height as the old aqueduct. That had been at a height far too low to allow ocean-going ships to pass under. The solution was a 300-foot trough that could rotate through ninety degrees, carrying the canal. Gates at either end of the trough held the water – 800 tons of it – and any boats that were in it. After more than a century, it is still in regular use.

I crossed the Ship Canal on a road swing bridge, parallel to the Swing Aqueduct and took a closer look. The Barton Swing Aqueduct is all grey girders, beams, rivets, braces, struts and huge gears. It has a tiny wooden control cabin like a garden shed stuck high up on its sides, and a small waterfall of water leaking from one corner. Under its midpoint on an island is the massive iron turntable and teethed gears that both support and turn it.

I stopped mid-bridge, hoping for a large vessel coming up the Manchester Ship Canal so that I'd get to see the aqueduct swing. I could see the cityscape of Manchester upstream. A woman was negotiating the bridge's narrow pavement with a baby buggy, and I pulled my heavily laden bike out into the road to let her pass. 'It's a lovely view, isn't it?' she greeted me. 'Are you following the canal?' I nodded. 'I love walking it,' she continued. 'It's so peaceful. At the other end of the bridge it's easy to miss the turnoff down onto the towpath again. There's a little bandstand there.' She wheeled on. I was cheered by her sense of the towpath as a haven – not an edgy edge-land given over to drinking and toking, dumping rubbish, hanging out. Canals were no-go areas for decades in places like this.

I found the bandstand, surrounded by scraggy trees and rough undergrowth. Across the water there were the kind of cement, corrugated iron, broken glass and barbed wire walls and fences that hide breakers' yards or scrapmerchants. The bandstand looked as incongruous as the streetlight in Narnia's Lantern Waste, looking out on plastic bottles bobbing along the

Barton Swing Aqueduct – one of the Seven Wonders of Manchester.

banks, and a nicely self-referential piece of graffiti on a black metal girder – 'paint the street'. A narrowboat chugged along the tranquil waters of the canal towards me. I watched as it puttered past and into the channel of the aqueduct, sending up a little wash from its propeller, so it looked like a leaf being washed along a length of zinc guttering. It seemed inconceivable that the whole length of canal, water, boat and all, could pirouette through the air. I imagined Brindley would have been impressed by the technology that had replaced his own innovation.

Brindley's success with the Bridgewater Canal brought him fame and a modest fortune. He became the 'Master Canal Engineer', called upon to oversee ever more ambitious canal projects. He added lock-building to his repertoire for subsequent waterways, allowing him to extend the Bridgewater Canal to Runcorn, thus connecting it to his next major work, the Trent and Mersey Canal. He proposed and championed the idea of the Grand Cross – an 'X' of major canals linking the four significant rivers of England – the Thames, Severn, Trent and Mersey. It has been suggested that the canals Brindley built and inspired, and their importance in accelerating metalworking (guns and cannons, bullets and balls) and the production of bulk chemicals (better and more explosives and gunpowder), were as crucial in the coming Napoleonic Wars as the leadership of Nelson and Wellington.

Certainly, the ability to move coal over long distances cheaply and efficiently had wrought the greatest change in England's fortunes since the Norman Conquest. And canals had effects – and indeed benefits – beyond armies and industry. They became a nexus of communication, spreading ideas, moving people around, and supplying increasing amounts of manufactured goods locally and further afield. More people had more things: clothes, cutlery, pottery, glassware, furniture, ornaments. There was more work, and more wages, and so more buying power and more jobs making things to buy. The growing canal system was like a slow physical internet, connecting nearly everyone in England to nearly everyone else, and at the same time delivering 'online' shopping to your business, town or village. Within a few decades of the Bridgewater Canal being built, it was estimated that half the English population lived and worked less than five miles from a canal.

Cycling the Bridgewater, a century and a half from its decline, I had imagined that following the towpath into Manchester through its industrial areas and suburbs might have been a grim commute. But I passed people slipping out of offices and from business car parks through gates or holes in fences or gaps in the hedges or breaks in walls to walk, eat their lunch, talk to friends. There were joggers, even a couple of optimistic fishermen ('fishermen' is a word that rarely requires gender equalising). The canal infrastructure remained impressive, too, with elegant red-brick bridges allowing the towpath to cross from side to side. My attempts to cycle the small-wheeled bike up and over these humpbacks often ended with my stalling on the rough bricks. On one bridge I met on the crest a Lycra-clad cyclist doing the same. 'That caught me by surprise,' he laughed. 'I'm trying to get fit. Not sure it's working, but the towpaths are great – no traffic, no stress or aggression.'

At that point a growing yammering, like lawnmowers running too fast, drew our attention to the towpath. Three mountain bikers came into view, but there was something unsettling about them: the hoodied lads weren't doing nearly enough work for their speed. As they passed, soaring up and over the humpback, with a flurry of cheery waves, I saw that they had jury-rigged small petrol motors onto their bike frames and had run drivebelts to the back wheels, powered by Coke bottle fuel tanks gaffer-taped to the handlebars. My new friend and I watched transfixed and perhaps a little envious.

A little further and I found myself in the shade of Old Trafford, Manchester United's vast ground, where food stalls and parking attendants were preparing for the evening's game, and then on past Liverpool Warehousing, a pair of enormous sheds dated 1925 and 1932, their old chains and hooks now welded together into a solid sculpture. The docks were off to one side, no longer busy but still used, and from there the canal path led on into the centre of town, reaching a basin near Deansgate. There you could connect with the River Irwell and the Rochdale Canal, whose initial stretch cruises through the heart of Manchester's Gay Village, the canal providing a focus for the terrace cafes and clubs, enhancing afternoon drinks and night action.

Given the luxury of time travel, the (men-only) Duke of Bridgewater would have been an amusing extra on this scene. In his day he would arrive at Deansgate Basin in immaculate dress, on board the *Duchess-Countess*. And on occasion he might have been accompanied by Brindley. There is a portrait of the great engineer in the National Portrait Gallery in London, painted by Francis Parsons in 1770, when his celebrity was at his height. It shows him dressed in a practical brown coat with lines of brass buttons, a waistcoat with more brass buttons, a flash of white shirt and cravat, and a froth of ruffled cuffs. Fancy clothes, but still workmanlike and sober, showing his importance and seriousness. He would have been in his late forties – a man in his prime and at the height of his success, burly and red-cheeked from an outdoor life. One of his arms is draped over a brass instrument – a theodolite for measuring inclines – and in the background is a landscape of his greatest triumph, the Barton Aqueduct. That being easier to portray than the 365 miles of canals which he surveyed and engineered.

Brindley became an obvious figurehead as a canal pioneer, but his celebrity overshadowed the achievements of many other canal builders. Some, like Henry Berry, who designed the Sankey Brook, were more renowned for other works – in Berry's case, the building of Liverpool Docks. Thomas Telford also eclipsed his extensive canal work with other successes in a long career of road, bridge, harbour, tunnel and other civil engineering projects.

James Brindley – in an engraving after Francis Parsons' painting. The father of British canals was arguably as crucial to the national story as Nelson or Wellington.

Other canal men were as innovative, dogged and adept in building canals as Brindley, and have lapsed into undeserved obscurity. One such is the Huguenot Richard Cassels, who, twenty years before the first section of the Bridgewater opened, had combined his engineering skills and what he'd seen of canals on the Continent to design the Newry Canal in Northern

Ireland. Like the Sankey Brook, this is seen by most historians as a navigation – an 'improved' river – rather than a canal, but its fourteen locks stake a decent claim.

Following hard on the heels of Brindley came a series of capable and often brilliant canal engineers. John Rennie's long list of canal achievements include the Kennet and Avon, a challenging sixteen-year job, with its tunnels, aqueduct and flights of locks, completed in 1810. John Smeaton – often called the 'father of civil engineering' – was another 'Master of All Trades': a physicist who improved the recipe for concrete, part invented the diving bell, designed the third Eddystone Lighthouse, and experimented with steam engines. He was also a drainage expert, an improver of navigations and the builder of several pure canals in England and Scotland.

But my favourite canal engineer, the man I'd most like to have talked canals with over a drink, was William Jessop. He was himself a pupil of the brilliant John Smeaton, whom he worked with on several canal projects before taking on Ireland's Grand Canal – an eighty-mile waterway to join Dublin to the Shannon, which had to overcome a long passage across the unstable Bog of Allen. Having accomplished this feat, further projects followed, including the Grand Junction Canal, which was designed to improve on Brindley's Oxford Canal by providing a more direct route between the Midlands and London by joining with the Thames at Brentford. It was a pig of a route: three big rivers to cross required three big aqueducts, and there were long tunnels to build at Braunston and Blisworth.

Jessop was reportedly a sharer of his knowledge, contacts and experience with other canal builders, so it's not surprising to find that he helped the tyro canal builder Thomas Telford – of whom more in the following chapter. Jessop drafted in Telford initially to help build the Ellesmere Canal (now called the Llangollen Canal) and defended his ambitious designs for aqueducts to the doubters on the canal committee. Those aqueducts included the

Pontcysyllte, which at 126 feet remains the highest in Britain, which Telford made light and airy by using a metal trough held up by eighteen hollow pillars. And, being too busy himself, Jessop recommended John Rennie for the Lancaster Canal, which established the latter as an engineer.

In this, Jessop was unlike most engineers – and particularly Brindley, who couldn't say no to new projects, let alone bear to pass them on to rivals, and would take on canal work relying on 'resident engineers' and assistants to oversee work on the ground. In effect this meant that long stretches of canals were built by forgotten men, many of whom felt a sense of injustice at being overworked and under-rewarded. One assistant, looking for a payrise, complained: 'my master Brindley never paid half the attention to all the canals he was concerned in as I pay to this one; he neither set out the work or measured it as I measure it, yet he received near £2,000 a year.'

Master canal builders, however well rewarded as consultants, still had a tough life, with constant travelling in the saddle or by carriage to oversee far-flung jobs and nights spent in lodgings of very variable comfort. It was a life that killed Brindley before his time. As the go-to canal engineer, consulting on the building of too many canals, he was out in all weathers, and a severe drenching whilst surveying a branch of the Trent and Mersey, together with a cold damp hotel room at the end of the day, gave him a chill. He was attended in his illness by Erasmus Darwin, grandfather of the evolutionist Charles, who discovered that the engineer was severely diabetic – a diagnosis that seems to have sent him into a decline. He lingered some months at home before dying, aged forty-nine, leaving two daughters and a twenty-six-year-old wife. He hadn't lived to see completion of either of his great works – the Bridgewater's continuation to Runcorn, and the Trent and Mersey.

4

In Praise of Navvies

I STARTED OFF ALONG the Huddersfield Narrow Canal on foot but boating with Kate Saffin had given me the idea of hitching lifts. I saw myself as one of the 'hobblers' of old; men who'd hire themselves out to help crews through locks in exchange for a few pennies. With its seventy-four locks, the Huddersfield Narrow seemed a good canal to revive this traditional form of casual work. And I was cheap; forget the pennies, I was happy to be paid in canal stories, mugs of tea, time on the water and less walking. My rucksack was stuffed with a sleeping bag and bivvy bag (I could sleep on the towpath), campfire coffee-making kit (tin-can alcohol stove, titanium mug and a 'coffee sock'), a change of clothes, and pen and notebooks. I also had a guitar, its strap hooked over one shoulder. I was willing to both 'lock wheel' – work the locks – and entertain hospitable crews.

The Huddersfield Narrow Canal was conceived as a shortcut to join East Yorkshire waterways to Manchester and other growing industrial towns on the Cheshire Ring. Its construction started in 1794, less than twenty years after the Bridgewater Canal's route from Worsley to Runcorn was opened, but in those two decades canal technology had accelerated in ambition, in scale and in technique. Fired by the success of his Bridgewater Canal, the ambitious and able James Brindley dug out, experimented with and perfected a lock design in the grounds of his own new estate at Turnhurst Hall. He used Leonardo da Vinci's mitered, double gates at the 'downhill' end of the chamber, where the greatest water pressure fell, and a single beam gate at the upstream end. The lock chamber's dimensions were just long and wide enough to fit a boat based on a Bridgewater 'starvationer', the basic craft he was familiar with from the Bridgewater mines. This was enlarged to carry as much bulk and weight as one horse could comfortably pull, and would morph into the narrowboat still in use today. In turn the size and design of lock would set in stone – literally – the pattern of those built on most canals.

The Huddersfield was typical of the small scale of most of Britain's canals. Brindley and his cohort engineers and surveyors created a toolbox of snap-together modules for building a narrow waterway across any kind of landscape; straight and curved pounds and cuts, fixed and swing and lifting bridges, aqueducts, viaducts, locks and flights of locks, winding holes, wharfs and tunnels. It was a superbly efficient model that led to rapid growth – indeed, to the 'canal age' – though it would have practical and financial repercussions in the late nineteenth century, and lead to the waterways' industrial demise in the twentieth. Hindsight would have dictated bigger-scale waterways, like the ship-sized, modern industry-friendly canals of France and Germany.

Britain's early canal building was nonetheless a substantial, indeed extraordinary, feat of engineering, in the spirit of the age. In little more than fifty years it would create a nationwide water machine of friction-free conveyor belts, geared and levered and powered by locks and reservoirs, able to carry immense weights long distances, and up and down hills, with maximum efficiency. And by the standards of the day, canal transport was swift. It was as if the whole landscape of parts of England were being turned into a giant factory. Canals were – until the coming of

The Huddersfield Narrow – not an extraneous inch.

the railways (arguably just a reimagining of the water roads and wooden boats as steel rails and steam engines) – the greatest homogeneous piece of technology conceived.

Yet the canals were built with little more technology than had raised Stonehenge, the Mayan temples or the Pyramids: levers, fulcrums, rollers, simple derricks and, above all, human muscle and hand tools. Plus a little gunpowder, courtesy of the Chinese. And quite a lot of horsepower, thanks to the Central Asian tribes.

This didn't stop the floating of ever more ambitious projects, and the Huddersfield Narrow was one of the most ambitious. Or, perhaps, foolish.

A short – less than twenty miles – southerly route across the Pennines, the Huddersfield Narrow was planned along an almost straight line to save on both locks and the scarce water required to fill them. But, to do so, it needed a three-mile-long tunnel to be driven deep below the Pennines.

Benjamin Outram was the consulting engineer. A keen technologist, who, as well as overseeing a number of canals, diversified into ironworks, quarrying and building tramways – which he was already calling 'railways' and which used his iron foundry's products. He had the usual canal engineer's vice of spreading his considerable abilities too thinly across too many projects, and even his wife described him as 'hasty in temper, feeling his own superiority over others'. Several years into its building he resigned from the Huddersfield Narrow Canal claiming illness (though he seems to have been healthy enough to continue with his many other works). Perhaps he suffered from a creeping malaise when he realised that the ambitious underground canal was proving – not surprisingly – difficult, slow and costly to build.

It was bound to be slow going. Acts of Parliament were needed to purchase land for canals, draw off water from rivers and streams, and compensate businesses, whilst canal financing was equally complex in the 1790s, with cabals of hard-nosed lenders scrutinising wild promises of returns. Then, once the permissions and finances were sorted, the engineers, lawyers, politicians, surveyors and financiers' lofty plans had to be dug into, excavated from and blasted through actual rock and earth.

Perhaps because I've never been a lawyer or an accountant but have worked a bit with pick and shovel, it was the muscle work needed to create these early canals that most interested me. As a nineteen-year-old I spent a winter in Dublin on a building site, putting up a school extension. I was a country boy used to mucking out stables and piking bales of hay, so I thought the job would take similar brawn, but brain ... well, not so much. I expected to be digging out foundations, and shovelling cement and barrowing blocks and earth around in the rain and the frost. What I didn't anticipate was the emphasis on speed and efficiency. My new job was not just about turning the calories from a full-fry breakfast, cheese sandwich lunch and mutton stew supper into units of dig, lift and shift. It needed thought and learning.

The ganger was a hard man from Mayo. 'Are you a fecking eejit? Are you? Turn the fecking barrow around before you fill it. You'll be turning it full otherwise. Sweet Jaysus'. And thus began a course of learning how to read a lump of rock and hit it in the sweet spot with the pick, so it broke neatly apart rather than sending bone-jarring vibrations back up my arms. Knowing when to shift my hands down the big 'Irish' spade's handle to get more leverage, and how to put a knee under a forearm to really get some heft.

We worked eight hours a day with an hour for lunch in a corrugated iron shed. For the first month I was so wrung out at six o'clock knocking-off time that I was asleep by seven. But then I 'got' labouring. I became far fitter than I'd even been, before or since, but more: I'd learnt how to handle the tools of the trade; I worked smarter and harder. Even today, decades later, people who understand labour see me use a shovel to dig out a blocked drain or mix cement and know I've done time on the sites. Less usual in the trade, I learnt not to start drinking on Saturday at midday when we knocked off and were handed our brown pay envelopes in the ganger's brother's pub down the road. There were men in their forties working on the site who'd have 'got out years ago' if only they weren't broke by Sunday night and back working with a hangover on Monday morning.

I imagine it wasn't very different back in the 1790s for the men building the canals as they developed their earth-shifting, rock-breaking, accurately measuring, ground-reading skills. The early waterways were built with local manpower, aided perhaps by a handful of fenmen who understood digging channels and water levels, or labourers who had experience of digging leets and flumes for mills, and miners who knew about tunnelling, shuttering and blasting. But very quickly, the growing number of canal projects created a need for experienced, dedicated workers to make 'the cuts'.

It was the age of the 'navigators' – or 'navvies' – the men who built the navigations. Strong, intelligent men found a full-time career. 'I've been a canal cutter upward of forty years,' claimed one such navvy, John Walker, interviewed in 1801. 'I worked upon the Duke of Bridgewater's Canal, and since have worked upon several.' Not all canal gangers and engineers wanted such experienced men. Some reckoned them too difficult to control, and liable to up and leave if they heard of better paying work. One early ganger boasted that he got the best work out of farm workers, though not young men, who he reckoned weren't hard enough for proper digging work.

Agricultural workers, used to hefting hand tools in all weathers, were often tempted onto canal workings as they passed within walking distance of their homes. Most then returned to farm work, but some were tempted to follow the waterways as they pushed on, for better wages, and this competition between farms and canals for manpower led to a 1793 motion in the House of Commons to ban canal digging at harvest times. It was defeated, with one MP arguing that hundreds of men came from Scotland and from Ireland 'for the purpose only of working on the canals and [who] know nothing of corn harvest'.

Popular history has the navvies as predominantly Irish, though records suggest they rarely accounted for more than ten percent of the workers – and most were English-speaking Ulster Catholics. Possibly the Irish bulk large in the narrative because they moved around and lodged in gangs, and earned a reputation for working and drinking hard. Though even that may have been something of a myth. Thomas Carlyle, writing in the 1840s about railway navvies, observed: 'The Irish are the best in point of behaviour. The postmaster tells me several of the poor Irish do regularly apply to him for money drafts, and send their earnings home. The English, who eat twice as much beef, consume the residue in whisky, and do not trouble the postmaster.'

There were other identifiable groups who moved around in mobs to work on the canals. Highland crofters and lowland

Victorian canal navvies, 1890s.

farmers were prepared to travel south of the border to work and, later, to build Scottish waterways. The money was welcome to subsistence farmers, though their hearts were at home. Gangers complained that the Scots might leave at any time, to fish, or for the potato harvest or peat cutting. Thomas Telford, who employed such men to build the Caledonian Canal, wrote in 1818 with some exasperation: 'The herring season has been most abundant, and the return of the fine weather will enable the indolent Highland creature to get their plentiful crops and have a glorious spell at the whisky-making.'

I think the Highlanders had their priorities right. They did what I would have done; headed south to work in the Scottish winter, when work and money and comfort was scarce, and then returned home for the summer days of whisky and herrings. But such happy-go-lucky, seasonal approaches to life didn't suit the new go-ahead age. What were needed for big canal-building projects, and for the mills and the potteries they serviced, were large amounts of men – and women – who worked set hours, six days a week, for fixed wages. Over the decades social ups and downs shrank and grew the amount of labour available: agricultural crashes, the Irish potato famine, troops disbanded after wars (and especially after Cardwell's 1870 army reforms recruited men into county regiments for six-year terms), and changes in the Poor Laws drove men to canal work, whilst jobs in the mills and factories and potteries lured them away.

Merely being in need of work didn't necessarily make one a professional navvy, though; there was a distinction between a labourer and a navvy. William Mylne, who worked as an engineer on waterways in the early nineteenth century, reckoned that it took a year to turn a labourer into a proficient navvy. Such a man was a mix of craftsman and strongman (on the building sites in Ireland I often heard the expression 'he's a horse of a man'), someone able to dig accurately to a fixed depth with minimum supervision. A navvy would know how to use the spoil to build up berms, and buttressing, and how to solidify the towpath for the coming heavy horse traffic. He would know different soils and how to pack and firm them to form the strongest banks, and to gauge the angles and dimensions needed to keep a channel from breaching outwards or collapsing inwards. Masons did the actual stonework for locks and wharfs, but navvies would set to facing earth banks with rocks. And those brainy engineers were continually coming up with novel ways of speeding up the processes with bucket cranes and hoists, windlasses turned by horses to pull barrows up inclines, tipping carts, and the like – all of which had to be mastered.

The memorial to the navvies' very real skills is that the canal system of today – bar the odd breached bank, and those waterways abandoned and let decay – is still much as it was built two centuries ago.

I arrived in Slaithwaite, a few stops south of Huddersfield, on an early evening train. Talking with the conductor as we arrived at the station, and then chatting as I picked up oat biscuits and a block of cheese in a Co-op, I pronounced Slaithwaite as 'Slaythweight'. Locals thought I was talking about some southern town, very possibly in the Cotswolds. They, it seemed, chewed the name down to 'Slow'at.' The first syllable rhymed with 'cow', a fellow drinker in the Little Bridge Wine Bar suggested, half an hour later, as I was having a couple of Platinum Blondes to fuel me through the evening's stroll and a night sleeping out.

I told my new pal that I was walking up to Standedge Tunnel. Again taking its spelling as a guide, I pronounced it 'Stand-edge'. He puzzled over this for a while as if solving an anagram. Then, triumphantly: 'Oh! Stun'ije! You're going up Stun'ije?' Like Slaithwaite, Standedge had a number of completely unnecessary letters lounging around in its middle, doing nothing useful.

I swung on my rucksack, shouldered my guitar and walked off through the town, along the canal. Edging into the country-side, the 'narrow' canal seemed almost model village in scale, its components compact and pocket-sized. There had been a sharp fall of rain whilst I'd been in the pub, and the locks and bridges and towpaths with their copings and arches, edgings and levels and cobbles were sleek and wet-gleaming. There were bridges, steps, blocks set into the end walls of the lock to climb between the beam platform, ridges to give horses grip, ramps up onto bridges and dark passages below them. When bridges and locks and towpaths abutted each other, there was an Escher-like complexity, a jumble of dimensions, as if following the wrong path down might bring me back up to where I'd started from. It was poetry in masonry. The North of England may have missed out on Brindley's practical way of spelling words the way they sounded, but it had benefited from his canal building.

As well as the navvies and labourers who were digging the canal cuts and lock chambers, and excavating reservoirs, there was work for masons, block cutters and quarrymen. Carpenters were needed for making lock gates, and boys to run between navvies and the forges with picks to be resharpened. Thousands of workers, of all ages and both sexes, worked across the country on tens of waterways at any one time (small beer, admittedly, compared to seventh-century China where it is recorded that there were five million men and women working on the Bian Qu extension to the Royal Canal). And the wealth that canals were creating really did trickle down in some Panglossian everything-for-the-best apology for rampant capitalism. The money when a canal was being built paid not just for the navvies but spread to the boarding houses, cooks, tailors, cobblers, brewers, cheesemakers, bakers, farmers, washerwomen and the rest who serviced their needs.

Lacking a boarding house I spent the night in a patch of mature woodland on a hill above the canal. I was very nearly suffocated by clouds of midges. Like the canal builders of yore, they too were go-getters, prepared to do overtime, with a rare tenacity and strength of spirit that despite the chill drizzle urged them on to renewed attacks on an earlobe, my hands, an ankle or any other exposed flesh. The onset of hard driving rain in the early hours finally beat them. I made a mental note to pack insect repellent and a more waterproof bivvy bag for future expeditions.

It was too wet and bleak the next morning to brew up coffee on my tin-can alcohol stove. So just after dawn I began walking towards Marsden. I began feeling a bit bleak myself, not so much from the weather, but from the solitary tramping. In several miles of walking I neither passed nor was passed by any boat. I realised, of course, that this might have something to do with my walking at the same speed as a moving craft. But it was not just that. There simply didn't seem to be any boats on this stretch of canal. I walked on.

The canalsides were thick with the segmented stalks of horsetail; sedge grass and ferns matted the banks and alders and hawthorns threw dark shadows. Canals can sometimes have a gloomy atmosphere. Perhaps it's the preternaturally still water, which can seem more sinister than a bubbling river or a raging sea. I found myself musing on their dark side – on canals' associations with crimes and corpses.

The murderers Burke and Hare, both from northern Ireland, first met whilst working as navvies on canals in Scotland in 1818. A decade later, when Hare was running a lodging house in Edinburgh, they began supplying no-questions-asked bodies for medical research. Others might have used the navvy's skills with shovel and pick to dig up freshly interred cadavers, but cemeteries were closely guarded and so Burke and Hare shortened the supply chain and began killing victims, first in the boarding house and then on the night-time streets of Edinburgh. It was thought that they had killed sixteen or seventeen people by the end of their career. They used suffocation as their chosen method of murder. It was easy, didn't damage or disfigure the body and allowed surgeons, anatomists and students to pretend innocence as to the provenance of the corpses.

The canals themselves were often killers. A knowledge of the many drownings – especially of children – when the waterways were a busy workplace are disquieting. Building canals claimed many lives from collapsed banks, flash floods, lock chambers caving in, underground explosions. And then there were the fights – over drink or gambling or women or money. One can easily deduce the effect that work-hardened men with money jingling in their pockets had on local girls, and speculate on how local lads might have resented this. Often Irish workers moving from job to job or caught alone or in small groups were 'hunted' – and fought back to avoid being beaten up by locals who accused them of taking their women or their jobs.

In an 1839 interview with the *Liverpool Mercury*, one navvy, Peter McDonough, complained that he had been defrauded of his wages for work on Ellesmere Port, and claimed that he had been told he was a 'fortunate kind of Irish animal because I was not driven from the place with sticks or stones'. He told the paper that he had witnessed a few Irishmen hunts, including one where 'a poor fellow who got employment and began work was attacked in a dreadful manner; he ran, and was pursued with stones, from which he received a severe cut on the head'.

As I approached Marsden, the climatic gloom – and my own – was lifting. The clouds were three-dimensional now, up in the sky. There were still sudden slashes of rain but they were being parried by flashes of sunlight breaking through from the east. My step was becoming jauntier. Lack of breakfast seemed the worst, indeed the only, problem in my life, and something that could be remedied by some brisk walking. The few last miles to town were measured out in pounds and locks, and in my freshly upbeat mood I saw the bright side of not being afloat. I strode past lock after lock unhindered, whilst to have locked a boat through each one might have cost me ten minutes or more apiece and turned my date with breakfast into a late lunch.

There was more to slow down a boat. Above one lock the water had drained almost out of the pound, exposing a shallow 'V' of mud and leaving only a narrow – less than a narrowboat's width, I thought – ribbon of water down the centre. Without the flesh of water I could see the exoskeleton of the cut. The stones of the bank, and the sloping mud sides. Workers would have puddled the bottom with clay. This was Brindley's invention, or at least his adoption of a technique used in dew ponds and other waterworks, for sealing the channels against water leakage. It was cheap, quick and lasted for decades or longer without maintenance. But it was more work. Tons of suitable clay had to be found, dug out, transported and shovelled into the canal cut. Then it had to be pounded down and compacted. Sometimes strings of horses or flocks of sheep would be brought in and milled around to tread down the clay, though usually it would be done by men working with heavy pugging sticks, beating the earth hard underfoot.

Seeing the almost empty canal made me marvel at how much work it would have taken to dig out the channel, throwing up the spoil to make the towpath and buttress the banks. And this was an easy stretch across regular ground, not built into the side of a hill, nor being excavated tens of feet deep through rock to create a chasm to keep the water level.

Workers in the 1950s 'puddling' a breached section of canal.

Where the waters were high the canal's surface was two-dimensional, like a reflective ribbon, with the sky replicated on the surface and the underwater world hidden as if behind a one-way mirror. But they had been built through three hard-won dimensions, cut out of the soil, the clay, the earth, the roots, the rocks and the stones of the land.

Marsden was spread out to one side of the canal. The place has given its name to the Marsdenian era – a 320-ish-million-year-old sub-stage of the Carboniferous period when strata of coal were laid down. Geology, the canal and industry had come together in the huge water-powered and steam-driven mills that spread out beside and below the towpath. Built in 1824, they were famed for turning out flawless woollen cloth and in their heyday, at the end of the nineteenth century, ran 680 looms. One supplied most of the British army uniforms in the First World War and remained in operation as late as 2003. Now the tall chimneys were cold. In its early years, local Luddites fearing the end of craftsmanship, and the rise of machines that the canals were integral in creating, had attacked the new shearing frames. Ironically, the same Marsden blacksmithing brothers, Enoch and James Taylor, had made the machines – each of which could do the work of ten hand finishers of cloth – and the Luddites' sledgehammers.

The coming of the industrial age and of consumerism had to navigate some choppy waters. After the relative simplicity of an agricultural economy, this new world was complicated: mills and canals competing for water, yet the mills needing the canals to bring coal and raw materials and carry off the finished products; the need for more labour pushing up wages yet leaving the jobless comparatively poorer; the money made by navvies and mill workers creating 'things' then being spent on buying 'things'. For many communities there was a triskele of legs running ever faster; more work, more money and more things. Canals were the key to everything. Coal became cheaper. Household goods like pottery became readily available and affordable to many. Josiah Wedgwood, a friend of the

Marsden Mill in its heyday.

young Brindley (he rented a workshop to the latter when he was establishing himself as an engineer), saw the benefits of not only being able to bring in coal and clay to make pottery, but just as much in being able to distribute the end product with far, far fewer breakages than on packhorse.

Staple foods, too, could be moved around, sometimes finding the highest bidder, sometimes filling a need. The idea of the self-sufficient local life was disappearing. Or perhaps 'local' had expanded to include a far wider geographical area. Industry could be included amongst the big forces – wars, weather, health, trading – that affected whole communities and ultimately whole nations and continents.

Escaping the drizzle, I dried out over breakfast, the rashers hanging over the edge of the plate for lack of space, a mug of coffee so full it was only stopped from overflowing by surface tension. I was noting how 'local' the full English was – some areas included black pudding, others beans. I'd become a fan of tinned tomatoes over the halved and fried 'natural' tomato. In the dark-stone streets, there was an ice-cream cafe called 'A Month of Sundaes'.

Marsden was also home to the Mikron Theatre, the first canal company, who since the early 1970s have been touring plays in their 1936-built Grand Union Carrying Company narrowboat, the *Tyseley*. Being midsummer they were away on tour. One of their first plays had been called *Puddle It – A Musical Story of the People Who Built the Canals*. I noted that they hadn't confined the story of the navvies to men. Apart from the ancillary jobs filled by women, many actually laboured on the early canals. Burke and Hare's landlady, and later Hare's wife, reputedly spent time as a ganger on the Union Canal.

The entrance to Standedge Tunnel lay only a mile up from Marsden, a cluster of hundred-year-old, refurbished buildings nestling under a steep wooded slope which was broken by the canal waters running into a semi-circle of darkness. I sat outside the cafe in what had once been the Canal End Cottages, accommodating tunnel maintenance men. In the early 1800s the building of the canal and its tunnel, and then keeping it running, had created a permanent community here. The canal had been completed in 1799, all except for the Tunnel, which took a further thirteen years to finish.

Whilst the navvies and miners (the workforce swollen by men used to working underground) laboured in the depths, cargoes brought up the canal to the tunnel entrance were trans-shipped at a large warehouse (now the visitor centre) and onto

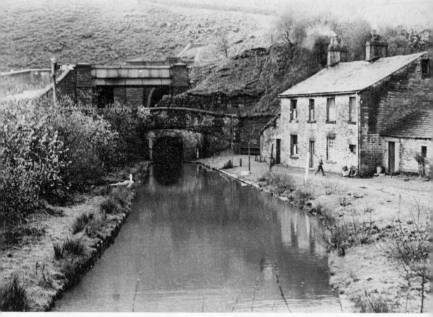

Canal End Cottages and the entrance to the Marsden Tunnel in the 1950s. The tunnels above the canal are for the railway.

packhorses to be carried up and over the Pennines to the other side, where they were reloaded onto boats.

Outram had been far too confident about the ease of boring three and a quarter miles through rock. In his defence, predicting what might lie underground was only accurate as far as instinct, surface strata and test borings allowed. Geology was a new science. William 'Strata' Smith's geological map of the country, showing the different kinds of rock in a beautiful marbling of sandstones, granites, gneisses and so on, wouldn't be published till 1815. Smith had worked as surveyor, with two other titans of the canal age, John Rennie and William Jessop, on the Somerset Coal Canal, gaining his first ideas on geology from observing the strata of rock that the cutting exposed. Smith noted that mineshafts and the deep cuts through hillsides for locks exposed layers of rock – and in the same relative order, however angled, shattered or twisted. He realised you could identify which strata contained particular minerals and types of stone, and that a seam of coal, say, that was at ground level at one location would run on and, if slanting, would still exist many miles away hundreds or even thousands of feet deep. His map would make fortunes in mining and save months or even years for canal builders. But the Standedge navvies were tunnelling into the unknown and were constantly threatened by what they might find in the depths of the mountainside. Groundwater flowing between hard and soft strata could pour out as an engulfing flood. Soft rock might irrupt as cave-ins and subsidence. Blasted rocks could create sinkholes.

Trudging up from Marsden, I'd found myself musing on which would have been the least hellish alternative – working in the dark Satanic mills or labouring in rain, snow, sun and wind on the canals? I concluded that I'd have fared better as a navvy, but I was doubtless overestimating my own toughness and willingness to be broken-bodied by the time I'd reached my forties. But tunnelling – navvying in the dark – was the absolute worst of both indoor and outdoor worlds rolled into one dangerous, noisy, asphyxiating Hades of an occupation.

Outram resigned from the Huddersfield, due to ill health, and in 1807, after some years of struggles by interim engineers, a new consulting engineer was commissioned to drive the Huddersfield Narrow on. Thomas Telford was at the height of his powers. As much of a successful inventor, problem-solver and ambitious thinker as Brindley, and with a meticulous eye for detail and head for planning, Telford had already engineered the Ellesmere Canal and designed the revolutionary Pontcysyllte Aqueduct that carried boats high above the River Dee. His work also included roads and bridges (rebuilding London Bridge was one consultancy, the Menai Suspension Bridge another almost visionary creation), and his refinement of Tarmacadam for surfacing highways earned him the nickname 'the Colossus of Roads'.

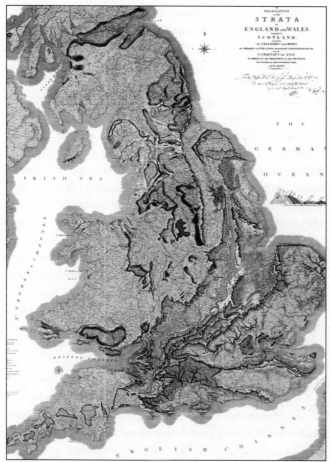

A Delineation of the Strata of England and Wales with Part of Scotland:
the first geological map of Britain, published by William Smith in 1815.
It was, literally, groundbreaking: a key that could lead to immense
wealth. Though not, alas, for Smith. Plagiarism of his map and his own
sloppy book keeping and over optimistic business speculation had him
in debtors' prison at the age of fifty, though he was rehabilitated late
in life and given a pension. His observations went further than geology,
too. Smith's discovery of fossils contained in certain, deep strata
showed that life had begun in very different forms to the prevailing
beliefs, giving Charles Darwin material on which to build his theory of
evolution. The building of canals had advanced science.

At Standedge, Telford came up with a plan to finish the tunnel in as short a time as possible and for the least addition to its already inflated budget. He discovered that the two ends already started on were at different heights and running on different axes. The necessary adjustments, and a kink in the tunnel's course, sorted that out. It is said that Telford's original plan proved correct down to the last bucketful of waste material.

Telford did, though, cut costs and tunnelling time by cancelling the towpath that would have run beside the waters underground, ensuring that until the invention of engines all boats would have to be 'legged' through, pushed along by men lying on their backs and 'walking' along the tunnel's uneven roof, whilst the horses were led over the top. Standedge may have been – and remains – the longest, the highest and the deepest tunnel on the whole waterways system, but with only four passing places in its depths, and every boat legged through, it was a bottleneck that both reduced numbers of boats and slowed them down. It was one of the least successful canals commercially – and one of the most expensive. The tunnel alone cost £160,000, an astronomical sum for the time.

If I hadn't spent so long in Marsden walking the streets looking for a cafe, then lingered over breakfast reading a book on local history and generally waiting for the rain to stop, I might finally have got a lift on a boat. Or so I was told by one of the two Canal & River Trust workmen in high-vis orange work clothes, opening their lunchboxes – polystyrene takeaway cartons and insulated coffee mugs – in weak sunshine outside the cafe. Three boats had gone through the tunnel earlier that morning, they said. 'There was one couple who were very nice – they'd have probably liked some company in the dark.'

That had been my only chance. Because of the length of the tunnel, and to avoid the buildup of fumes from engines, only three boats in either direction were allowed through every second day. The next boats going this way would be in forty-eight hours' time. The two men worked on the canal's maintenance, and were happy to sit in the sun and talk of how the 'Everest of Canals' had a brief heyday. From its opening in 1811 until 1840, it was used by forty boats a day. But railway routes led to a swift decline and the last commercial trip through the tunnel was in 1921.

The canal was officially closed in 1943, but after the war a few boats – and once a whole flotilla of unlikely craft – inched their way through, piloted by canal enthusiasts keen to assess the waterways for leisure. By then unmaintained, the tunnel provided an assault course of low water levels, rockfalls, subsidence and cave-ins. One boat got seriously stuck and the Standedge Tunnel might have formed its sepulchre but for offloading ballast, pulling with other boats and pushing with poles. The tunnel was seen as both too tempting and dangerous for future self-styled Indiana Joneses to explore, and in the 1960s both its mouths were barred.

But for canal restorers the Huddersfield Narrow was always going to be an attractive challenge, and despite decades of dereliction (one account described water rushing through the gateless locks in 'cascades'), volunteers with little mechanical help, recalling the manual skills of the navvies who built the canal, pulled off what was dubbed the 'impossible restoration' and brought canal and tunnel back into service in 2001. Sixty-nine locks were restored, five new locks added, twelve new bridges constructed, and two new short tunnels put in under buildings that had been built across the canal.

When the tunnel was first reopened, cruising boats were linked together, like a string of sausages, and pulled through by an electric tug. Owners objected to the inevitable scrapes, bumps and dents this caused in their boats, and in 2009 policy was changed and leisure boaters were allowed to drive their own craft through using their own engines. Tunnel rules stated that all pets were tied or caged below, that crew who couldn't

A Standedge Tunnel gateway commemorating the 'leggers'.

negotiate steps and ladders and slippery tunnels in the event of a breakdown in the darkness were sent ahead by taxi, and a compulsory tunnel 'chaperone' accompanied each boat to offer 'navigational advice'. (I imagined something along the lines of 'You want to keep going straight through till you see light ahead, and then keep going a bit more,' would cover that).

The biggest risk in a tunnel of the Standedge's length was a buildup of engine fumes in the confined space. In the days after legging, when commercial boats nose-to-tailed through the Standedge, there are accounts of people rendered unconscious by the fumes. The atmosphere was made even more noxious by the steam trains pounding through the parallel passages, smoke and steam rolling through the cross chambers. A modern limit of eighteen boats a week – nine in either direction, three one way, three the other on Mondays, Wednesdays and Fridays – had lost me the chance to hitch through the tunnel.

'There'll be a few boats coming up from the Diggle side later today, then nothing either way tomorrow, so your next chance for a trip through the tunnel is the morning after tomorrow,' the maintenance man told me. If it was a weekend (it wasn't), then there might have been one of the centre's electric tourist boats going through, but today's trips only went a short distance and then back out again. I was going to have to walk over the top.

Still, walking over the Pennines to the other end of the tunnel at Diggle was a part of canal history, too, the CRT men assured me. Back in the days of horse-drawn boats, the narrowboats would be legged off into the darkness and the animals would be led high up over the Pennines by a spare man or two. The horses would be accompanied by the Traffic Regulator.

The CRT engineer told me that the first Traffic Regulator, appointed when the tunnel finally opened in 1811, had started in the job at the age of twelve and continued without a day off, except for Christmas, for the following thirty-seven years. Thomas Bourne – the 'Standedge Admiral' as he became known – was the son of the first Tunnel Superintendent, who had in turn started work on the tunnel as a miner. To avoid jams in the narrow tunnel, he oversaw an alternating one-way system. Boats were sent off from one end in a group to leg their way through. As they emerged from the other mouth several hours later, boats from that end would then enter and make their way through. The Traffic Regulator walked or rode from end of the tunnel to the other locking a chain behind the last boat going through. And then he would travel back to open the chain at the other end, count the boats out, let more boats in to go the other way, and so on throughout the day. 'He did that four times a day. Every day. For thirty-seven years. Never a day off.'

It was around four miles over the moors from one end of the tunnel to the other. By my calculations that was thirty-two miles a day. Had Thomas really done more than 300,000 miles in all weathers over the moors in his working life? Probably not – bad weather and frozen waters would have stopped traffic for weeks in hard winters. But one informed reckoning has put the figure at a very precise 215,812 miles walked in his capacity as the Standedge Admiral.

The Admiral's job was made redundant when a new policy was instituted – a Victorian automation – with the last boat through being handed a certificate of passage and a red light, which was handed over to the last boat of the flotilla coming through from the other direction. Thomas lived only a few more years after his enforced retirement and was dead at the age of fifty-two.

The Standedge Tunnel – as far as I got.

The CRT engineer was explaining the old boater's scam of covering up high-toll cargoes, like coal or grain, with manure or other low-toll materials when his phone rang. He listened, nodding, then, 'Right, we'll be there.' He rang off. 'C'mon,' he looked at his offsider. 'Sounds like a breach or some problem on one of the pounds.' It was my turn to contribute. 'That might be just below Marsden,' I chipped in. 'The water was very low there a few hours ago.' They looked anxious. On the slow waters of the canal a breach is about as big as dramas get. A burst bank, a broken lock gate – if it gets out of control – can cause catastrophic flooding and real danger to communities below the canal. At the least, lack of water can close a canal. In the case of Standedge a drop in the water level could lead to boats grounding far into the mountainside, and within a few hours three boats would be starting through from the Diggle end. They set off.

I walked off in the opposite direction, following the horse's trail up onto the moors. It was steep climbing. And strange to leave the canyons and corridors and level pounds of the canals and climb up into space and winds and rolling lands. It was poorly signposted, as those of us who get lost like to say.

I got lost. A shepherd, a dog whistle on a cord round his neck, a spaniel darting at my ankles, gave the clear directions of a man who knows gorse bushes, tracks, rocks and streams as others know a city's streets. I kept climbing, bowing around a wide shoulder of yellowed upland. The clouds were high now, and had lumped together into thick cumuli leaving a wide stretch of blue for the sun to cross. It was hot. Sweat ran down into my eyes. The guitar was an ungainly package to carry. And I was tramping hard uphill. The tunnel had entered the hillside at 643 feet above sea level and the top of the moor was the same height again above the tunnel. Along its course shafts had been sunk so that horse-powered cranes and windlasses could raise huge buckets to clear the waste from the works below. There were still heaps of spoil, like tumuli, covered in heather and bracken.

Building the canal tunnel had been such a costly, time-consuming, difficult affair that it was strange to think that far below there now ran four tunnels. In 1848, and again in 1871, and once more in 1894, railway tunnels had been driven through, parallel to (but higher) than the canal's underground corridor, and joined to it by cross-chambers – adits – so that the spoil dug out for the railway passages could be shipped out in boats. The youngest passage still carried trains; I'd heard and seen them rushing past from Slaithwaite and Marsden and up to Tunnel Mouth, where I'd met the CRT engineers, and then throwing themselves at the mountain side where the railway lines and the canal's route crossed each other. One of the older railway tunnels had been adapted for vehicles so that ambulances, fire engines or other services could get through to even the deepest sections. That presumably was the route, reached by ladders and clambering and underground walking, that boaters had to be able to negotiate if their boat got stuck or broke down.

The roads and tracks over the Pennines were nearly as great feats of engineering as the canals below. The Romans had laid early roads to march troops and supplies across. Then had come ad hoc trails for lines of medieval pack ponies, then a coaching road was built and, later on, tracks for the horses that carried the canal cargoes over the unfinished tunnel's course. Those same tracks were finally used by the boat horses when the boats were legged through the tunnel.

There was a joy in climbing higher and higher, being buffeted by fresh wind, sun-baked then splash-soaked in a shower and being breeze-dried again. Down in the valleys loomed the dark mill towns. Up here I could understand why the millworkers and miners had been such enthusiasts for spending their few free days on the moors – ferreting, courting, poaching and, later, rambling. The navvies, who'd been out in the weather all their working days, were, I supposed, keener to cluster in a pub or one of the common-room huts that canal companies provided in their camps.

It was a different world up high. Ahead I could see the silhouette of a woman fell-running up a steep slope, appearing and disappearing with the fall and rise of the land. I plodded on heavily. A rough wooden sign to Hades Farm pointed off up a track (I had found my way onto an unpaved farm road). I wondered at the name – descriptive, humorous, a past family of hellfire-preaching Methodists? Far below there were flat pewtery reservoirs in the valleys. Far far below, the manicured links of a golf course. Then, climbing higher and bending around a rise there was only moorland, for the full 360 degrees. I'd been given a leaflet by the tunnel information centre which described – in broad brushstrokes – the walking route. It seemed that quite a few modern leisure boat crews split up, with the troglodytes taking the boat through and the claustrophobes heading into the hills. A raven swept overhead, grunting and cronking. On a lower stratum of air a kestrel rode the breeze. Off to one side there was a large reservoir with a flotilla of beached sailing dinghies. It made sense to put a sailing club where there was no lack of wind.

Coming up from a dip onto a long straight I met a woman with three greyhounds cantering in wide circles around her. 'They love it up here ... no traffic ... and they can run and run; I love it up here too, because I have it all to myself.' She paused as it sank in that she had met me, and waved her arm to encompass the space around us, generously giving me a share in the Pennines. This had been the Roman road, she confirmed, but had been rebuilt as the coach road by Blind Jack in the late 1700s. Intrigued, I pressed her for detail, but her knowledge beyond the name was hazy.

Only later did I learn that 'Blind Jack' Metcalf lived a lifetime of dogged achievement eclipsing even the persistence and abilities of the canal engineers. Blinded by smallpox as a six-year-old boy, he had started life as bar-room fiddler in 1770s Harrogate. After walking to London and back, alone, doing a bit of horse dealing and gambling, and navigating a complicated love life that included illegitimate and legitimate children, he began to trade as a carrier, using horses, carriages and carts to move stones, fish and people across the moors. To add spice to his life, he often took the reins of his passenger coach. In an unexplained career change he took up road building in Scotland with the military, becoming an expert on moving heavy guns across boggy ground. And then he started building roads across the Pennines.

The track I was walking was apparently one of the routes that Blind Jack had intuited, using his heightened senses, crossing bogs with a foundation of wood, brush and stones, and feeling out the best and driest route around the high ground's contours. He retired when the growing numbers of canals opening up at the end of the seventeenth century began to compete with his road-building projects. The water roads made land roads – unreliable, often impassable in bad weather – seem old-fashioned.

I decided to stay up on the fells for the night. I'd crossed the watershed, and as dusk began to fall I found a tiny quarry, cut into the hillside like a balcony. There was a tumble of rocks and amongst them a patch of flat turf just big enough to take my bivvy bag. I lit my stove in a sheltered recess, like a stone cupboard, and set water to heat for packet soup. I hadn't planned on sleeping out here, rather had imagined myself with a pub supper before a night spent in a wood or along the towpath, so my supplies were basic. A few oat biscuits, cream of chicken soup, a block of cheese, and coffee. It was cold, and so I half got into my sleeping bag, propping myself up against a perfectly angled rock as a backrest. I could hear the wind sifting through the gorse above the quarry lip. There was a sudden rattle of chain on gear, and scriffle of gravel as two mountain bikers racing the dusk plummeted down the track a few hundred feet below me. I watched them swoop down, bucking and clattering across the rough stones of the packhorse road, to a cluster of

'Blind Jack' Metcalf, the Pennine road builder.

small houses, and then – the map told me – lanes, roads, Diggle, Saddleworth, and pubs.

There was the bleating of sheep. Several had grazed their way up the slope to the quarry forecourt, black-faced with a white streak under their eyes like cartoon tears. Just before dark, there was a sudden dart of movement across my peripheral vision. A scurrying in the air as a little owl pitched up on a rock – bobbing like a tiny skittle that wasn't quite going to fall. It gave a sharp little bark and scudded across the room-sized quarry, flying back and forth and yipping in the last of the light, before falling silent. Into the night I watched as darkness filled the airy chamber of sky. There was a glow of reflected light from Manchester, on the fair horizon. A brisk morning's walk from where I lay. Or a more circuitous boat trip from where the Huddersfield Narrow exited at Diggle.

Not surprisingly, I had ended up walking the towpath from Slaithwaite. There had been no boats to hitch. No chance to become a 'hobbler'. Not that hobbling was ever a career choice. It was, a canal expert told me later, the last resort of old navvies, broken-bodied, but still wedded to the waterways. And, in today's canal world, I had overlooked one thing in my hopes of getting a lift on someone's boat, if there had been any. I should have remembered from travelling with Kate, and from the tens of moored craft I'd passed, that a boat is more a home than a form of transport. Rather than sticking my thumb out and hopping into the passenger seat of an aquatic truck, I had been intending to knock on someone's front door and trusting they'd invite me in.

I lay back in my own home for the night – the dark tumble of rocks under the stars – and fell asleep.

5

Horse Power

WALKING BLIND JACK'S TRACK over the Pennines set me thinking about droving – and whether I'd have enjoyed being a drover. It was hard, uncomfortable and dangerous work, but drovers appeared a swashbuckling lot, with new horizons each day and evenings of high spending, drinking, feasting and flirting in remote taverns and hill-farm stopping houses. It would surely have been a better lot in life than labouring in fields, digging down a mine, or indeed building a canal. And at the zenith of their trade, in the seventeenth and early eighteenth centuries, drovers were an important part of Britain's economy, transporting high-value goods – china, wool, cloth, gunpowder, salt and metals.

The classic drover image is of a packhorse train wending its way over hilly country. A line of twenty or so ponies, each with a pair of panniers slung across their backs, trot over a stony track. The animals have wooden bows hung with jingling bells arching over their necks and accompanying them are mounted drovers dressed like Spanish *hidalgos*, wearing heavy cloaks, high boots and wide-brimmed hats decorated with plumes.

They ride spirited, high-stepping horses. And one just knows there are rapiers and flintlock pistols under their capes.

Packhorses, however, had severe limitations. They couldn't carry much weight, fragile goods were likely to get broken, or damaged by weather, and they were easy prey for bandits. Which meant costs were high, and for heavy, bulky goods like coal or grain, hugely so in relation to their final value. Pack trains worked best when Britain's major economic commodity was wool. Fleeces and cloth were relatively light, unbreakable and weatherproof – and valuable enough to make the cost of transport between far-flung flocks, spinners and weavers, city markets and shipping ports worthwhile. Ten or so animals could carry a ton of goods, and under the guidance of experienced drovers they moved fast and could get virtually anywhere. Horses and ponies were

The romantic image of droving – a caravan of packhorses crosses the Pennines in the early 1600s.

even relatively efficient for moving the small amounts of coal, iron ore, limestone and other elements needed for the fledgeling industries of the early eighteenth century, especially when old tracks and ways were improved and better roads built to allow the use of horse-drawn carts. But the amounts of heavy goods that could be carried were still small, and in bad weather (much of the year in mountainous or rough country where most of the coal, stone and ores were mined and quarried) wheeled transport and even packhorses could be held up for days or weeks.

If the transport of coal and other bulk goods had remained reliant on packhorses and carts, the Industrial Revolution would have been highly constrained. Canals changed that decisively as they repurposed horses – and ponies, mules and donkeys – into a far more efficient unit of power, working in harmony with the almost friction-free tracks of the water machine. A single horse could pull some twenty to twenty-five tons of coal loaded into one of the improved 'starvationers' of the Bridgewater Canal – some forty to fifty times as much weight as it could haul in a cart on a reasonable road surface. If there was an equivalent development in modern road surfaces, your car would be able to do around 1,200 miles to the gallon. That's the distance from London to Naples. On a *single gallon* of petrol.

There were transport boats, of course, before canals. But river transport was no more reliable than tracks, as waters varied through the seasons and were prone to droughts and floods, as well as rapids and currents. The boats used for river transport varied in shape and size to suit local conditions, from small punts through to large sailing boats, and often had to sacrifice efficiency for seaworthiness. Canals by their nature were calm, uniform and shallow – water roads that could be built to exact specifications, and so could carry the biggest cargoes for the minimal amount of boat, year-round, in safety.

With the building of dedicated canals, Brindley and other engineers experimented with lock sizes, and the dimensions of 'narrow' canals that would use the least water for the greatest efficiency. Looking at the dimensions of Britain's early canals, you realise that the starting unit of measurement – the canal's Golden Mean that dictated everything from the size of the boats to the dimensions of the locks and depth of the canals – was extrapolated from the work a single horse could do in a day. And the weight that a horse could pull efficiently in a boat was about twenty tons. So the length-to-width ratio of the proto-narrowboat was streamlined with rigorous efficiency, and canals likewise. There was only one flaw, which was that Britain's early canals did not have a uniform standard and the length and width of the locks and breadth and depth of a canal varied. Sometimes it was just a matter of a foot or two in length, or a few inches in width, in a lock. But it was enough to cause problems later, when boats built for one waterway wouldn't quite fit the lock widths or lengths of another.

The incredible return on horse power worked only on the still waters of canals, and – crucially – only those with well-made, dedicated towpaths. Horses had been used before the age of the canals to tow vessels against the currents of rivers, but not over great distances. The hedges, fences, trees, floods, shallows and incoming streams along the banks of most natural waterways meant it was impossible for a horse to get far along a riverbank, even in summer, let alone keep a tow rope clear of obstructions. The poet Robert Southey, in a letter written in 1815 from Namur (in modern Belgium), reported seeing 'a horse in the middle of the river, towing a vessel against the stream', whilst a second horse was kept on the vessel to take over when the first was exhausted.

To cope with the varied challenges of natural waterways, early inland cargo boats were as often sailed, let drift on currents, or poled along like a punt. Frequently boats were 'bow-hauled' by teams of men – a hard, slow task. It took seven or more men to pull as much weight as a draught horse, but they had the edge over animal power in that, where the bank of a river was over-grown or flooded, they could clamber over hedges and fences and pass the rope around trees and over shrubs.

A well-surfaced towpath, with cleared banks along a canal's side, transformed horses into efficient units of pulling power. Indeed, the historic word for machines originally driven by horses – such as mills and threshers, or the lifting windlasses used in mining, tunnelling and excavating canals – was 'horse gins', or 'horse engines'. And it could be argued that, along with locks, and an independence of rivers, it is a towpath that defines a canal.

The importance of a dedicated towpath for horses to pull from might have passed me by if I hadn't been invited to White House Farm in Suffolk for its Alde Valley Spring Festival. I planned to spend the time writing and researching, but it seemed unlikely that in the flat agricultural lands of East Anglia, far from any coal mines or mills, I'd find any local canal culture to study. I couldn't have been more wrong. Though detached from the main network of British canals, East Anglia had waterway traditions a-plenty.

The East Anglians, it turned out, had embarked on their own agricultural revolution, predating Britain's Industrial Revolution by several decades and then kept pace with its developments. It was a revolution that improved crop yields, breeds and variet-ies of stock animals and staple plant foods, and invented ever more efficient horse-drawn ploughs, reapers, binders and other machinery. All of which were essential to produce the huge amounts of cheap, reliable food essential for workers newly deployed in industry and crowded into cities.

Prosperous farming meant that East Anglia's land and labour were differently allocated compared to the rugged and far less fertile coal country, where the main canal network was constructed. Where manpower and horsepower were already employed to the full in tilling, reaping, harrowing, ploughing and harvesting, it made no economic sense to set men to dig canals through valuable growing land. But as I explored Suffolk I realised that over the centuries a lot of canal technology had been trialled on the region's navigations. Indeed, most farms were served by water routes, and the Anglian waterways struggled with the problems of inland boat transport before the emergence of canals.

No river illustrates this history better than East Anglia's Stour, where we have the good fortune of a series of near-photographic records of the river and its locks, painted by John Constable in the early nineteenth century. Britain's greatest landscape painter, Constable was the son of a Stour mill owner and waterways commissioner and illustrated in great detail, and from close observation and knowledge, its rural and river life.

The Stour was one of England's earlier canalised waterways, brought into serious transport use during the reign of Queen Anne in the early 1700s, when, as at Exeter 150 years before, its weirs and flash locks were bypassed by short channels with pound locks. Its importance as a navigation was for transporting food to the rapidly expanding markets of London. Farms along the river sent wheat, flour, peas, barley, oats, malt and bran down to the estuary port at Mistley, where the cargo was transferred to Thames barges and Spritsail barges to be sailed down the coast. And goods were similarly carried back upriver to the prosperous farms and market towns. A 1750 document lists the rates levied on commodities carried though Sudbury, including oil, pitch, vinegar, rosin, paper, glass, osiers, grindstones and sugar. Coal, mainly for domestic use, also spread inland from the ports, via the river. And immense amounts of manure, from both horses and humans, was carried out of London daily, to be spread on the Anglian fields.

As an early 'improved' waterway, and one with good farmland on either side, the Stour, however, lacked one important aspect of canals – a dedicated towpath. Access to land along the river

The Stour's unique lintel locks at Flatford Lock. The lintels stabilise the locks, preventing the weight of the gates from collapsing the lock in the absence of balance bars. Originally there was no towpath.

had been overlooked in the 1705 act granting navigation rights. This meant that, while the river became ever more practical for transport, as locks, weirs, staunches and wharfs were built, there were major problems in pulling the boats. Stour tow-horses had to jump fences that came down to the water's edge – some 123 of them along the twenty-five-mile length of the river. And worse than that, the towpath changed from one bank to the other thirty-three times, with only sixteen bridges, meaning that for the other crossings horses had to be coaxed onto the deck of a boat and poled across the river. Often it was easier to bow-haul the boats with men, though crews had to be prepared to punt the

Detail from Constable's *The White Horse* (1819), showing a barge horse being ferried across the Stour, and *The Leaping Horse* (1825), in which a rider urges a barge horse to jump over a barrier on the towpath.

boats, ride the current (always dangerous) and hoist crude sails to take advantage of any favourable winds.

It was a world, depicted in Constable's paintings, that seems closer to the medieval life of a Brueghel painting than to the slick, uniform canals being built across the rest of the British Isles. The finest of Constable's paintings of the Stour's working life is a series known as the 'six-footers' – big expansive landscapes in which he catches with almost uncanny precision the interface between land, water and sky. *The Hay Wain* is the most famous of the series but for anyone interested in the history of the waterways it is two other paintings – *The White Horse* and *The Leaping Horse* – that are most compelling.

The White Horse is interesting in terms of water transport as it shows, at a glance, the difficulties of the inadequate towpaths, with a horse needing to be transported from one side of the Stour to the other. A trio of boatmen work together, poling off the bank, while the horse gets a brief rest from its labours standing on the foredeck of the barge (and on the Stour there were 'barges,' beamier and heavier than narrowboats and more reminiscent of Dutch *tjalks*).

Even more curious barge-pulling practices are shown in *The Leaping Horse*, which centres on a young man jumping a bay horse over one of the many stiles, fences and hedges beside the Stour, with another figure leaning over the sluice gate beside him, apparently handling the tow rope across it. The detail of this fascinated me – the two-man team, and the fact that the swingletree (the heavy wood and iron bar that connects the horse's traces to the tow rope) is attached by such long ropes that it's lying on the ground rather than hitched up close to the horse's haunches.

Constable, the normally meticulous draughtsman, had, it seemed, sacrificed accuracy for artistic drama and composition. Attached to the trailing lump of wood, as depicted, there is no way that a horse could have jumped safely over fences. Not even once, let alone the tens of times required along the length of the river. And Constable's painting *The White Horse* shows clearly how the swingletree should have been, held up by straps close against its hindquarters, clear of the ground and the horse's legs.

As to the rider, Constable's own notebooks and large sketches for the finished picture bear out his uncertainty over what to portray. Some show the horse jumping riderless, others with the boy aboard, as in the final painting. On canals with proper towpaths a working boat horse was never ridden. But the Stour, with its numerous obstacles for horses, was an anomaly and a rider was often needed to urge the horse over the fences. This was a disadvantage – having to jump and also carry a rider tired horses out quickly. One carrying company, Allens of Sudbury, made it a rule to employ boys or very light young men to make the horse's task a little easier; other carriers outlawed riding horses altogether.

Constable's *Boat-Building on the Stour* (1814–15). The boatbuilder is using a dry dock, which could be flooded once the boat – a traditional Stour Lighter – was completed.

And, in a nod towards equine welfare, a local worthy petitioned to have stiles and hedges along the towpaths reduced to under three feet – high enough to keep in stock but less onerous on the leaping horses. Then, finally, the navigation's committee, the Undertakers, did away with the stile-jumps and put in double gates.

One of the great pleasures of walking along the Stour is that the landscape has barely changed in the two hundred years since Constable painted it. You can still pick out locations featured on his canvases and in sketches. I went in search of them after talking at the festival with Otis Luxton, an instrument maker and woodworker who had worked on a project to restore the remains of a Stour Lighter – the river's traditional craft. He pointed out the shipwrighting detail in another Constable painting, *Boat-Building on the Stour* – a scene replete with adzes, boiling pitch for caulking, hanks of tow and hammers. Otis recognised the different tools and went on to tell me how the lighters were often worked in pairs, steered in a unique way. Both boats were close coupled, with the bow of the hindmost boat almost up against the stern of the front boat. A massive 'tiller' – more a long heavy pole – fixed to the aft boat ran forward to a steerer amidships on the front boat. By pushing the pole one way or the other, the whole of the back boat was turned into a massive rudder, giving exceptional manoeuvrability as both boats articulated around tight bends in fast-flowing waters.

The Constable scenes of water transport powered by horses came to life in my imagination as I walked along the Stour. But, for an understanding of how horses once worked on Britain's waterways, I'd learnt most from a day on the Grand Western Canal, at Tiverton in Devon, where the Brind family have run a traditional horse-drawn passenger boat since the early 1970s.

The Grand Western Canal was conceived as one of a series of linked waterways that would join Exeter to the Bristol Channel and so to the port of Bristol and the network of inland waterways, allowing cargoes to avoid having to travel around Land's End. Indeed, if things had worked out, Exeter would have been connected to London via the Kennet and Avon. A route was originally surveyed by James Brindley in 1796 but it was another project that he failed to live long enough to see finished – or, in this case, started. His ambitious route was never, in fact, completed but stretches of canal were opened linking Tiverton and Taunton to the River Parrett and thence to Bristol, and local quarries kept these busy through the nineteenth century, supplying stone for building and for lime kilns. When the quarry trade died down, the spring-fed waters of the Grand Western were used for a time to grow water lilies that were harvested and sent to London to dress Victorian funerals. After that trade, too, collapsed, the canal at Tiverton was abandoned, until it was revived in 1971 as part of a country park.

Engined boats were initially banned from the restored Tiverton Canal, but permission was granted for a horse-drawn passenger boat, the *Tivertonian*. This was both practical and an attraction in itself, as well as reviving the almost forgotten traditions and skills of horse-boating.

My first visit had been a few years before, on a commission for a horse magazine. It was a perfect summer day and I arrived at the canal's basin above the town just as the horseman, David Poxon, was leading Dandy, a large 'red roan' Clydesdale round from the stables. At 16.1 hands (there's four inches, the width of a man's palm, to a 'hand'), Dandy had the steady pace and 'saving my energy' attitude of a mature working horse. He was also well used to being patted and photographed by the *Tivertonian*'s passengers, who were being boarded for the two-and-a half-hour round trip up the canal.

As the boat was readied I talked with Phil Brind, dressed like Dave in traditional horse-boater's clothing – waistcoat, heavy leather belt, high-waisted trousers and braces, stout boots, Daz-white shirt, bowler hat and jaunty red neckerchief, all worn as much for comfort and practicality as for show. His knowledge had been gleaned from research, talking with old working horsemen and from his own experience.

'Everyone has the idea that in the old days canal horses were big shire horses,' he told me. 'But they were just as often smaller cobs, or mules, and quite a few boats were pulled by a pair of donkeys.' Like everything to do with canals, it came down to efficiency and saving money. Where cargoes, distances and other factors allowed smaller animals to be used, it meant that all the infrastructure could be scaled down. A canal might have tens of bridges along its length, so if the arch over the canal and over the towpath could be built a hand or two lower, there'd be a saving in maybe a thousand bricks on each bridge. And, for the carrier company, there was no point in fuelling a big, heavy horse if a lighter animal could do the same job for less feed. Indeed, on some canals there were particularly favoured animals referred to as 'half-legged horses', strong and powerful but on shorter than usual legs.

Phil pointed out that there was a considerable difference between the work done by a carthorse and a boat horse. A laden boat starts off as an immense dead weight, anchored to the spot by inertia, but once it is moving it takes relatively little effort to keep it going. As if on cue, with all the passengers aboard, Dave was hitching the tow rope to the swingletree (held up close against Dandy's hindquarters, I noted, not trailing behind on the ground as Constable had portrayed) and preparing to move off. I went over to join them on the towpath and watch Dandy's technique for getting the seventeen-odd tons of laden boat moving. Rather than lunging into his collar, as he might have done if pulling a carriage or a plough, he leant his weight against that of the boat, then shuffled forward to get momentum, accelerating slowly and smoothly up to walking speed. At that point the water had reduced nearly all friction and there was little work for him to do beyond walking and keeping a bit of pressure on the tow rope. It was a pretty neat demonstration of Newton's first law of motion. And it was the reason why boat

115

horses could work far longer hours than coach or plough horses, whilst doing less actual 'work'.

But, just as boats are hard to get started, Newton's law ensures that their immense laden weight is difficult to stop. Coming into locks, approaching wharfs, passing other boats – all took planning and experience to do safely. Ropes would have to be dropped over strapping posts by the crew and used to brake the moving boats, or the horse eased up well before bridges and locks so that a boat slowed in time. In the days of horse barges, getting things wrong could be disastrous. When we'd been talking, Phil had pointed out a ramp cut back into the opposite canal bank. Here, in the basin where boats had to be halted or turned, the chance of a horse being pulled into the water had been high, and the ramp was needed to get them out safely. Out on the cut, a horse that slipped or was pulled into the canal might have been drowned, or have to wade through the water for miles before finding a spot that allowed it to scramble back onto dry land.

An interview with one of the last working boatmen, recorded for a BBC 1969 oral history LP, recounted just such an accident. The boatman told of his horse being pulled into a canal, in December, and getting bogged in deep mud as it tried to climb back out again. He had to leap in and push the horse out into the middle of the canal, where the water was deeper, and then swim it up the middle of the channel until it got to a point where it could heave itself out. Then it was back to the stable to dry the horse off. 'Oh, yes,' he concluded. 'You'd do a lot for your horse.'

For a canal horse, life could be a lottery. Owner operators, 'Number Ones', as they were called, looked after their horses well. Another boatman interviewed for the BBC LP recalled of his fifty years of canal work: 'You wouldn't be a good boatman in those days unless you had a love of horses. Your horse should

The *Tivertonian* on the Grand Western Canal – Phil Brind on the boat and horseman David Poxon walking on the towpath with Dandy.

be your first consideration, 'cos he's the chap that makes your coppers for you. He should be fed, cleaned, looked after, bedded down for the night before we should look after ourselves. If he's been out in the wet, you wouldn't put on a damp collar in the morning; you'd have the collar dry before putting it on, like putting on your own socks.'

Life wouldn't have been nearly so good for the horses used by carrier companies of earlier times, when well-being or even common-sense welfare for the units of pulling power was rarely considered. Instead of a horse and boat being one unit, animals were pressed hard and changed at the regular staging posts when exhausted. This was especially so in the case of the fly and express boats which ran night and day and had priority at locks, to speed up transport of high-value or perishable goods such as cheese. Undoubtedly, many boat crews drove those horses hard. Writing in the 1780s, in his *History of Birmingham*, William Huttons described the lot of the canal horses bleakly: 'the boats carry about twenty-five tons, and are each drawn by something like the skeleton of a horse covered with a skin; whether he subsists on the scent of the water is a doubt; but whether his life is a scene of affliction is not; for the unfeeling driver has no employment but to whip him from one end of the canal to the other'.

For the fortunate horses looked after by their 'Number Ones', however, life on the towpath could be far better than farm work, or road transport. Such canal horses often worked and lived far longer than their agricultural and carriage pulling cousins. Indeed one canal horse on the Mersey and Irwell Navigation is said to have been the oldest known horse with a verified age. Born in 1760, just as work started on the Bridgewater Canal, Old Billy (once just 'Billy', presumably) died at sixty-two, twice the age of the average horse. Somewhat macabrely, his skull has ended up in Manchester Museum, whilst his stuffed head – brown with a white blaze – is displayed in the museum in Bedford.

As Dandy set off, driven on long reins from behind by Dave, I walked beside them, keeping well clear of the tow rope running to the *Tivertonian*'s looby pin, set back along the boat's roof so that (like the centre rope I'd used on Kate's *Morning Mist*) the pull came from closer to the boat's centre of balance, making it easier to steer in a straight line out from the bank. Dave pointed out the gaudily painted wooden 'bobbins' – round rollers threaded on the rope traces looking like a string of sausages – where they ran back along Dandy's sides to the swingletree behind him, to which the tow rope was attached. With the boat following one track on the water, and the horse following another parallel track along the towpath, the hundred feet of white cotton tow rope was always pulling off-centre. Though the angle of offset might not have been great, it was still the equivalent of carrying

David Poxon walking Dandy along the Grand Western.

a heavy bag of shopping in one hand and the lop-sided strain would throw a horse's musculoskeletal system out of whack if not evened up. Thus the towpaths on longer canals switched banks at frequent intervals, so that horses drew first from the left and then from the right.

That, of course, created its own problems, necessitating bridges to take a horse across to the other side. And if the horse went up, over and down the bridge, and then on along the other side, whilst the boat went under the bridge, what would happen to the tow rope? Solutions to this conundrum – it was too time-consuming to unhitch the tow rope at every bridge – were imaginative. The

119

Stratford-upon-Avon Canal introduced cast-iron 'split' bridges which had a gap running across their widths, as if someone had sawn them in half, leaving an inch-wide slot for the rope to pass through. On other canals there were bridges called turnover, roving or 'snake' bridges, shaped like stone pretzels, with a ramp leading up onto the bridge from one side, then another ramp coming down in the same direction on the other bank before looping round and under the bridge's arch. So, to follow the boat's route under the bridge, the horse's track threaded the tow rope back on itself as if it has been carried around a Möbius Strip.

As boat numbers increased, more and more canal horses were needed. Wars, poor harvests for fodder, agricultural booms and busts all kept the markets for horses in flux, and it's

The snaking path of a 'turnover bridge' on the Macclesfield Canal, designed to allow horse and tow rope to change bank unhitching.

hard to know how many thousands of horses were working on the canals in their busiest era, before engines began competing against four legs. And it's also hard to compute the extent of the secondary trades and employment provided by the canal horses. This included farriers, of course, who often had to work on Sundays to shoe horses on the animals' rest day. Then there were harness and collar makers. Rope layers. Ostlers. Vets. Horse breeders and horse breakers. And, at the end of the line, knackers.

There was also a sizable physical infrastructure. Horses used as units of power and worked to maximum efficiency couldn't just be put in a field to graze at night. They needed stabling, which was provided at regular stops. At busy urban wharfs or major junctions, stalls might be across two or three floors, with the horses accessing the top levels by ramps, like a multistorey car park. Then they needed straw as bedding, hay as fodder and grain as hard feed. This meant that a whole sector of agriculture – also powered by horses – was given over to fuelling canal horses. The Industrial Revolution transport of fossil fuels was itself powered by bio-fuels.

New working patterns had to be developed, too. Agricultural horses, used for ploughing or harvesting, were fed early in the morning, left to digest their hard feed, then harnessed and worked hard till midday, fed and rested again at lunch time and then worked through the afternoon before being brought back to their stables and fed and left to recover for the night. But boat horses might work ten or twelve hours in a day. It may have been light work but it was non-stop and didn't allow breaks to eat, so instead of the soft nosebags of farm horses a tin feedcan was buckled onto the horse's head, so it could eat on the move.

Walking with Dave along the Grand Western Canal, on that summer's afternoon, I noted the light crunch of his boots and the heavier tread of the horse on the towpath gravel, the shading branches and leaf-dappled waters, the coots and ducks scooting out of the way of the *Tivertonian*'s bow.

It was an almost perfect rural idyll. But, in the days of the working horseboats, canals across the nation were rarely peaceful. They were a workplace with boat crews competing to be first through locks or the narrow channels under bridges to save precious time. There would have been shouting and arguing over who had right of way. Scuffles and fights weren't uncommon. Most of the commotion, though, would have come from the steerers, who kept 'smacking' their whips on the cabin roof. Not for the horse, who was a hundred feet of tow rope and the length of the boat ahead, but to crack (three times, was the code) in warning to other boats. One imagines that the whips were used a lot, the explosions increasing in intensity as boats approached blind bends. This is well proven in that canalside shops stocked spare 'crackers' or 'thrums', which boatmen kept tucked in their hatbands to replace the whip's tips as they wore out.

The same shops sold replacement white cotton tow ropes, too. These were a significant expense for the owner-operators, who would knot, macramé and weave the lengths of worn and broken rope into fenders, mats and other practical and decorative boat accessories. The ropes would wear out quickly from rubbing on bollards, running around the corners of bridges or from being dragging along the towpath. They picked up gravel and mud when wet and then became highly abrasive, wearing deep grooves in the walls of bridges, even where protected by metal guards, which can still be seen today. Ropes also snapped under pressure – a danger for the horse, who could be thrown to the ground or into the canal, and for the horseman as the rope whipped through the air.

The real difficulties for working boat horses in the past was the intense busy-ness of the waterways. With Dandy and the *Tivertonian* we were just one boat moving along an empty

Joe Skinner and his mule, Dolly, in the 1950s. The Skinners operated one of the last working horse-drawn boats, on the Oxford Canal. In the background is his narrowboat, *Friendship*, loaded with coal.

canal, with the odd fisherman pulling in his rods, or walkers stepping off to the side to let the horse pass. But visualise how it would have been with maybe five or six boats on a stretch of waterway, travelling in both directions and having to pass each other. There would have been a cavalcade of horses going both ways, even as boats jostled for water in the cut and tow ropes stretching in all directions. As with negotiating the bridges, it was the long tow ropes that made things complicated when oncoming boats passed each other. For reasons of cost, most canals only had a towpath on one side or the other, though Thomas Telford, when improving sections of canals like the Grand Union, insisted on a track on both sides to allow a two-lane system.

With all the horses on the same side of the cut, tow ropes had to be crossed over by horses and boats, and it was too easy to become entangled, and risk animals being pulled into the canal, vessels dragged into the bank, or expensive ropes having to be cut. So there were agreed rules for passing. Normally the boat going 'downhill' would take the 'inside' (as the water nearest the towpath side is always called) and its horse would keep on pulling steadily. Meanwhile, the oncoming boat would steer to the 'outside', even as its horse stood off to the outside of the towpath, its rope slack and lying across the ground for the oncoming horse to step over. And at the same time the slacked rope would sink in the water for the inside boat to pass over.

It was a system fraught with problems. If the towpath was narrow or the edge degraded, there might not be room for the horses to pass. Whip-cracking and shouting. And sometimes boatmen didn't like sinking their tow rope for the other boat to pass over, as it could get caught on submerged debris or, worse, under the hull of the oncoming boat, plucking their horse into the waters. In which case, the inside horse would move away from the canal, stop enough to let its own rope slacken to the ground, allowing the oncoming boat's horse to step over it, whilst someone on the inside boat picked that horse's tow rope up at the bow and then passed it down over the whole boat's length. But mess that up, and the rope would sweep everything off the topsides of the boat – water pots, buckets, mops, the chimney, possibly the helmsman, too. And if things did go wrong, one had to hope that the rope could be unhitched from the swingletree fast enough to avoid real disaster.

Horse-boatmen needed skill, authority and bravado, and an ability to communicate their intentions. Passing tens of boats a day on a busy stretch of waterway, one couldn't turn each meeting into a drama of whip-cracking and shouting. It was a necessary sign of professionalism to be able to work out who was going to take precedence and whose horse was going to slow to slack off the tow rope. It was the kind of thing learnt from childhood, for in early horse-boat teams there were usually two men on board and a young lad to lead or drive the horse. When in later years families ran boats (more on which in the following chapter), it was invariably children who walked the towpath with the horse, in all weathers, and for hours on end.

Walking peacefully along the Grand Western, as Dandy strode along, occasionally following the towpath under a bridge, David mentioned that 'sometimes the horseman would need to be on board the boat to help with something, or to eat. And I've been told that one trick was to tie a boot onto the tow rope, just behind the horse, so that that it banged on the ground as the rope moved up and down and the horse thought someone was still walking behind.' We fell into a doubtful silence, pondering this old canal tale. Surely only the dumbest of horses would fall for such a trick, and canal horses were known for being smart.

Indeed, David told me, in canal towns, where flights of locks and tunnels were so tightly spaced that there was no room for a towpath, the horse was often unhitched and left to make its own way through the streets to meet up with the boat on the far side. Some reliable horses – known in boat lore as 'backers' – apparently learnt to do almost all their work on their own, without anyone guiding them along the towpath.

We associate canal boats with slow travel – with the plod of one horse power, not to mention the obstruction of tow ropes. But this has not always been the case. If you had a private canal, like the Duke of Bridgewater, you could operate a packet boat with a scimitar blade mounted on its bow to cut through tow ropes not cleared away fast enough. And by putting several horses to pull, you could get up to a higher speed by brute force. But that had its drawbacks, tiring out horses. On some fast boat routes, teams of animals had to be changed every two miles, and if they went too fast the boats threw up a huge wake, damaging the canal banks and tossing around boats they passed, putting them and their fragile cargoes at risk.

However, in the 1830s canal transport made a great (if short-lived) technological leap with the discovery of hydroplaning – the waterways' equivalent of the invention of the jet engine. This seems to have been discovered by chance. As canal boats became popular, various accounts from around the country told of a horse bolting when pulling an empty boat, at which point the vessel pushed up a wave of water ahead of its bow and then accelerated onto the rapidly moving wave, where it skimmed along behind the galloping horse. So far, so exciting. Or indeed terrifying. It took a canny Scottish boatman, William Houston, who, having had such an experience, saw the 'mercantile advantage' of light boats, designed to skim along at the speed of cantering horses, and set up in business.

Houston's boats were built of light iron plate and, though seventy feet long and six wide, weighed just thirty-three hundredweight (1.6 tons). Even fully laden with passengers, they could be accelerated by a pair of horses to the speed needed to create

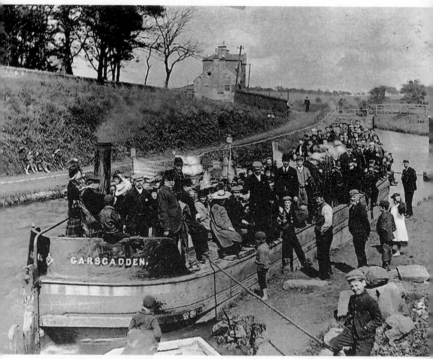

A steam-driven passenger boat on the Ardrossan Canal, still in service in Glasgow in the 1890s.

a wave and surf along on top of it. The horses would pull the boat along, almost friction-free, more on top of the water than in it. Light boats, skimming along with scarcely any resistance, meant very little disturbance of the water, and so none of the destructive waves and wakes that damaged canal banks from speeding heavy traffic.

Through the 1830s, Houston ran a light boat passenger service over the eight miles of the Ardrossan Canal between Glasgow and Paisley. Canals were already in regular use for passenger traffic, but the speed of this new service turned it into a regular commuter route, carrying nearly 400,000 passengers a year. The sheer volume of his business allowed Houston some Ryanair-style price slashing, to the point where one could skim along at ten miles per hour – an almost inconceivable velocity – for 6d (2.5p) inside a cabin, or just 4d in steerage.

Houston's technology was copied elsewhere, though not always with success. Like aircraft, the boats needed experienced crew – pilots and co-pilots, as it were – who knew just how to accelerate the horses and boat to create the wave, and then the right speed to pull the boat up on top of it for 'take off'. And there was another factor: the wave could only be created and its energy kept intact when the dimensions of the canal were uniform and narrow over long distances.

The science behind the solitary wave and the surging boats was little understood until John Scott Russell, another Scot, did some experimentation and rigorous observation. Watching one of these soliton waves breaking free from the bow of a boat in a narrow canal, Russell galloped his horse in pursuit of it for several miles. On other occasions he used horses and boats to create soliton waves, pinning down the technique needed for the horse-boats to build up the wave and accelerate onto it. He scribbled down formulae and addressed the Edinburgh Royal Society, leading to the foundations of a complex science that has led to a modern understanding of tsunamis, suggested ways of sending lightwaves down fibre-optic cable speeds, and hinted at the manner in which signals pass through neurons. All pretty cutting-edge science for something that started with runaway horse-boats.

Science and techniques aside, there were problems operating high-speed boats. They needed a waterway narrow enough to contain the soliton wave and allow light boats to achieve full speed behind teams of horses, and an unobstructed towpath. Most narrow canals were unsuitable, being congested with other craft, their horses and their cats' cradles of tow ropes. Nonetheless, fast cargo and passenger boats became a transport revolution and if a few of them mastered the soliton wave, the efficiency of boats when pulled by horses could still be turned into speedy services with fly boats run for passengers as well as cargoes, especially if operated on less busy waterways, run at night or having secured passage rights that forced all other craft to pull into the side and loosen their tow ropes as soon as they heard the bugles or horns announcing the approaching horses pulling boats at express speed.

Ireland's Grand Canal was one such waterway with a reliable, fast passenger service. This had relatively few goods boats and there was profit to be made in running speedy 'passage-boats' between Dublin and the Shannon River, from where passengers would be transferred on ferries down to the Atlantic port of Limerick, effectively crossing Ireland. Launched in 1788, the Grand Canal fly-boats increased in efficiency and popularity over the next forty years, and by using four horses – changed frequently – the fastest boats kept up an average of eight miles an hour. This was a remarkable progress, since it included travelling through forty-odd locks over the canal's eighty miles.

One winter weekend, when the water was frozen and the path glazed in thick frost, I had set off to walk the towpath from Dublin to Shannon Harbour. It took me nearly three days to get as far as Mullingar, fifty-two of the canal's eighty-two mile length. The fly-boats did this stretch in a little over seven hours.

James Johnson describes much of the experience of crossing Ireland by fly-boat in his *A Tour in Ireland* of 1844: 'The dress of the postillions, the measured canter or gallop of the horses, the vibration of the rope, the swell that precedes the boat, and the dexterity with which the men and horses dive under the arches of the bridges without for a moment slackening their pace, all produce a very curious and picturesque scene such as I have never seen equalled in Holland or any of its canals.'

Anthony Trollope, who was postal surveyor in Ireland in the 1840s, travelled on fly boats, too, and wrote about them in his novel *The Kellys and the O'Kellys*, where he has a character, Martin Kelly, take a twenty-hour journey from Dublin to Ballinasloe, complaining of 'the misery of the canal-boat' and registering a complaint at the catering, a 'half-boiled leg of mutton, floating in a bloody sea of grease and gravy, which always comes on the table three hours after the departure from Porto Bello'.

Trollope perhaps pokes fun at the discomfort of the fly-boats because he's writing at a time when they were beginning to be superseded by railways. For, inevitably, it was rail that doomed this brief reign of supersonic canal travel, and led to nearly all canal boats returning to transporting cargoes at more prosaic speeds by the end of the nineteenth century. Still, for a period in the 1800s, one could fly along at a dizzying ten miles an hour, powered by horses, sipping wine and eating (albeit from a rather restricted menu) in comfort. Fly boats are surely due for a heritage revival.

Canal horses and their boats survived the expansion of the railways, as there was still work in moving slow, heavy cargoes, especially coal, the old canal standby trade. And a handful of fly-boat services kept going for a few more years, too, offering specialist transport of valuable, perishable and urgent goods, using teams of horses changed at staging posts and crews who took turns to sleep on the move.

It was perhaps more of a surprise that horses continued to work the towpaths long after the coming of the diesel engine at the end of the nineteenth century, doing away with the webs of tow ropes. But the horse had left a permanent mark on the canal system since Brindley and the other canal engineers had fixed the dimensions of the boats, the size of the locks and the widths and depths of the canals based on what a single horse could pull. No-one had imagined that another power source – a metal horse that could fit inside a boat and that could be made as powerful as one liked – would be invented.

This legacy meant that, despite the rapid improvements in engines, boats couldn't go much faster than a horse in almost all of Britain's narrow, shallow canals. If the speed of boats was increased by even a few miles an hour, the propellers either sucked all of the water out from under the boat's hull, grounding it, or the wash from the boat slapped the banks of the canals into pieces. Despite every modern development, boats were forever tied to around three miles an hour. For that reason, and because horses were cheaper to run and replace than engines, and perhaps also because many boatmen preferred working and walking with them, horses remained in use for a good number of canal boats well into the twentieth century. And on London's Regent's Canal 'barge' horses worked into the 1960s, as an effective way of moving 'lighters' – engineless carrier barges – from one place to another.

Horses came into their own, too, at times of frozen weather, when they were pressed into service to pull metal icebreaker boats. These were basically heavy iron hulls with a handrail down

Marbury, an icebreaker built for the Shropshire Union Railways and Canal Company, in 1900. Men stood either side of a central handrail and rocked the boat from side to side.

their centre and would be pulled by long lines of horses, whilst men standing either side of the bar would rock the boat violently from side to side to smash through the ice. In another of those BBC oral history interviews an old boatman recalled the hard freeze of 1893, when 'in Snearsdon they had twenty-six horses for the ice boat', before adding that the ice boat had been sunk there and three men 'went down with her', although he did not reveal whether they merely got a chilly ducking or worse befell them.

Horse-boats also remained popular for Victorian Sunday outings, when of urban families escaped the crowded and grimy cities to go on picnics or to rural fetes or country meetings. Dressed in their best clothes, they packed themselves into boats that perhaps carried coal during the week, but had been swept clean and maybe lined with sacking and benches, and were towed out to the country. It was the kind of thing that fixed the romance of the horse-drawn 'barge' and its big 'Shire' horse in the popular imagination.

Talking with Phil Brind, and walking with David and Dandy along the towpath of the Grand Western Canal, had shown me how integral horses and horse skills had been to the establishing of the canals as the most efficient transport system known in the early nineteenth century. But it also demonstrated how the dimensions of the canals and speed of boats, based on what a horse could pull, had been frozen in time. As industry accelerated and the steam train, and then the internal combustion engine, were invented, the canals were going to be outpaced. But not for another century. And the restricted speed of the boats, set in Brindley's time at the dawn of the golden age of canals, provided perhaps the one thing that makes the waterways so valued in our own leisured time. As slow ways, forever fixed at a horse's steady plod.

6

Rise and Fall

ONE OF THE FEW MODERN horse-drawn passenger boats operates on the Llangollen, one of Britain's loveliest canals, with a series of breathtaking engineering feats spanning the English and Welsh borders. It was packed with passengers at its start point in Llangollen, as I paid my respects to its bay cob and began pushing my folding bike along the towpath. My panniers were laden with wet-weather gear, a bivvy and sleeping bag, ready for a couple of hundred miles of pedalling towpaths in search of what have been dubbed the canal's 'golden age'.

In the period between the opening of the Bridgewater Canal in 1761 and the arrival of efficient railways in the 1840s, Britain's waterways powered huge changes in the social, industrial and rural lives of the British. Arguably they created the modern country. Living in the times before the canals would be inconceivable for most of us now but there is something much more familiar about post-canal Britain, with its expectation of regular work and food, the manufacture and spread of essential and fashionable 'things', the contact with other parts of the country. And the canals of the northwest – the Manchester Ship Canal, the Trent and Mersey, the Shropshire Union and what had once been the Ellesmere but had shrunk to the Llangollen – tracked the history of the canals' golden years, and beyond, into their losing battle with railways and roads. Along their lengths were illustrations of every stage of the canals' importance as water roads, and it felt appropriate – and also fun – to start a journey at the top of the Llangollen Canal, now one of the busiest leisure waterways, and once, despite its rural remoteness, a driving force in manufacturing, chemical works and canal innovation.

Before setting off along the Llangollen towpath, I called in at the offices of the Horse Drawn Boat Company. The boat in question the *James Brindley*, was just picking up pace outside, as it edged away from the wharf and reached full one-horse power speed. Rather cunningly, it had been built as a double-ender – with a bow at both ends – so that the tow rope could be changed from one end to the other as the journey was reversed. This was essential, in fact, for there was no winding hole to turn a boat around at the deadend where the canal took its waters from the Horseshoe Falls on the River Dee and started its journey to the Shropshire Union Canal, forty-six miles downstream,

In the boat office, Lee Jones told me the rollicking history of the trip boat, which had been launched in 1884 by one Captain Samuel Jones. The captain was a genuine seadog, who had been 'pensioned off' for being drunk in charge of a vessel and, becalmed on land, had invested in a couple of old lifeboats and some horses to take tourists from Llangollen up to the Horseshoe Falls and down towards the spectacular Pontcysyllte Aqueduct. The horse-drawn trip boats had run ever since. The captain had clearly stumbled on a good business proposition, for nineteenth-century Llangollen was a magnet for wealthy, poetic-minded tourists seeking wild landscapes, rustic beauty and exotic peasantry. It attracted, among other notables, Queen Victoria, William Wordsworth, Sir Walter Scott and Charles Darwin.

The importance of tourism to Llangollen's canal over the past century or so could easily obscure the real purpose of the canal, which was to promote industry. The area around Llangollen had coal, slate and other minerals, and was close to the burgeoning industrial areas of northwest England. But it was hard country for transport and the canal was seen as an essential for the region. Work started in 1791 with the generous-hearted and diligent William Jessop as engineer, and Thomas Telford, working on his first major waterway, as resident agent. It was opened in 1806.

The canal carried slate and agricultural produce down to England, with staples and luxury goods coming in the opposite direction. Some must have found their way to the 'Ladies of Llangollen', Lady Eleanor Butler and Sarah Ponsonby, two Irish aristocrats who in 1780 had set up home together at Plas Newydd, outside the town, to escape being married off. Plas Newydd, their home and gardens, became a calling place for people as varied as Lord Byron, the Duke of Wellington and Josiah Wedgwood. Reading descriptions of the metropolitan-style salon life they maintained it becomes clear how much canals underpinned the great social changes across Georgian England. The canal age was a watershed era when styles of houses and furniture, and fashions and foods and comfort, at least of the wealthy, seem surprisingly modern. Read Thackeray or Jane Austen and much of the background to the stories – a maid laying coal fires through a house, china on the table, rich fabric curtains, heavy furniture – has been put in place by canal traffic.

As a commercial waterway, however, the Llangollen was closed to traffic in 1944 and would probably have been allowed to decay if it hadn't been needed to carry water from the River Dee to Hurleston reservoir. Since its post-war revival and restoration, it has gone from strength to strength, with its first eleven miles given UNESCO World Heritage status, and is one of the most popular cruising routes on Britain's waterways. The busiest canal in Britain, I'd been told several times. Indeed, experienced boaters blow hot and cold about the canal's charms – one of the prettiest but frustratingly busy in the summer months, seemed to be the general verdict. Lee had told me, with relish, of the boat jams of high summer: 'arguments, shouting, fights over right of way – when, boats meet head to head ... well ...'

In May there weren't many boats on the waters but Llangollen was busy celebrating a 'Victorian weekend' with steam trains. People had dressed up in the spirit of the occasion, with a light dusting of top hats, deerstalkers, capes, crinolines, muffs and Malacca canes. A male voice choir, uniformed in claret blazers and grey trousers, were singing lustily till they were drowned out by a shrill whistle and then the chuffing and squealing as the steam train pulled out, leaving the smell of boiling water and coal smoke behind. The restoration of heritage railways and canals, I'd noticed, often went in hand in hand, and because they followed the flattest routes they often ran next to each other.

I had a late breakfast in the Cottage Tearoom before following the towpath east out of town, towards Shropshire. Pedalling along the narrow path as it contoured off to follow a line through hilly countryside the throngs of people thinned out and within a few miles I had it to myself, save for a fleet-footed runner in pink Lycra who moved at about the same speed as my bike and stayed on the horizon as I bowled along under the trees.

It was so quiet that I heard the low, steady thumping heartbeat of an engine before I saw the *Lodestar* – a shining example of a traditional narrowboat, all polished brass, neat signwriting and rope-work fenders. At the helm, Neil Ecclestone was as effortlessly 'traditional' as his boat, sporting a well-worn boatman's peaked cap, a denim smock and just the right level of concentration needed to steer the acute turns of the Llangollen, expecting an oncoming boat around each corner. Seeing Lodestar navigating the twists of the contour line, I marvelled, as always, at the precision demanded of the designers, engineers

Neil Ecclestone steering the impeccable *Lodestar* along a narrow
stretch of the Llangollen.

and navvies when creating the most efficient waterway possible. A plaque back in the town had suggested that when making the Llangollen twenty-five men could dig a mile of canal a year, but that was in good soil, and a lot of the Llangollen's course had been cut out of steep, rough hillsides or blasted back into the rock face. Naturally it had been made as narrow as possible both to save water and the man-hours of construction. I could see how, in the busy months, a pushy or inexperienced boater could jam the whole canal up when forced to reverse back around the bends to rare passing places. I wondered what it had been like when the original horse-drawn boats had navigated this stretch, and time was of the essence. This first length of the canal had never been as busy for cargo, so perhaps the boaters had worked together to create a system of waits and advances to avoid boats ending up nose to nose and having to be stern-hauled back.

Modern boaters, I'd found, loved discussing strategies for navigating the Llangollen. Have someone walk ahead to report back on the blind bends and narrow stretches, was common advice – and, ideally, use two-way radios. Or make up a convoy with other boats, some suggested, forcing right of way by sheer numbers; like poker hands, three boats in a row would beat two oncoming, while tucking in behind the trip boat (whose right of way was paramount) was the equivalent of a straight flush. One pragmatist suggested leaving your boat moored in Trevor and then walking up the towpath to Llangollen, allowing a dose of schadenfreude as you watched more determined boaters reversing, tail-gating and crawling the final four and a half miles to town, only to have to turn around and come back again.

Canal historians might point out that the channel from Llangollen to Trevor – the narrow stretch I had been cycling alongside – was never intended as a full navigation and was built to supply the water for the canal and Hurleston reservoir, and that it was the latter purpose that stopped the canal being destroyed or filled in when it was briefly decommissioned in 1944. Those same historians might also point out that the Llangollen Canal was a modern name, a rebranding if you like, and originally it was just a part of the Ellesmere Canal, an ambitious and never fulfilled plan to build a waterway between the Mersey and the Severn, joining the mineral supplies of north Wales to the manufacturing bases of the Midlands.

I arrived at Trevor in time for lunch at the Thomas Telford Inn. From the mid-1790s this had been the house that the engineer had kept rooms in as he worked on the canal and particularly on the Pontcysyllte Aqueduct. William Jessop, recognising Telford's genius as a civil engineer, had given him free rein to solve the problem of how to get the canal across the deep, wide valley of the Dee. Bravely, Jessop backed his man when Telford came up with a design for the Pontcysyllte Aqueduct – an airy scalloping of eighteen arches, carrying a metal trough 125 feet above the river. The Pontcysyllte was the highest navigable aqueduct ever built and to save materials and costs, Telford designed

The Pontcysyllte Aqueduct over the Dee, drawn in 1823 by Captain Robert Batty, not long after its completion in 1805.

light pillars which supported cast-iron brackets to carry the channel of water. The components were made to key together and actually get stronger under the weight pressing down on them. An inscription on the sculpted monument at Trevor Basin records that to seal the joints in the trough Telford used 'Welsh flannel impregnated with lead dipped in boiling sugar and set with mortar made of lime, water and the blood of 1,700 oxen'. Not unreasonably, perhaps, the canal committee were sceptical that any of this could work. But Jessop stood by his man, and two hundred years later you can still motor a narrowboat across it. Or cycle along its towpath.

As I approached the basin, I stopped to chat with two local-looking men standing by a moored boat, and asked them how to pronounce Pontcysyllte. 'It's easy enough,' one man said, uttering something that sounded like 'Ponth-ker-sertay'. I gave it a shot. 'That's about right,' his mate allowed, 'though if you're not a Welsh speaker, you haven't got much chance really. "Llangollen" is worse. Whenever I hear a holiday person trying to say "Llangollen" I'm always worried that they're choking and I'll have to give them ... what's it called ... ah, the Heimlich manoeuvre.' I congratulated him on his German pronunciation and headed into the pub for a pint and a sandwich.

The Thomas Telford had the nostalgic decor of pubs from my past – Windsor chairs, plain tables, and the kind of pub artefacts that are already being sold on eBay as antiques. There was a blackboard, too, not with dishes of the day but gnomic sayings – 'Whose coat's that jacket?' 'I'll be there now in a minute.' Thinking they might be the preserved wisdom of some local character, I asked the young woman pulling my pint about their origins. 'To be fair now, they're from *Gavin and Stacey.*' I looked blank. 'The television show – though we do say them ourselves now, even though it's more South Wales.' Endearingly she prefaced most sentences with 'to be fair now', and a smile, as if I might not believe her. The canal and tourists, she said, kept the pub busy year-round. 'To be fair now, we do close for half a day on Christmas day,' she added, 'then we close by four.' Trevor, it seemed, was making up for time lost when prohibition had sent local drinkers over the border by boat to England.

In the golden age of canals, the Llangollen was at the heart of a lucrative local industry of quarrying and associated trades. Slate was exported to make billiard tables, morgue and operating slabs, and whisky vats. Cefn stone, from which the aqueduct is built, was used for Bangor University and Liverpool's Walker Gallery. Fine clays and marls were turned into tiles, decorative bricks and architectural terracotta shipped all over the country. There were brickworks and iron foundries.

The Llangollen Canal and its hinterland illustrate many of the stages in a canal's life, and the huge contrast between their time as working waterways and their modern roles as a nature park for leisure travel. I looked over the tranquil basin and its hire boats, and at the strollers and at the families sitting in the warm afternoon sun outside the pub, and read writer George Borrow's description of the view at dusk in 1854: 'Enormous sheets of flame shot up high from ovens, illuming two spectral chimneys as high as steeples, also smoky buildings, and grimy figures moving about. There was the clanging of engines, a noise of shovels and a falling of coals truly horrible.'

But that was the sight, the sound and the smell of progress during and for a while after the golden age of the canals.

Waterways historians like Charles Hadfield define the golden age as 1760 to 1840 – from the opening of the Bridgewater Canal to the start of competition with improved railways. It was coal that underwrote the capital costs of building canals, and it remained their main cargo, though everything from foodstuffs to chemicals, manure to road-building materials were transported on boats. Double-decker barges would arrive in London carrying live sheep for the meat markets. And, as we saw in East Anglia, boats left the capital daily laden with horse dung destined for the fields, collected from the thousands of cab, cart and dray horses powering the city. Other canal boats carried barrels of urine, needed as a mordant in dying cloth in the Yorkshire mills; embarrassed boat crews might deny that was their cargo and claim to be carrying something more prestigious, but those in the know would meet the fibs with 'you're taking the piss'.

The building of canals involved acts of Parliament. These acts often had clauses allowing local agricultural produce, building and civil engineering materials to be moved either toll-free or at reduced rates. Private companies established waterways for profit, but there was an acknowledgement of their public good in the Parliamentary acts. That said, canal building was capitalism at its most rampant – a boom and bubble of feverish investment to match any in Britain's history. And there were plenty of losers among the canal investors, for the success of a waterway project was not easy to predict. Many proved to be overambitious and needed to be refinanced, or had their final profits reduced by compensation clauses paid to already extant canal companies for their loss of business or the use of water or connections. The legalities of competition were complex and led to anomalies like the 'bar' – a barrier between the near-touching waters of the Birmingham Canal and the newer Worcester and Birmingham Canal that forced goods to be trans-shipped between boats.

Cabals of canal financiers would often operate a closed shop on the more lucrative projects. Public meetings for investors might be changed from venue to venue at the last minute, or even from one town to another, with speculators keen to cash in on the 'canal boom' riding at full speed in pursuit. Other companies were scams. Or woefully ambitious. Few canals, even the successful ones, came in close to budget, as we saw with the difficulties of the Huddersfield Narrow, for example, when tunnelling wasn't as straightforward as hoped, or rock rather than earth had to be dug, or local materials weren't suitable for the infrastructure and expensive alternatives had to be brought in. Sometimes canals were never finished; either because the need for them was overtaken by events or the money ran out and further funding couldn't be raised.

Some projects changed with circumstances, as here with the Llangollen, which was originally planned as the Ellesmere with a promised route from the Mersey to the Severn. Parts of a canal – or, in the case of the Llangollen, a branch line – might be completed and prove profitable, and then later become incorporated into another canal route. The canal companies had all the hallmarks of modern finance, so perhaps it's no surprise that when the London Stock Exchange was established in 1801 – changing from a coffee-house enterprise to a (relatively) ordered and regulated money market – they made up half of the listed companies within ten years.

Acts of Parliament aside, canal companies were independent of any central control, which led to a confusing lack of harmony over their widths and the sizes of their locks. There were different bylaws affecting each waterway, too. This meant that running a reliable long-distance carrier service was challenging, though again a successful operation could turn high profits. And, as the waterways network expanded, there were attempts to regularise the individual canals' toll rates, the provision of professional lock-keepers, and the rights of express and fly-boats to operate around the clock. Often these efforts were driven by the more ambitious carrying companies.

Pickfords, which remains in business today with its removal lorries, started in the carrying trade nearly four hundred years ago with packhorses in Cheshire, before moving into carts and light 'fly wagons' that in the 1700s cut the journey time from Manchester to London to four and a half days. Pickfords were early adopters of the canals, seeing their potential for speeding valuable and mixed loads between major destinations, and by the beginning of the nineteenth century had a fleet of boats, serviced by hundreds of horses that were changed out at staging posts to keep the craft moving round the clock. They also built dedicated facilities for accepting, sorting and labelling cargoes, and sending them on

The Pickfords shed on the Regent's Canal, at Southampton Bridge, Camden, painted around 1842.

from wharfs. When in 1801 Paddington Basin was built as a major trans-shipment terminus for goods coming into London by canal, Pickfords turned this into a bustling 24/7 enterprise. The sorting of individual consignments was done aboard the moving boats, and manifestos sent ahead for clearance, so that goods arriving at Paddington could be loaded immediately into light carts and delivered throughout the city in hours.

In the canals' boom years, boats were mostly owned by carrier companies and operated by several crew. On slow cargo boats it was mandatory to have two crew, though it might well be a man and a boy, the latter working the horse (and, literally, learning the ropes). On the Stourport it was a legal requirement to have a three-man crew when passing locks, speeding up the process and saving tailbacks by having one man dedicated to working the gates ahead of the boat. Horses had to be stabled at night, and so it was usual for crews to sleep ashore in inns or lodging houses. On the fly boats, which ran twenty-four-hours-a-day, relief crew were carried and there was a small cabin for them to sleep in.

There were a few live-aboard husband and wife teams in the canal's dominant years, but family-run boats didn't become common until the waterways were in decline from railway competition, and costs were cut to the bone. Until then, working the boats was a hard but well-rewarded skill – a job like long-distance truck driving today. Though far from a nine-to-five occupation, it was paid well enough for the men to maintain houses for their wives and families, traditionally owned or rented in boating communities at key junctions like Stoke Bruerne on the Grand Union, Hawkesbury (where the Oxford and Coventry canals meet), Stoke on Trent, London or Birmingham. The boats' cabins were thus little more than small, functional cuddies, to get out of the weather, and to cook and doze in when necessary.

The early canal boats were kept functional in all respects. Again, like a fleet of trucks they might have identifying company paintwork, but rarely any other decoration. They were uniform, too, their size imposed by the dimensions of the canals and locks, though the lack of precise uniformity in the sizing of locks between different canals – it might only be few feet difference in length, or inches in width – caused problems where boats built to the maximum size of one waterway to carry the maximum load, were unable to transfer onto another company's canals.

The canals of the golden age – and, indeed, throughout their working life to the 1940s – were not places of leisure. Aside from an enthusiasm for Sunday outings, using cleaned-up cargo boats, or the regular passenger-boat services, the canals and their towpaths were exclusively for business. Often, they were off limits for non-commercial traffic, or pedestrians, and they could be dangerous places for outsiders. Even where the canals looked inviting, access to them was often prohibited: a bill published in 1800 imposed a fine of one guinea on trespassers on the Trent and Mersey towpath, and three boys caught swimming in a canal had to publish an apology in poster form, a form of fine. Swimming in most of the early canals would not, in any case, have been an attractive proposition, with the waters often used to flush away chemical and industrial waste.

It's hard to imagine, on today's leisure waterways, that for 150 years the canals were as much a part of the Industrial Revolution as mills, foundries and potteries. The 'water machines' might have passed through some of the most rural and remote parts of Britain, but their effect was not so much to transport the countryside into cities as to take the industrial and urban into the remotest corners of Britain. Indeed, some of the most resolute objections to canal building came from landowners who neither wanted the bustle, noise and pollution (horse manure and worse) of boats crossing their estates, nor the boat crews who they suspected would poach or steal at every opportunity. For this reason some canals had to be sunk deep into cuttings to hide them from view, and further bylaws enacted to stop boats mooring next to private lands, and to prohibit outsiders from their towpaths.

Throughout the new industrial age, factories were either established next to canals, sometimes spreading out into corridors along them, or had branch channels and wharfs built to transport materials and products in and out. The six towns that made up the Potteries in Staffordshire were an illustration of how an industry changed and grew in response to opportunities provided by the canals. In the 1720s, John Astbury had discovered that finely ground flint added to the local red clay made a delicate white ware. Initially the flints, mined in the southeast of England, had to be brought by sea and then by packhorse to the grinding mills and thence to the potteries. Josiah Wedgwood, founder of the pottery dynasty, was a friend and early supporter of James

Brindley (who is also credited with improvements to the flint-grinding process) and he was quick to see the advantages of canal transport, making it possible to bring materials – coals, clays, flints and chemicals for slips – more cheaply to his factories, and speeding distribution of finished products across the country, with far fewer breakages than by horse carts. Wedgwood was a major backer of the Trent and Mersey Canal and dug its first sod in July 1766 in Burslem, where he had his factory. Over the following decades, water transport meant that Wedgwood and other pottery firms were able to centralise production, create an elite workforce, share (and steal) new processes and discoveries, and export their wares across the world. Canals were key to the economies and innovations of centralised industries.

And so it was at Trevor on the Llangollen Canal. Heavyweight raw materials were dragged from quarries and moved around on tramways, or hoisted up and down slopes with massive cranes, to get them directly to the Trevor Basin for onward shipment by canal, or into local factories to be made into products that were transported out on the waterway. And in the 1860s, when the Ellesmere Canal, as it was still called, began losing its monopoly to railways and roads (Telford had gone on to engineer the London-Holyhead road, arguably the first modern highway), it got an extension on its useful life when Robert Graesser established a factory making disinfectants, soaps and explosives from tar acid extracted from coal; it was far safer sending these volatile products onwards by canal boat than by road. Graesser's Chemical Works went on to become Monsanto Europe.

I left Trevor by the same route as the morgue slabs, terracotta tiles and explosives of the past. Pushing the bike past a discreet Samaritans' notice fixed on a wall, I walked out onto the narrow towpath of the aqueduct. To my left there was light metal railing of the kind you might find in a park, and a dizzying view down

Narrowboats crossing the Pontcyssyllte Aqueduct – a ribbon of water in a metal trough, 125 feet above the River Dee.

onto the tops of the trees below. To my right was the trough of water, running off into the distance, just wide enough to take a narrowboat, and with no safety rail on its far edge. A boat was chugging slowly towards me, the water gurgling under its bow, and the engine burbling. As it passed, the man on the helm seemed to be gliding through the air with nothing behind him but the hundred-foot drop to the fields, the woods and the river down in the valley. Miraculously, Telford had created his 'stream through the sky', as it was dubbed. Miraculously it had lasted two centuries. And, most miraculously, people – sane, sensible, perhaps even cautious people – were still happy to float a ten-ton narrowboat across a ribbon of water held more than a hundred feet up in the air by airy arches, linen and ox blood.

Only a few miles beyond the Pontcysyllte, the canal plunged into the quarter-mile of Chirk Tunnel. Telford had designed the tunnels along the Ellesmere Canal with towpaths, in one of those economic balancing acts between greater construction costs set against the future savings made when instead of slowly legging boats through the tunnels the horse-boats could plod through. The Chirk Tunnel towpath was challenging – long and narrow enough to force me off the bike, to walk through the darkness. I wondered at the sangfroid of the old canal horses who one moment were plodding through the air a hundred feet up on the Pontcysyllte and then squeezing themselves through this dark, dank corridor. And then – like me – coming out into the light and finding themselves atop another aqueduct.

The Chirk Aqueduct, though more solid in build than the Pontcysyllte, felt almost more precarious, with a railway viaduct running parallel, and higher still, above. It was like a vertiginous reflection of the bridge of stone I was cycling across, carrying a stream of water high above the tops of the mature trees.

In the air I crossed from Wales to England. And my *Nicholson's Guide No. 4* – every bit as useful for towpath pub-finding as *Guide No. 1* had been for steering *Morning Mist* – showed that a few miles further along the towpath was the Poachers Pocket, where thirsty passengers on the prohibition drink-boat trips would come in from Wales to get their Sunday pints. Mentally I contrasted their sober trip down from Wales over the aqueducts and through the tunnels with how it must have been, after an afternoon's and evening's drinking, on the return trip from England. I imagined the luminous dusk of a summer evening with the last of the sunset and a warmth in the air, and assumed, hoped, that the voyage would have felt like a slow-motion fairground ride, Welsh voices raised in choirs of song.

It was hard to keep the idea of crowded, working canals in my mind as I pedalled further into the Shropshire countryside. Perhaps the contrast between the busy transport hubs and the bottlenecks at lock-flights and aqueducts with the long days through tranquil countryside was one of the attractions to working boatmen. Like cattle droving or seafaring – periods of slow travel bracketed by bustle and carousing. I moved along at a regular canal pace. A folding bike isn't the best transport for rough towpaths and it was often more pleasant to walk and push into the Shropshire countryside.

In the evening I moored, so to speak, at the canalside Jack Mytton Inn. The eponymous Regency eccentric, 'Mad Jack' drunk a bottle of port whilst shaving, set his own nightshirt on fire to cure a bout of hiccups, kept a bear called Nell (with which he would surprise guests by leaving it in their bedrooms), and made his way through a very considerable fortune from keeping racehorses, gambling and drink before being committed to a debtor's prison. The inn's licensee, David Mandell, was a Mytton enthusiast and had commissioned a signature Growling Bear beer, its label showing Mytton in his best-known prank, dressed in full hunting costume riding Nell into dinner to liven up a party at his nearby estate, Halston Hall.

David had designed his own pub coat of arms, too, and talked me through the escutcheon's symbolism. 'Top quarter is a sheaf of barley for beer, that one's for America where I'm from, there's the Union Jack, and in the bottom corner is a narrowboat because we're

Jack Mytton, the bear-back squire.

right on the Llangollen.' And the motto? *Quocumque ieri ibi sunt.* 'Wherever you go, there you are.'

Later, much later, fuelled by pints of Growling Bear, I pedalled into the dark along the towpath before finding a place out of the wind within the encircling horse ramp off a turnover bridge, laying out my bivvy bag as if within the walls of a roofless, stone igloo. *Quocumque ieri ibi sunt* indeed.

The next day was a Sunday. A warm, blue-sky day. The towpath and canal were busy as boats chuntered past walkers and dogs and cyclists. After finding a full-fry breakfast in Ellesmere – the town where the original meeting to establish the Ellesmere Canal was held (but *not*, confusingly, the Ellesmere Port where the Shropshire Union Canal meets both the Mersey and the Manchester Ship Canal) – I stopped for coffee sold from a moored narrowboat. The couple on board dealt in 'all things Spanish', as well as toys, signs and artefacts crafted from stainless-steel sheet.

The back-of-the-boat coffee bar tinkled with a line of shiny metal cut-outs illustrating the different sizes and combinations of shot and milk in ten kinds of coffees. I perched with my Americano nearby – actually, inside one of the Ellesmere Sculpture Trail pieces. This one was a representation of a boat's bow, set on end so as to form a sort of seat inside a sentry box; further along, I came across a bench in the form of the Pontcysyllte aqueduct and, later, in a corner by a bridge, a 'shoal of fish' – sprigs of twisting fronds, made of rusted, interlocking metal.

I had begun to note how often canals around towns had been turned into alfresco art galleries and outdoor exhibitions. Sometimes these celebrated a waterway's local history; near Chirk, I had been captivated by a striking piece made of salvaged miners' pickaxe heads. Other times, it was just 'art' and often, too, there was art on display in the boats that I passed. Sometimes the art was unconscious. A narrowboat named *Destiny*, which I cycled past just outside Ellesmere, could have been the title and degree show installation of a conceptualist: piled along the length of its seventy-foot rooftop were logs, tyres, a cat box, a bicycle, a rusty wok, pots of herbs, a deflated lilo, folding chairs, a dog's ball thrower, an oriental rug and a kettle.

Some miles further on, beside a farm, there was a coolbox on the towpath, full of eggs and home baking. I put a pound coin into the honesty box and took a slab of treacle flapjack. Chewing away happily, I watched as a hired narrowboat, decorated with ribbons and a 'Just Married' sign, sidled around a tight curve, the strong breeze blowing it off course. I had a perfect vantage point to see the look on the new husband's face as another boat came into view from the opposite direction. He was standing to one side of the tiller (I could hear Kate Saffin's voice in my head at this point) and desperately trying to get his boat out of the way. It was almost too late. Fumbling for the gear lever, he threw the engine into reverse and a mad bubbling came from under the stern. As damage limitation, it worked, driving the boat into the bank rather than the oncoming craft. A jolly blonde woman had already hopped ashore from the stern of her just-missed boat and, without apparent hurry, was suddenly on the bank at the bow of the newly-weds' boat, giving it a hearty push off. 'Just married, are you? Distracted?' she called out to them in saucy tones, leaving a number of punchlines hanging in the air.

Since the canals' change from the watery conveyor belts of industry to the slow hydroways of leisure, they have come to fulfil a number of functions. One of the most important is how they form wildlife corridors. The canal network is, in a sense, a 2,000-mile-long (if very narrow) national park, its (mostly) clean waters, green banks, thick hedges and mature trees connecting woodlands and meadows, hills and rivers, allowing fish, amphibians, insects, rare mammals such as bats, water voles and otters, and numerous bird species, to move in safety or to make their home along the canals themselves.

My main wildlife interest is birds, particularly birds of prey, and in my travels along the canals I'd often hear the sudden silence of songbirds, broken by the high-pitched chitter of a blackbird's alarm call, as a sparrowhawk flew the towpath or a hovering kestrel over a nearby field. I had seen buzzards mewing and wheeling above the Huddersfield Narrow, and most nights when I slept out I'd hear tawny owls. But what I was hoping to see, somewhere along the canals, was the rare and beautiful hobby (*Falco subbuteo*), a jolly little Hussar of a falcon with red breeches, blue wings that hang like a cavalryman's cloak, and a rake's mustache. As befits such a dashing bird, it specialises in hunting dragonflies, snatching them from the air and holding them with one foot to eat on the wing.

Past Ellesmere, the Llangollen crossed Fenn's, Whixall and Bettisfield Mosses National Nature Reserve. The canal had been driven in 1807 through this 10,000-year-old raised bog, which had later suffered from drainage, peat cutting, use as an army firing range, and monoculture pine planting. Then in 1991 a halt was called by Natural England and Natural Resources Wales, and work started to save the habitat. It had been a slow process but the bog was now re-established and home again to rare mosses, crowberries, cotton sedge, raft spiders and curlews. Best of all, an information board pronounced it one of Britain's best habitats for dragonflies – four-spot chasers, red and emerald and azure blue damselflies, black darters and, Britain's largest species, emperor dragonflies. This constituted a fly-through takeaway menu and the information board suggested looking out for 'the acrobatic hobby catching dragonflies summer long.' I spent a warm, sunny afternoon scanning the sky with binoculars in the hope of spotting one, before giving up in disappointment and wheeling my bike back onto the towpath.

A few miles further I heard a high shout – 'Come on, boys!' – from a large sprawling farmyard. On the steps leading to a loft door, a brawny farmer held out a bucket as he called racing pigeons down from the sky. Were they back from a race, I asked. 'No, they're youngsters getting some exercise' he told me, 'but I had others out racing yesterday 120 miles to get back home.'

The farmer's love for his pigeons had made him an observant naturalist and his taciturn speech flowered as he talked about seeing the first cuckoos each year – 'I always see them before I hear them, they look like sparrowhawks in flight'. Did he see peregrines, I asked? 'Often'. Goshawks? 'I've not seen them since I was a boy, and I'm sixty-four now.' What about hobbies? 'I do – but they won't be here for another few weeks. They come when there are young swallows. They love swallows.' It's wonderful to watch them fly, I suggested. 'No, not really ... well they do fly well, but they snatch the swallows. There was a woman standing where you are now saying just that – how nice to see them fly – and then one dropped a swallow's head right onto the boards next to her ... she didn't like them so much after that.'

The golden age drove canals through wilderness, connecting hundreds of remote rural communities, and joining up cities at opposite ends of Britain. Its canals brought vast social change in their wake and, for many, a degree of prosperity. They also encouraged an exponential growth in technology and provided the blueprint, finance, materials and much of the science for the next development in transport – the railways.

The railways, of course, would eventually destroy the canals, and at quite a pace. Richard Trevithick built *Puffing Jenny*, his first steam locomotive in 1801, and Matthew Murray, George Stephenson and others experimented with steam train designs over that decade and the next. By 1825 the first public rail line, the Stockton and Darlington Railway, was opened, using Stephenson's *Locomotion No. 1*. In 1830, the Liverpool and Manchester Railway opened, transporting people and goods, and the golden age of canal building – and, within a century, most canal transport – was at an end. The Liverpool and Birmingham Canal (now the Shropshire Union Canal), which I was heading towards, was opened in 1835 and turned out to be one of the last significant new British waterways.

It might have been otherwise if the early canal engineers had imagined the horse might be replaced by some other form of motive power. They might instead have carved out fewer but broader and deeper navigations, like those of France and Germany, which remain important routes for modern freight transport. But the British, in their enthusiasm for routes, had stayed narrow, carving out canals that would retain an eternal one-horse power speed limit.

When railways began to get going in the 1830s, many canal companies thought that steam trains could ever serve as a useful adjutant to their (obviously superior) waterways. After all, the plateway, the earliest form of railway line, had been developed in the previous century to bring ore in horse-drawn trucks from mines to canal wharfs. But the efficiency of those tram rails, with their smooth surfaces that allowed horses to pull profitable weights, and the comparatively low cost of laying rails, gave railways a huge advantage. This was soon recognised by many of the canal engineers, if not the canal owners. Benjamin Outram, engineer of the stalled Standedge Tunnel project, made his principal focus his own iron foundry, where he began forging 'L-shaped' plateways for ever longer 'railway' mileages. The carriers, too, were open to change. In the 1840s, Pickfords – one of the main national canal carrier companies – defected to rail, lending its backing and finances to developing train routes, at the expense of the canals.

Railways, like canals, needed to take the flattest route between two points, and so the two often ran parallel to each other for long distances, with canal boats used to transport many of the bulk materials needed to lay railway tracks and construct embankments, bridges and tunnels. Canal navvies moved seamlessly from digging waterways to laying rails. And the new railway companies, riding a fresh investment boom, began to buy up canals. They may initially have intended to integrate the best of canal and rail systems, but whenever there was a conflict of interest a railway company would close down its canal or confine it to cheap bulk cargoes. Independent waterways found themselves involved in cut-throat price wars.

Nonetheless, Britain's canals didn't die overnight, and the largest and mightiest of them all, the Manchester Ship Canal, opened nearly half a century later in the 1890s. Steamboats could operate well on the ship canals, or on big river navigations like the Ouse, Trent, Mersey and Thames. But steam technology didn't quite fit the traditional canals, however inventive its exponents. Steam tug trains were trialled on some towpaths with limited success, and a steam paddleboat took a twenty-ton load by canal from London to Birmingham in 1826. In the mid-century, a number of steam-driven narrowboats were constructed, too, but the engines, boilers and coal bunkers took up a disproportionate amount of a boat's space, reducing its cargo, and experienced mechanics were needed to run them. Until the invention of the smaller, reliable and easy to master diesel engine, at the end of the nineteenth century, most canal boats remained horse-powered.

For those businessmen who still believed in the canals – and there were many – improved infrastructure was more often seen as the way to fight the competing railways. When Thomas Telford became chief engineer on Birmingham's canals, he made use of high embankments and cuttings to keep the lines as direct and level as possible, shortening distances and avoiding all but essential locks. As the go-to engineer, he also widened Brindley's Harecastle Tunnel on the Trent and Mersey and, when improving the Birmingham Canal, put a towpath on both banks to separate horses and boats going in different directions. Elsewhere, the new steam technology was co-opted to drive pumps, like the one built at Crofton on the Kennet and Avon in 1812 (and still in working order today), to get water up to high pounds and keep busy canals in operation.

If it was too late to change the dimensions of the country's whole waterways system – though some of the most important canals were widened – engineers realised that what really slowed down boat traffic were the locks, with crews having to wait their turn. Where there were long flights of locks on busy canals, jams could take hours or even days to clear – as can be the case with canal leisure travel today. So, inventive minds of the nineteenth century set their minds to coming up with alternatives ways of getting boats up and down hills, to save time and, as crucially, to save water. For many years – indeed since small boats and their cargoes were lowered between different levels inside the Bridgewater mines – experiments had been made with various kinds of lifts. Winching boats like sleds up and down slopes was tried with little success. Tub boats fitted with wheels, so they could be hauled up rails, fared a little better.

There was more hope in the proven technology of huge tanks – caissons – which boats were floated into, then the end doors closed and sealed, and the whole caboodle winched up and

GRAND JUNCTION CANAL. LEICESTER.

Foxton Locks, (Old Style).

Foxton Lifts, (New Style).

The short-lived Foxton Boat Lifts on the Grand Junction Canal.

down slopes from one level to another. Key to this was using two tanks that balanced each other out, the descending one acting as a counter weight to the rising one, like a funicular railway. These 'inclined planes' sound like huge operations, and they were, but, once installed, stationary steam engines required relatively little energy to raise fully laden narrowboats tens of feet, and far more quickly than working them through a flight of locks.

By the end of the nineteenth century, there were ten inclined planes in operation across Britain. The most impressive of them all was built at Foxton on the Leicester line of the Grand Union Canal in 1900. It ran parallel to a flight of ten locks, rising seventy-five feet up the hillside, which previously took forty-five minutes to work a boat through. The inclined plane's two caissons could, by contrast, take two narrowboats each and, rising and falling in just twelve minutes, effectively moved a boat through every three minutes. This was a massive saving in time and water. Working a boat through the flight of locks took 25,000 gallons of water, while the inclined plane used virtually no water at all. What it did take, though, was fuel, a skilled workforce and expensive maintenance, which needed traffic to pay the necessary tolls. The lift lasted just eleven years before being mothballed and in 1928 it was sold for scrap. The flight of locks remains in use today, two hundred years after they were built, a testimony to the simplicity and practicality of the canal's oldest technology.

Pedalling along the Llangollen and then the Shropshire Union, it felt as if I had journeyed through the golden age of canals, through the prosperity and industry they had bought to a remote area of Britain, and out the other side, passing an array of big projects created to keep waterways relevant.

At the end of the Shropshire Canal, I cut across country to Northwich, on the Weaver, a canalised river which links to the

Mersey estuary. I admired the town's black-and-white 'Tudor' houses which, I learnt, were actually built in Victorian times; their timber frames meant that they could be jacked up and levelled, or even moved to new locations, when the continual subsidence from underground salt extraction threw them askew. The salt mines here, first developed by the Romans and still active today, were one of the reasons that the River Weaver was made navigable at the early date of 1721. And nearby was the Trent and Mersey Canal, the one where Josiah Wedgwood turned the first sod, opened in 1777 to serve the Potteries with clays and flints and carry off the finished products.

These two waterways were interesting in that both were founded on commodities other than coal. And, in the nineteenth century, they offered great commercial opportunities if they could be joined together. That was difficult because, though they ran within a few hundred yards of each other at Anderton, just to the north of Northwich, the canal was fifty feet higher than the river. Most of the trans-shipments went downhill to the river and its larger boats, so salt was sent down from the canal by chutes, while pottery – up to 30,000 tons of it in an average year in the 1860s – would be carted and craned. The obvious idea for joining the two waters was a flight of locks, but this was rejected as too slow, and as using too much water from the canal. Instead, this being the Victorian world, with big engineering feats becoming the norm, an 1872 act was passed for the construction of a vertical lift – a massive affair that could take two boats in either of its two self-balancing caissons and raise and lower them vertically fifty feet on hydraulic rams. By 1875, it was built and operational.

Cycling along the towpath of the Weaver, I turned a corner and got my first sight of the Anderton Boat Lift. If Brindley's canals, locks and aqueducts had the precision and simplicity of Lego pieces snapped together, this struck me as a mega-sized Meccano structure (indeed, I later discovered that the Anderton boat lift was the March 1949 cover illustration of *Meccano*

Magazine). The original frame had been made even more bulky and complex when, in 1908, the hydraulic rams had been changed to electric winches. Additional huge pulley wheels and A-legs were installed to take the weight of all the new machinery.

Pushing my bike up a steep path – and feeling sympathy for the wharf labourers who had wrestled laden barrows – I reached the

The Anderton Boat Lift, one of the finest bits of engineering infrastructure on Britain's canals – and a fiend to build with Meccano.

161

Trent and Mersey towpath. From a vantage point on the bridge, I could look down over the aqueduct that joined the lift to the canal, just in time to watch the dark blue hull of a narrowboat, the *Tumzul Cloud*, ease its way into the chamber fifty feet below. The gate closed behind it. Moving round to the bridge over the channel, I was able to see the tank rising slowly, with the boat floating inside it. Machines can be things of genuine wonder.

In the background, dwarfing even the bulk of the boat lift, was the Winnington Works, now part of Tata Chemicals Europe. This had once been an ICI chemical works and in 1933 experiments in high-pressure reactions had by accident produced polythene. It seemed a miracle product, when discovered, but, with its plastic cousins, had now become one of the defining pollutants not just of the oceans but along the waterways – bottles, bags, cable ties, discarded toys, string, cups and cartons inhabiting the waters, banks and hedges like some alien fauna.

As the caisson reached canal height, and the gate opened, *Tumzul Cloud* emerged from the chamber, moving slowly across the aqueduct and into the tight bend leading under the bridge and into the Trent and Mersey Canal. There was a quick burst of reverse to kick the stern round, but still the bow just kissed the wooden rubbing strake on the wall underneath my feet. I could see a grimace of self-annoyance on the steerer's face as the length of his boat smoothly slid past.

The bold idea of a hydraulic lift at Anderton was conceived by the Weaver Navigation's engineer, Sir Edward Leader Williams. Leader Williams was the man you needed for hubristic vision and big-machinery solutions to canal redundancy, and ten years later he was appointed as designer and engineer of the Manchester Ship Canal, Britain's last great waterways project.

On the continent, big navigations were profitable (and still are today) because they could take ever bigger boats as steam, and then diesel, engines improved in power and efficiency. As we've observed, all British canals and most British navigations were too small for this option and engineers realised that to be commercially viable new waterways had to break away from the old 'one horse power' scale and build big. The Manchester Ship Canal was the biggest of all, conceived to make the manufacturing city an actual seaport, despite being thirty odd miles inland.

I spent a rainy day in the splendour of Manchester Central Library – a 1930s building inspired by the Pantheon in Rome –reading Sir Bosdin Leech's *History of the Manchester Ship Canal*. A future lord mayor of the city, Leech had been involved in all aspects of the canal's building and his heavy tome covered everything from the rush to invest in the canal to the detail of its construction. The financing was surprisingly egalitarian. Although Rothschilds and Barings were both involved, locals also bought shares and Leech recalled a lad at Manchester Grammar School collecting pocket money from fellow pupils to apply for '£2,000 worth of shares'. The construction – which began in 1887 – was a last hurrah for the canal navvies, though by now most of them would have been familiar only with railway building.

Thousands of navvies were employed, and unions – which had never had much success in the canal age – agitated for greater pay. There were police raids on drinking shebeens in the shanty towns and Leech chronicles accidents and injuries of all kinds. An engineer had both his feet taken off. Two boys smoking in the dynamite store blew the whole lot up (though, remarkably, no-one was killed). One Thomas Edwards was awarded a Humane Society medal for jumping in and saving the life of a woman who had fallen into the canal cuttings, though he failed to find the body of her sister.

The strongest and most skilled navvies worked the 'horse barrow roads', hooking their laden wheelbarrows onto ropes attached to horse 'gins' that pulled them up steep, narrow planks to the top of the banks. They returned by sliding down, crouched, with the barrow behind, using their boots as brakes.

A long way from narrowboats – the yacht *Norseman* opens the Manchester Ship Canal in 1894 with the canal directors on board (from a painting by James Mudd).

'Navvies', in those newly mechanised times, was also used as a term for huge steam-driven machines. There was competition between crews working Whittakers crane extractors, Ruston Proctor steam navvies, and French excavators. One August, a Ruston Proctor filled 557 wagons with 2,500 tons of spoil in just twelve hours. But where the digging was easy the French machines were shifting 3,000 tons a day. The works captured the imagination of the city and sightseers flocked to gawk at the works, taking tea at the Ferry Hotel, which could serve 1500 teas at a time. A Mr Cullis of the Gloucester Engineers claimed, after a tour of inspection, that the excavated material would make a six-feet-high, two-feet-wide wall around the Equator. The canal was opened on 21 May 1894. There were knighthoods, medals, bonuses and celebrations all round.

The canal was used extensively through the twentieth century but it was never a huge financial success and almost closed in the 1980s, when Britain lost so much of its industry. Perhaps the recent plans to open and expand a container shipping port will make it relevant again. Or perhaps not. At one time ship canals and big river navigations had seemed to offer new hope for the declining waterways. The Gloucester and Sharpness Canal, opened in 1827 and financially ropey for decades, became busy with bulk oil carriers in the early twentieth century, before suffering the indignity of being diverted for the A430 Gloucester bypass. Perhaps the most successful is the Aire and Calder Canal and Navigation, which connects Leeds with the Humber ports and still carries two million tons of freight a year.

Hopping aboard my bike and riding alongside the Ship Canal was a little anticlimactic. I stopped to admire Sir Edward Leader Williams' innovative Barton Swing Aqueduct, which carries the Bridgewater Canal across the Ship Canal, and which had swept away James Brindley's equally innovative 1761 Barton Aqueduct. It was a reminder that there was no room for heritage nostalgia on working canals. It was to take several more generations for nostalgia to paint the memory of the waterways in rosé hues rather than sepia.

7
Canal Folk

AFTER THE BIG HARDWARE of the Anderton Lift and the Manchester Ship Canal, I looped back to the Shropshire Union Canal. It was good to be on a small waterway again and I was in optimistic mood as I locked my bike outside the Shroppie Fly pub at Audlem, next to a quartet of big motorbikes. It was still only mid-afternoon but it was a hot day and after a good stint of cycling I felt I deserved lunch and a pint.

One of the bikers was leaning on the bar – or, more precisely, on the hull of a narrowboat. The Shroppie Fly, a new pub in an old warehouse, had declared its canal credentials by cutting an old wooden narrowboat down the middle, like a baguette, and turning its starboard half into the bar counter. A woven rope fender hung off the bow from chains and the name plate – Shroppie Fly, of course – was picked out in traditional yellow, red and green.

Whilst we waited for our pints to be pulled, my new biker friend asked if I was there for the evening's music. 'It can be a good session,' he said. 'Good players, traditional and folk.' And, yes, he replied in answer to my question, they probably would play a few canal songs. I'd been intending to pedal south towards Staffordshire that evening, but the chance of a session, playing a bit myself perhaps, and maybe hearing a few waterways songs, was too good to pass up.

Canal songs had become something of an obsession on my travels. When I'd begun researching waterways history I imagined finding a rich seam of songs from the 150 years of working boat people – ballads and verses that would bring the world of navvies, tunnelling, lock-keeping, tow-horses and boats alive. But to my surprise and then puzzlement, I drew a blank. There *were* canal songs, but most of the ones I had come across were written by folk musicians and leisure boaters (the two often overlapped) in the 1960s and '70s, or were best-behaviour songs, commissioned to be sung at ceremonial canal openings. The ribbon cutting of Croydon Canal in 1809 prompted a 'gentleman' to come up with such lines such as 'Long down its fair stream may the rich vessels glide, And the Croydon Canal be of England the pride.' Not quite the gem of oral history I was after.

A day spent in the library at Cecil Sharp House, the home of folk music, had produced only a handful of songs that felt in any way authentic. Two of these were navvies' songs. 'The Tommy Note', published in an early nineteenth-century broadsheet, felt like a true labourers' song, complaining about companies paying workmen with 'notes' that could be spent only in their own 'tommy shops'. Another, which specifically references the waterways rather than railway or road work, was 'Paddy Upon The Canal', one of whose verses runs:

I learnt the art of navigation,
I think it's a very fine trade,
I can handle the pick and shovel,
Likewise the wheelbarrow and spade

and concludes with a toast to every 'true-hearted Irishman that's digging upon the canal'.

And then there was an absolute chiller, 'Tom Beech's Last Trip', the tale of a boatman and his family snowed in on the pound high above Napton Locks, where the local farmer refuses them food and fuel, so that the man, wife and children die of cold and starvation. The song seemed to have an actual event at its root – the big freeze of the winter of 1893–94, which locked canal craft solid in ice for weeks – and it had a proper oral pedigree, too, having been scribbled down after being sung by an old boatman in the Greyhound, a famed canalside pub at Hawkesbury Junction, one November night in 1962. And, finally, there was a jolly if undistinguished ditty called 'Shake Them Bobbins', which I came across in accounts of boat-horse barges, a walk-along song hummed to encourage man and horse.

These were thin pickings for the folk who for a century and a half had built and worked on the canals. I shared my frustra-

The Dead Rat Orchestra, bearded purveyors of authentic and 'awful' canal songs, touring their show, 'The Cut'.

tion with Nathaniel Mann, whose band, the Dead Rat Orchestra, toured a show called 'The Cut' on the waterways, and he agreed. He put it down to the fact that 'the communities that inhabited canals were largely transitory; a lot of the navvies that built them came from Ireland, and many of those who worked the canals were ex-seamen. So, it's not to suggest that the canals were silent, but that the songs and tunes harked from other places.' Nat and his fellow Rats had researched the archives for their show and had ended up performing many of what he described as 'corporate' canal songs. 'Which we ended up really enjoying,' he added, 'even though they are awful songs!'

Other people I talked to about canal songs mentioned the rootless and isolated nature of boat people's lives – and that of the navvies who built the canals. The canal age had emerged with great suddenness in the mid-1700s across Britain, and its new workforce, unlike farm workers, or even seafarers, didn't have obvious origins, either cultural or geographical.

Not that this stopped writers from inventing them. E. Temple Thurston, a flamboyant Edwardian writer and playwright, wrote a romantic account of a trip in 1911 on a hired narrowboat, in the company of an old boatman and his horse. His book, *The Flower of Gloster*, recalled a journey along the Thames, Severn, Stratford-upon-Avon and other navigations and canals, and declared that boat people were gypsies, with 'ideas of colour [that are] very southern ... and in their habits, their appearance and their minds ... they are no less than water gypsies'. The book (published twenty years after Jerome K. Jerome's *Three Men in a Boat*) was a bestseller and brought the (supposed) life of the waterways to a wide public, creating the romantic idea of boating families as of Romany background.

There may well have been Roma on the canals. Why not – for everyone *else* was there? And the idea has permeated through to the literature of our own times. Philip Pullman begins *Northern Lights*, the first of his *Dark Materials* trilogy, with the adventures of his heroine, Lyra, with the 'Gyptians' – working boat people on the canal at Jericho, in Oxford. Pullman, in interviews, has talked about drawing more on myth than local history, though he himself became active in community protests after the sale of the Jericho boatyard to developers.

And the 'water gypsy' background is one that Ronnie Wood, guitarist with The Faces and The Rolling Stones, embraces. In his autobiography he writes that his parents were born on the boats and came from a long line of boaters, working on narrowboats up and down the country, and, when he was a child, around London's waterways. Ronnie and his brothers were the first generation to be born ashore and he recalls his grandfather, Sylvester, dressing like a 'Chicago gangster dandy' and reputedly keeping a second family up the canal in Stratford-upon-Avon, and quite possibly a third in Manchester, suggesting both a rock'n'roll lifestyle and fashion sense. In a set of portraits of the Stones' members, Wood drew himself as a Romany character with a gypsy caravan in the background and the stern of his mother's family's boat, the *Orient*, in the foreground.

The truth, most likely, was that canal work drew people from all backgrounds and created new communities who, over the generations, became the 'boaters'. However, there were some particular groups whom history and the number of agricultural and sailor songs sung along the waterways suggest as being the stock that produced early boat crews. A lot of navvies, especially those living local to the diggings, switched shovel for tiller when the cuts that they had dug were filled with water and the boats began to move. They would have understood the water's workings, known the landscape, and wages were good.

Another large group of boatmen – and in the early days crews were predominantly men – came from the professional carters hired in on the workings to move materials and excavated soil. Once the boats were running, the canal companies needed horses to pull them, and skilled horsemen to work them. And, with the canals then transporting the loads that horse carts had once drawn, the canal was where the work was. The canals would also have attracted soldiers – fit men, but unemployed after campaigns – and sailors looking for a life ashore, although there is almost no crossover in skills, vocabulary or traditions between canal folk and seafarers. This is a point gleefully lampooned in a mid-1800s comic song, 'Voyage of the Calabar', in which a trip along the Rochdale Canal is inflated into an epic adventure on the high seas, along with stormy weather, the dangers of running into an 'unmarked lump of coal', a collision in the narrows, and finally a full-on battle with 'pirates' (the crew of another boat carrying cobblers' wax).

It seemed likely, as Nathaniel Mann had suggested, that the canal folk brought the songs from their old pasts with them. Carters might sing harvest songs; sailors, sea shanties; navvies, Irish songs. And the movement of boats between cities and rural areas would mean that songs from other traditions – broadsides, ballads, music hall, factories – were picked up along the way.

If the canal age had developed too quickly to build up much of a body of specific waterways songs, there was of course singing on the cut. A journalist writing in 1858 reported that 'the boatmen at the tillers nearly all sing' and that their song 'generally contains a story, and is written in a measure that fits easily into a slow, drawling breath-taking tune which all the lower orders know'. During long hours travelling with horses, I often fall into slow hoofbeat-paced singing, possibly even drawling, when on the move, in a 'Shake Those Bobbins' kind of way. As well as passing the time, good singers would have been welcome in pubs and might even have made money. In Roy Palmer's book about transport and music, *Strike the Bell*, there's a story of a navvy's wife making the equivalent of a few days' pay, when she

Working boat people in traditional dress, photographed around 1910.

sang for an hour in the streets of Warwick whilst the couple were tramping between work.

Some boaters were said to be able musicians, usually on the concertina, the traditional instrument of the seafarer, and well suited to stowing on a narrowboat. But, unlike sailors carousing on shore leave in harbour inns, or sharing life aboard, boat people moved as families or crews and moored up in a different place each night. And, though this might be beside a canalside pub, these were often low-key affairs, attached to stabling for their horses. There were a few canal junctions, wharfs and docks, where a number of boats might moor alongside each other, but in general the stables and pubs where they moored were set apart, and needed to be in order for the boats to make an early start and to avoid queues at locks. It was often the canal workers on the banks – lock-keepers, lengthmen, gaugers or other officials – who provided the most regular interactions with boaters. Messages, news and even letters might be left with lock-keepers to pass on, and they would possibly read letters aloud if the boaters were illiterate, as most were.

The families that lived and worked for generations on the cut, and who intermarried and looked out for each other, formed very definite communities – but communities with very limited chances of actual communing. It was difficult for boat families to celebrate even the big events of life. Gatherings for christenings, weddings and funerals were popular, but family and friends might be too far-flung to attend. Plans could be easily frustrated, as boaters were tied to work that kept them on the move, laden with cargo that couldn't be left unattended and working schedules that allowed almost no time away from the cut. And, even on the cut itself, actual contact could be elusive, allowing only for a few words to be exchanged across the gunwales as boats slid past each other and onwards.

Not that it was easy for families to talk to each other on the boats, either with a husband and wife or child almost out of earshot on the end of a long tow rope tramping with the horse, or steering the butty towed on an equally long rope, and this for all hours of light. The working day could be twelve hours or more (one of the disadvantages of diesel engines was that there was no longer a need to stop at dusk and stable the horses), and boat people were always at work, handling the tiller, walking the horse and working the locks.

None of this left much time or energy for music, especially in the confines of a boat cabin full of children trying to sleep.

Still, as I sat in the Shroppie Fly, writing up my notes over a beer, I had hopes for its evening session. Musicians began arriving in the late afternoon, carrying odd boxes and bulging bags and more obvious guitar-shaped cases. There were greetings and chat as they pulled chairs into a rough circle and began pulling out their instruments. Unboxed and unbagged, a fairly eclectic folk orchestra was revealed: three fiddles, three guitars, a set of Northumberland pipes, bones, a hurdy-gurdy, a bodhran (the Irish frame drum) and tin whistles. There were good singers, too, who led on Irish ballads and traditional English folk songs, once they got going.

In proper session style, the floor was given to one person after another to sing, or play, and those who knew the piece would join in. I took out a harmonica from my rucksack and played along with a few songs, and then borrowed a guitar and played and sang 'Ain't Misbehaving', with an apology for tainting the purity of the session with cod-jazz.

I thought we were getting closer to the waterways when one musician struck up 'Blow the Man Down', and another followed it with 'The Last of Barrett's Privateers', a rousing seafaring song. And then somebody did sing a canal song, 'The Tommy Note', which another singer followed with 'The Single Bolinder':

And then she burned a gallon a stroke,
titty-fa-la, titty-fa-lay,

You could see sod-all for smoke,
titty-fa-la, titty-fa-lay,
The motor went so fast,
I wound her up full blast,
She pulled out the butties mast,
titty-fa-la,titty-fa-lay,
Tra, lah, la-la-la-la,
Smackin' it into the cut.

The song was a kind of homage to Bolinder, the Swedish diesel, with its slow, percussive thudding. In Cecil Sharp House I'd listened to an LP called *Narrow Boats*, recorded for the BBC in 1969, and one track had been a boatman singing along in time to the loping drum of his engine.

Then it was the turn of a singer who, with his tattoos and Fender guitar, I'd taken for a local rocker. But it turned out he was a boatman through and through. His songs were straightforward and simple tales. One was 'Charlie Atkins', about a boatman who carried chocolate crumb to the Bournville factory on the edge of Birmingham, and I realised from the detail that he was singing about someone he'd known first hand. Then he launched into his own song about Joe and Rose Skinner, their mule Dolly and *Friendship*, the last horse-drawn narrowboat on the Oxford cut. I had heard the Skinners talked of before, always with great fondness and respect, as one of the last boating families. They had retired for the last ten years of their life to a cottage at Hawkesbury Junction but still preferred to sleep aboard their boat and with the growing number of waterways rallies held in the 1960s they were happy to tour the festivals, where they were celebrated as a connection to a disappearing traditional way of life.

As the hurdy-gurdy and the whistles started on a new tune, the boatman-singer stepped over to the bar, where I joined him. 'Mal Edwards.' He extended a thick-knotted hand. 'It sounded like you knew the Skinners,' I said by way of introduction.

'Oh, I did, and Charlie Atkins, too, I knew him. He taught me a lot.' Mal had written the songs, he said, because 'there aren't many good canal songs' and, since he knew the people, he felt he could fill the gap as well as anyone.

As I travelled the waterways and discovered museums along their length, I had been finding that, although the building of the canals is well documented, the boat people themselves tend to be either unrecorded or romanticised. The golden age of the canals had taken place long before photography, and, with the major exception of John Constable, few artists thought working boatmen an interesting subject. Photography arrived at a time when competition with the railways had left the canals at a low

Boat people on a working short boat on the Leeds and Liverpool Canal, around 1900.

ebb, so the pictorial records we have of working canal life are those of the industry's decline. There were still thousands of boats in the late nineteenth century, and indeed into the twentieth century, but payment for loads had been so reduced that the good wages and high status had vanished. While in the canal heyday a two- or three-man crew could own or rent a house and keep their families ashore, in the new pared-down reality the only economic way to make a boat pay was for a man to live and work on it with his wife and children. The reality for such working boat people was essentially that of zero-hour contracts, with a single wage to feed a family.

Many families worked on boats owned by large well organised carrier companies like Fellows Morton and Clayton. Others, known as 'Number Ones', owned their own boats, giving them independence but leaving them exposed to bad luck. With every resource focused on trying to bring in or collect another load, and where long delays or a disaster like a stoppage due to severe weather, this could spell the loss of their livelihood. For many families the threat of destitution was a constant and haunting fear.

Canal boatwomen, however, were invariably house-proud, fighting a battle against the clouds of coal dust, chemicals, filth or whatever else was carried in from industrial wharfs or from the cargoes they carried. Their back cabins – on average just ten feet long and only six and a half wide – became tiny shrines to cleanliness, with lace, linen, fine china and brass. For those who owned a boat, decoration became the norm on the exteriors, too, with panels of 'roses and castles' on doors. Chimneys had brass bands, polished of course. Water pails – known as Buckby cans – were also painted with flowers, as were the nose cans used for feeding horses on the move.

With the onset of the twentieth century, efficient diesel engines became available and, though some boats stayed with the versatility and cheapness of their horse, others changed over. Engined boats could tow an equal-sized engineless butty, doubling the load, and allowing more space, and opportunities for work, for the growing families. Steam engines had been complicated, space-consuming and unreliable, whereas the early diesel engines – Bolinders, Nationals, Gardners and Listers – had the slow beat, robustness and simplicity that endeared them to men used to working with horses.

As often happens with marginalised and cash-strapped outsider groups, the boat people cleaved to the traditional, old-fashioned costume of their forebears. In those BBC *Narrow Boats* recordings of working boatmen and women, one interviewee described traditional costume: 'A good boatman must have white corduroy trousers with bell bottoms, double-breasted waistcoat, with two rows of buttons, and a billycock hat sort of thing.' The hat and the flares were practical attire – the latter designed to gutter rain over, and not into, one's boots. Another interviewee added that the shirt should be handmade and white, and trousers should have a velvet ribbon down the leg seam and 'diamond' stitching. Tucked into the belt would be the heavy windlass for working locks. Spare whip lashes (whips continued to be used as warning sounds after the advent of diesel boats) would be threaded under the hatband.

The women were even more conservatively dressed, with layers of petticoats, heavy skirts, aprons, shawls and bonnets with fold upon fold of material under a heavy curved brim. So much trailing clothing might seem impractical for getting on and off boats but had its value as weatherproofing and for warmth when standing at the helm all day in all weathers.

Photographers at the end of the nineteenth century caught these costumed boat folk in sepia prints – over-romanticised images of simple traditional values, but useful ones when it came to campaigns to save the canals, a half-century later.

Books, too, often created simplified accounts of the families living on boats. As more boating families were forced by economics to live aboard – and children to help with their work, steering the butties, tramping with the horses and acting as general 'runaboats' for a parent stuck in charge of the tiller –

reformers became interested in their plight. George Smith was at the forefront, a former child labourer himself in the brick-yards, who had campaigned successfully to outlaw child labour in his own trade, and then turned his attention to canal families. His polemical and sensationalised books *Our Canal Population* (1875) and *Canal Adventures by Moonlight* (1881) describe filthy, crowded cabins, illiteracy and hints of depravity.

This stigmatising caused understandable offence to boat families already dealing with considerable problems. There were some realities they could do little about: the infestations of lice and fleas or rats, filthy and sometimes toxic cargoes, and the crowded conditions and ever-present hazards for children on the boats. And there were, naturally enough, strata in canal society, with boat-proud Number Ones, and those from the smarter companies looking down on unkempt boats, which they referred to as 'Rodneys'.

But the issue of children was difficult. Very few of those who worked on the canals could swim and, if a child 'took a look' (fell in the canal), the boat could neither stop quickly nor turn. Appalling accidents occurred, too, with children being crushed by shifting cargoes or between boat and bank or by being dragged under the propeller (just as equivalent accidents befell children in the mills and factories on the bank). But, as life began improv-ing for the children of mill- and factory-workers, boat children seemed to lag behind. For many generations they grew up learn-ing the skills of the waterways, rather than attending school, and at a young age would start a lifetime's work on the canals.

Smith's accounts of canal life sold in large numbers and helped promote the 1877 Canal Boats Act, which limited the number of adults and children who could live aboard a boat. In reality, though, the act brought little benefit to boat people; families, fearful of being split up, would on the rare inspections hide their children or loan them out on other boats. After an even more lurid book, *Rob Rat: A Study in Barge Life* by the Reverend Mark Guy Pearse, was published in 1878, a further act

A young girl walks the horse (with its feedbowl) along the towpath of the Grand Union Canal, around 1910.

charged local authorities with ensuring boat children attended schools. For families on the move, this was next to impossible to comply with and, before and after, few canal children spent more than the odd day in school, unless they were sent to board with family members ashore. Boat-living children were forced to attend different schools for an hour or two along their boat's route, and were invariably bullied by the other children and mostly ignored by the teachers. Some companies set up schools for their employees' children in the early twentieth century, but illiteracy remained common.

Harry Bentley, interviewed for Euan Corrie's *Tales from the Old Inland Waterways*, about his early twentieth-century childhood on the Trent and Mersey Canal, noted that his family had to work two boats to have enough accommodation for the children to satisfy the inspector. Regulations prevented children over the age of twelve of the opposite sex sharing a cabin: 'One sister was sent to live with my aunty, wife of a tugboat man. She ended up being a district nurse.' Though he became a boatman himself, Harry conceded that it wasn't much fun as a child – 'It was long hours with nothing to do.' Interestingly, though, Harry reckoned the wages, even in the declining years of the canals, in the 1950s, were not so bad: 'No house to rent, no fuel to buy, no lighting. We had £15 a week and nothing to pay out; that was a very good wage in the 1950s.' When he and his wife Sarah left boating, so that their son Colin could go to school, Harry ended up getting a job in a factory. He earned half the boating wage, with rent to pay, and he couldn't progress far as he had never learnt to read or write.

One effect of Smith's and Pearse's books and campaigns was to fix a view of canal families as outsiders. These tough, often dark portrayals become the norm in children's books. In Kenneth Grahame's *The Wind in the Willows* (published in 1908), Mr Toad disguises himself as a washerwoman after escaping jail, tricks a 'barge-woman' into giving him a lift on her boat; and when she sees through his bluster and throws him into the canal, the pair get into low name-calling, each giving as good as they get. In Edith Nesbit's *The Railway Children* (1905), it's seen as quite plausible that the eponymous children have their adventures on the railway lines, along embankments and in tunnels, getting involved in the stationmaster's life, whereas the chapter where they save a canal woman's child portrays the waterways as filthy and dangerous, and the woman as an angry drunk – a storyline that was dropped from the 1970s film.

In more recent years, the best-known book about life on the cut was Sheila Stewart's 1993 oral history, *Ramlin Rose: The Boatwoman's Story*. Having interviewed an Oxfordshire farm labourer for her bestseller, *Lifting the Latch*, Stewart attempted to find a boatwoman who could supply a similar story of canal life, but ended up interviewing a number of different boatwomen who had worked with their families as canal carriers in the first half of the twentieth century, and combining their experiences into her character, 'Rose Ramlin'. As a composite, Rose lives all the extreme experiences of the women's different lives – a daughter killed by lightning, an adopted son removed, a drowned horse, being iced in and short of work.

Stewart's explanation for why she had to cobble together a single character from several women is almost as illuminating as the book. Of the women she got to know well and who trusted her, she writes, 'I could not find a single one who could furnish me with enough memories to compose her biography, though each prided herself on belonging to a traditional boat family, remembered who was related to whom among the canal community, and never forgot a kindness.' She explains that, unlike other illiterate women living on the bank, the boatwoman was frequently isolated from her own community, with no neighbours, friends and relations to meet and talk with, no constant re-enactments of events to help bolster or contextualise her own memories, often no family photos to refer to, and few gathered mementoes. The boatwomen were nearly always on the move with little cabin space to store items from the past.

It's hard for us to see the geography of Britain as boat people saw it. They might have known every moorhen's nest, every bridge and waterside house along the cut, but either side of the canal the world was often unknown. Boaters, for instance, always described themselves as going 'down north' because the waters and locks were all downhill from the Midlands to the Mersey. This cut-centric linear geography, and the relentless demands of the boats as both workplace and home, is shown in a heart-rending way in *Ramlin Rose*, when Rose's sister, Suey, gets TB and is taken to a sanatorium near Banbury. Rose is able to visit her regularly when passing through the town, but then Suey is moved to a sanatorium in Farnborough, far away from

Working boat people gathered for a christening at Buckby Locks, on the Grand Union Canal, 1913. Boatwomen's bonnets were traditionally white, but they moved as one to black following the death of Queen Victoria.

the boat's working waters, and Rose doesn't see her again. For a woman tied to boat, work and family, with only a hazy view of geography beyond the waterways, Farnborough is off the map.

But there are biographical accounts of individual boaters' lives – again, notably in Euan Corrie's fascinating collection of interviews – which suggest how varied different women's experiences of the waterways were, and that possibly the Oxford Canal, where Stewart created Ramlin Rose, was something of a backwater. Corrie talks to Violet Mould, for example, who was born on land in Braunston during the First World War, and came from many generations of boaters. Her father was captain of a steam-engined narrowboat, a well-paid job allowing his family to live ashore and Violet to go to school. After her own marriage in 1938, she and her husband Ralph never had a house – 'just the boats' – and two of her four children were born on board. She recalls the inspector coming by regularly, but with only four children – and all daughters – on a spotlessly clean boat, Violet was always commended rather than sanctioned.

Violet lists the cargoes she and Ralph carried – buttons, bedsteads, chocolate crumb, metal tubes, dried milk and sometimes barrels of Guinness from Park Royal, adding that 'Ralph always used to keep one water can empty when we arrived and they'd fill it up for us.' And there was foraging. Her husband kept a gun on the boat for rabbits and hares, they had a fishing net on a handle for scooping up swans' eggs as they passed, and they picked mushrooms, watercress, raspberries and blackberries. Even when they retired from carrying, they lived on a converted narrowboat, whilst their three youngest children continued school.

The day after the session in the Shroppie Fly, I cycled out to meet with Mal Edwards on his narrowboat, *Becky*. The weather had changed again to blue skies and sharp showers. I found Mal in a yard full of craned-out and blocked-up boats, old winches and rusty machinery, under the eye of a benign guard dog. *Becky* had been ashore for work on her hull for the past month and Mal was still living aboard. I climbed up a ladder onto the back deck and he gestured me inside.

The cabin was mostly traditional, with a cushioned settle, small solid-fuel stove, and a fold-down table with hand-painted decoration on its 'up' face. The cabin's wood panels were covered in straps of horse brasses representing Victorian celebrities and a menagerie of lions, horses and bulls – an array as fascinating and unreadable as Egyptian hieroglyphics. Hung from the walls, and even pinned to curtains and hangings, were souvenir 'ribbon' and 'lace' edged china plates of the kind that working boat people collected (though breakable, they took up little room in cramped cabins) and which, despite the canals' connection with the Potteries, were often imported from Germany and bought at canalside fairs.

Mal got out photo albums, letters and cuttings and, as we went through them, I learnt about his life. 'Dad was born in the lock-keeper's cottage at Grindey Brook' (I must have cycled past it on the Llangollen but couldn't remember it). 'He came off boating ... He would never talk about the canals – "dirty ditches", he called them. Ashamed, I think he was. Great Uncle Jim was a canal policeman, policed the boatmen, they could be swine in those days ... he arrested someone for murdering his wife, mostly though it was arguments at locks, poaching ... Of course there wasn't much money around.'

Leaving school at fourteen, Mal found himself a live-aboard boat – 'no engine, bowhauling it' – and got a job as a length-man for British Waterways on the Shrewsbury and Newport Canal. His work was to keep the banks and towpath and hedges trimmed and tidy, and keep an eye out for potential breaches. Even a mole- or vole-hole at water level could enlarge and then blow through with the weight of water, and drain a whole cut, causing devastating flooding. One time he had to clear a derelict tunnel – 'I took out a dead sheep and refloated three sunk tub boats'. The canal (one of Telford's, and featuring an early inclined plane, as well as a thousand-yard tunnel with a wooden 'balcony' towpath) was later allowed to become derelict, though it is now being restored bit by bit by volunteers.

Mal's life on the waterways probably reflected that of many post-war working boatmen, changing from one canal job to another as opportunities waxed and waned. At eighteen, he was helping George Page, a carrier with a horse-boat. Later he worked with Charlie Atkins – the chocolate crumb carrier of the song from the night before. 'He taught me how to make fenders from ropework – how to make 'buttons' and 'puddings' – I still do those to sell to boaters. People think you knot the rope wet, but it's the other way round; if it's wet, it loosens when it dries.'

Photo after photo flicked past, prompting memories which took Mal back to the time of the working boats. "When we worked for Anderton, we would carry salt and stuff for ICI ... they used to have a fleet of boats, there was a coaster called *Polythene*. That's Caggy Stephens – he had horse-boats, taking rubbish. Oh, and, here, that's the Barton Swing Aqueduct – we were on it and the keeper says, "Here, do you want a thrill?" and he swung her round whilst we were on it ... tugs going by below ... He was just back from the pub.'

In the 1970s Mal had married Jill, a mathematician who had fallen for the life of the waterways – 'She loved horses, and she was an artist' – and together they had operated a horse-drawn trip boat. He pulled out a faded advertising flyer – 'Day hire twenty quid, and here's a picture of the boat and horse, Fred, that was on the cover of the British Waterways calendar, 1974.'

Somewhere along the way there had been seven years as a lock-keeper at Grinley Brook, where, although next to the lock-keeper's cottage where his grandfather lived and his father was born, Mal had lived aboard his boat. An official letter and a sheaf of paper cuttings heralded the MBE he'd been awarded a few years before, honouring his volunteer work with the *Glas y Dorlan* – a trip boat for disabled and disadvantaged on the Llangollen. 'Harry Secombe launched it, he flew in by helicopter, then, that photo's David Essex there – the singer, do you know him? He's one of the patrons.'

In search of another photo, we squeezed through a small door at the end of the cabin and into the covered cargo area, now a workshop, where Mal did his rope work. He found the one he wanted. 'That's me on my twenty-first birthday in Gas Street.' I saw a handsome beatnik with a guitar beside the canal in Birmingham. 'Donovan got me into singing. I got my guitar-picking from him. That's an Eko twelve-string – a bugger to keep in tune.'

A life on the canals – Mal and Jill Edwards with their horse-drawn cruising boat at Norbury on the Shropshire Union Canal, 1973.

I thought of Ronnie Wood, artist and guitarist, and his pride in his boating past. With a few changes in fortune he could have ended up with a life like Mal, on perpetual tour along the waterways, playing in canalside pubs and painting roses and castles and candy-striping swan-neck tillers.

'I always played, and I got into writing songs ... I've got songs everywhere', Mal gestured at boxes and folders. I had bought a copy of his *Songs from the Cut* the previous night – fifteen self-penned songs, the cover a black-and-white photo of a teenage Mal sitting on the cabin roof of his bow-hauled work boat on the Shrewsbury and Newport, its hold piled with sticks and logs from the waters.

He was reminiscing again. 'They vandalised that canal, took the bridges down so it couldn't be used. Took me off it and I ended up on the working boats. It was Beeching time on the railways. They'd have closed this one, too' – he gestured to the Shropshire Union Canal outside – 'if they could have.'

We'd been talking for several hours and Mal looked tired. I left him feeding ducks. 'Two lads with an airgun shot that duck in the head, but she seems to be recovering.' The duck and eight chicks came paddling towards the bank. 'Here they come ...'

8

Jules' Fuels

STIRRED BY MAL EDWARDS' STORIES of working life on the canals, I wanted to experience – as much as one could in the modern world – what life aboard a working boat was like. Once again, I was set on the right track by Kate Saffin, who was back in London with *Morning Mist*, setting up another waterways theatre tour. 'Jules' Fuels,' she announced. 'They're the people you need. They've got a boat and a butty – both heritage boats – and they do things properly. And they're good fun.'

The Jules' Fuels website seemed to bear that out:

> Julia Cook (Jules) and myself (Richard, I just lift heavy objects), sell solid fuel and diesel from our coal boat *Towcester* and the new addition butty, *Bideford*, on the Grand Union Canal. We are a friendly couple that enjoy boating and having a laugh with our customers.

And Jules's reply to my email was even more encouraging. 'Of course,' she wrote. 'Come along for a few days when we're delivering near Hemel Hempstead. You can help out humping coal – and you won't have to sleep on the towpath (as I'd offered). Our apprentice will be off for a week and there'll be a cabin free.'

189

A week later, I was riding the folding bike along the towpath from Apsley towards Bourne End where, Jules had messaged me, they'd be unloading coal in the early afternoon. Across the canal I saw their boats moored up: two traditional beauties, in red and black livery. On the butty was a woman – Jules, I presumed – lifting twenty-five-kilo bags of coal out of the hold and onto the gunwale. And a man – Richard – was piling a wheelbarrow and trundling them off through a gap in a hedge.

They spotted me waving, on the wrong side of the water. 'You can't get round to here. Wait there!' Smoothly Richard crossed to the *Towcester*, untied the rope that was tying her to the butty, and pushed off with a pole so the boat hinged on her stern rope and angled across the canal to make a bridge. Almost. The bow ran aground a few feet from the bank. 'There's not much water at the moment,' Richard said, pushing a gangplank across to bridge the gap. I handed my pack and bike across, and Richard reversed the process to get back to work. It had taken just a few minutes to get me across the canal.

I said a quick hello to Jules – there was no time for anything more, as, clearly, there was work to be done. 'There's a second wheelbarrow there ... See where Richard's taking the coal?'

I loaded a rickety barrow with bags that Jules was throwing with an easy swing onto the gunwale of the boat and trundled them off down the path. These were private moorings here, with allotment gardens behind, and the couple whose boat was moored behind us were stocking up winter fuel at summer prices. They directed me to a Portaloo beyond the vegetable beds, already stacked high with bags. Richard and I barrowed coal for another seven or eight trips, with snatches of conversation as we passed. 'The barrows are called Craig and Wayne – we named them after the guys at Jewson's who sold them to us.' And then after another load or two: 'You can see the boat rising as we unload – from the wet strip along the hull. It should be an inch to a ton.'

The holds of both boats were stocked with bags of different kinds of fuels, while platforms held tens of gas cylinders, and a veteran garage pump stood on top of a large diesel tank. Further boxes held those staples of the live-aboard life, Elsan Blue for toilets, Morris Stern tube grease, and litre cans of Brasso.

Our offloading finished, the coal-buyers invited us for tea and coffee cake at a picnic table. There was canal talk, with Jules and Richard passing on news from along their route. Talk about characters – so and so 'went by the other day, heading for Oxford' – and boats – 'that'll be for sale, then, a lot of work to do on it.'

It was soon time to move on and, as Jules sorted out the butty, preparing to cast us off, Richard swung down through a sidehatch and into the engine room on *Towcester*. I peered in at a green engine block, its exhaust pipe running up to the roof swathed in lagging, and over all the smell of bilge water and warm diesel. A water tank stood on a shelf, which after the engine had been running would provide hot water for washing. The obligatory tin of Swarfega sat beside it. Link rods for the gearbox and throttle ran high up under the ceiling, through into the next-door cabin and over to the stove, to join to two brass wheels that wound back and forth to engage gears – reverse, neutral and forward – and control the throttle whilst standing at the tiller.

'The engine? It's a Lister JP 2. JP for Joint Project.' Richard's voice kept time with the rotations of the handle as he cranked the engine. 'Joint Project ... with Rustons ... it's ... twenty-one ... horse power.' He built the speed up, giving momentum to the huge fly-wheel at the end of the engine. 'It's a quarter ... ton ... fly ... wheel.' He flicked at something on top of the engine and then, still crank-ing, reached back to a switch and the engine tumbled into life, and a loose-limbed beat rocked the metal box of the engine room.

I went forward to the boats' fore-ends, edging along the butty's side planks amid an assault course of stacked coal bags, serried rows of gas cylinders, wheelbarrows (and my bike), baulks of timber, bundled-up side sheets, coils of ropes and the snaking hose from the diesel pump. From the butty's foredeck I jumped down onto the towpath to undo the front mooring rope, push the bow out into the canal and hop back on board.

Jules waited as the boats pivoted out together. Then as the engine increased in noise and was put into gear she unlooped the stern rope from the bollard on the bank. We moved off 'breasted-up', the two boats side by side so that their bows formed two bosomy curves surging through the water. The two sterns of the boats were together so that the three of us could chat over the clatter of the engine.

Here the Grand Union was a wide canal and there was plenty of room in the cuts to move along breasted up and pass oncoming boats. And we could motor into the lock chambers side by side, too, making things quicker. At the first of these, Winkwell Locks, I marvelled as the boats exactly filled the lock chamber from side to side and end to end. Once in the lock, the butty's helm had to be pushed right over to bring the rudder to one side; otherwise it would have made the boat too long to clear the 'doors'. Richard was already up on the side, windlass in hand. I jumped off the other side. We were going 'downhill', so the water was high in the chamber. We closed the lock gates behind the two boats, then walked to the other end and opened the paddles, slowly at first, the water surging out below the gates, and the boats dropping fast. When the level in the chamber fell to the level of the water in the downhill cut, it was easy to push the gates open. Jules pointed out that they are in good condition on the Grand Union, with their beams and 'sets' – hard bricks or stones raised from the 'quadrant' to give boots a grip – nicely restored.

We moored up for the night just a little further on. The handle of the helm on the butty was taken out and reinserted upside down, so instead of arching over at waist level it curved up into the air, out of the way. The upturned tiller stick was the sign of a moored-up boat. It was one of the things I'd learnt to notice when looking through archive photos of more than a century before. I had begun to notice the design of things like tillers, too. Jules and Richard's engine boat had a 'swan neck' tiller – as had Mal's *Becky* and Kate's *Morning Mist* – with the metal 'S' ending

Jules' Fuels' traditional carrier narrowboats – the boat is on the left, the engineless butty on the right.

in a brass tube and at the end of that a turned wooden handle ('you appreciate that on a frosty morning'), attached to a smaller rudder under the stern. The butty, by contrast, had a big 'helm' attached to a heavy, long rudder hung off the back of the boat. Like a big vane, it was a design dating from the time of the horse-pulled boats, making it easier to angle the boat away from the pull of the horse and clear of the bank.

Jules assigned me the cabin on *Towcester* normally used by their apprentice. My luck was in. This wasn't just a roof over my head but an experience of a classic working boat – a setup and design very like much like that of Mal Edwards.

193

Just inside the door, by the throttle and gear controls, was the boatman's office with a 'ticket drawer' where passes and 'tickets' for using canals and locks would be kept. Beyond was the bench (making an extra bed if needed) and, opposite it, a blackened stove with a copper kettle on the hob, and hanging beside it a tiny tin bath painted with flowers and leaves and scrolls. The customary drop-down table had a leaf painted with a fanciful square-rigged schooner ploughing across a sea, and everywhere hung ribbon plates, folds of heavy crochet lace, and brightly-polished brass globes. There had been a craze for these 'bedknobs' amongst boatwomen and, like much of the traditional decoration, the idea was to add brightness – I could see the cabin's interior reflected in the golden orbs. Paradoxically, there was an illusion of space created by cluttering everything up with plates and brasses and ornaments.

Narrowboat living is by necessity about simplicity and downsizing. The cabin itself was a cubby shelf-bed across the back wall – handily, a narrowboat is just wide enough for a six-foot bed across its width – with heavy curtains to create a dark cave. It was like being in a Gypsy caravan, a Victorian railway carriage and an antiques stall all in one.

I changed into a clean shirt, combed my hair and walked up the towpath with Jules and Richard to the Three Horseshoes. The pub was a welcoming place, with snugs and uneven walls swathed in William Morris wallpaper. It had once been a farm cottage, with a shop and stables to provision boatmen and overnight their horses. A couple of houses away was a forge for shoeing horses. Later, I found that the Duke of Bridgewater was buried just up the road, at the family vault in Little Gaddesden church. The inscription reads, *Impulit ille rates ubi duxit arartra colonus* – 'He sent barges across the fields the farmers once tilled'.

Relaxing into our pints, Jules recalled that she had 'been potty about canals' since a child growing up in Stoke Bruerne – one of the important hubs, where many boat families moored up between jobs. She could just about remember the working boats and had met 'Sister' Mary Ward, one of the famous canal characters, who spent most of her life as nurse and midwife to the boat people, paying herself for their treatments until she was given a small stipend by the Grand Union Carrying Company. 'Sister' Mary (who wasn't actually a qualified nurse) was awarded a British Empire Medal in 1951 and featured on the TV show *This Is Your Life* in 1958, when she was surprised by a cast of boat families, some of whom owed their lives to her care. She was so saddened when the last carrier boats stopped running in the late 1960s that she left Stoke Bruerne and moved to London.

Jules herself was equally devoted to life on the waterways. Although she grew up as commercial boating came to a halt, she had always found ways to work on the canals, starting with a popular 'camping boat', *Charlie*, run out of Stoke Bruerne. As a new wave of leisure boaters and live-aboarders created a market for canal services, she and Richard saw an opportunity to work on vintage boats. They had sold fuels, and worked on restorations, patching all kinds of heritage boats together, There was talk of a busted engine block in 1989 whose mechanism was so old that the search for a replacement piece ended in Iran, and a memory of an old-style engineer who diagnosed crank problems by putting a spanner to his ear and up against the block like a doctor with a stethoscope.

'Then we needed the butty,' Richard told me. 'Oh, did that make economic sense,' I asked. The snug erupted into laughter. 'Don't be silly,' they chorused, 'Don't be silly.' I was gathering that anything to do with heritage boats was a labour, a constant labour, of love and involved never-ending maintenance.

And they were off again, into stories of the 1970s and 1980s, when there were still a few working boats trying to make a living on the waterways – the last of the characters, the last of the tribe, the last generation who knew how to do things properly. And about the tricks or skills (frowned on in modern canal times) used to speed through locks, like using a loop of rope off the moving boat to pull the gates closed when entering the lock,

Classic boaters' decorations: ribbon plates, rose paintings, brass bedknobs, copper kettles and lace.

and nudging the gates open at the other end. But even the old professionals had their mishaps. The last working boatmen often worked their craft alone and would leave the engine to crawl the boat out of a lock unmanned, whilst they dropped the paddles and hopped back on board from below the lock. 'People missed it sometimes and then their boat was off down the cut – and the boatman running after it. There was one fellow who had to run across the fields, over a bridge, and shin out along the branch of a tree to drop back on his boat.' These were the kind of stories that were traded up and down the canals. Individual boatmen got nicknames, and families got reputations, for being steadfast, hot-headed or pugnacious.

I slept deeply that night in the cocoon of *Towcester*'s sleeping-cave and awoke to the sound of light rain on the roof and a light knock on the door. On the door sill, I found a mug of strong coffee. Again, I was learning the proper way of doing things. On boats where cabins are small and moorings public, privacy is sacrosanct. There is a rule on the waterways. 'Never touch a rope unless you're asked'. Stepping onto someone's boat uninvited, or barging (finally, there's a correct use of the word) into a cabin, were almost unforgivable rudenesses. I was given a shout for breakfast, though, and afterwards Richard invited me into the engine room. The day was to be my hands-on introduction to working a boat and butty. These were the kind of skills that a ten-year-old boat child handled with expertise – but that child, I reflected through the day, had been born to a life of boats, and learnt from parents who in turn had lived a life on the canals.

My first task was to start the beast of an engine ... and that needed careful instruction. I had to crank the starting handle with both hands – not easy in such a confined space – and get the flywheel turning fast enough to pressurise the diesel. 'Now, keep her turning with one hand, and flip over the compressor on top of the engine.' I reached over with my left hand and flicked the lever over. The handle under my hand seemed to hit a sandbag, then stopped. I let off the compressor and tried again. And failed again. Crank, flip and ... stop. 'No, I'll get it,' I insisted, wondering if I would (I'd read about boatwomen not being strong enough to start engines – or was it perhaps their husbands telling them so?) The fourth time, I concentrated on keeping the flywheel turning evenly as I reached over to flick the compressor. There was a rumble inside the block, and off she went.

Richard assigned me to the tiller of *Towcester* and we moved off, breasted-up. 'It's a bit confusing,' he warned. 'Because it's a Lister, the gear and throttle wheels turn the wrong way.' As I had no experience handling controls that went the 'right' way, that wasn't a particular problem and, as we chugged along, I had the same sense of joy (and concentration) as driving *Morning Mist* with Kate. I realised that Jules and Richard knew what they were doing so perfectly that they could let me learn by trial and error, with the odd word of instruction. Spinning up the throttle cautiously, getting a feel for the lopsided pull of the two boats, with the engine pushing off centre from under *Towcester*, I was enjoying the experience and that alertness of the senses you get with slow canal travel. Moorhens scuttered out from under the stem of the boat. Ducks with lines of ducklings like a tug pulling a file of tub boats navigated the shallows. Suddenly there was a rich waft of coffee above the diesel and sun-warmed water – we had passed Smiths Coffee Roasters, whose back door opened to the canal bank. And then we were on to a lock.

We were still moving breasted-up, with me steering the two boats, so things looked very tight and quite complicated. Throttling up and down, and changing back and forth between forwards, neutral and reverse to ease the boats into the chamber was tricky, as the surge of water out of the lower gates tried to suck them forward. I was worried, too, that I might hook the butty's big rudder, turned to the side but still sticking back, on the sill. And I discovered that it was as easy to turn the control wheels the wrong 'right' way, whilst trying to remember which was the 'wrong' way that was right. But we made it.

After the lock, we undid the ropes to let *Bideford* slip behind, in single file, as the canal water was low and the engine boat needed to be able to take the middle water to clear its propeller. This felt even more of a responsibility, as I was now in control of two boats joined by an umbilical cord of white cotton. Not only did I have to position *Towcester* correctly but keep in mind where the butty was, ninety feet behind. And, though I might have an engine and could reverse to stop *Towcester*, Jules, at the helm of *Bideford*, had to follow wherever I pulled her. It was a tricky stretch, too. Or to me it was. We passed a marina of boats, all moored end-on ('throttle down, throttle down,' I could hear Kate in my head), then a snaking double bend under a low railway bridge, all the while passing oncoming boats. At least those oncoming boats meant the next lock was set in our favour, but going in I needed to keep *Towcester* well to one side so that Jules could drift the butty into the gap at the engine boat's side, whilst Richard, already ashore, slowed *Bideford* with the centre rope snubbed around a bollard.

The only raised words from Jules or Richard – and, actually, from both of them – came when I reached out from one boat to fend the other off. It was an instinctive movement and I knew it was wrong even as I was doing it. A boater's instinct should be never to risk any part of themselves – hand, arm, leg – being trapped, crushed and mangled between the slow-moving but steamhammer power of laden boats. This is, really, the one great danger of canals. I snatched my arm back inboard.

Jules mentioned that often on the bridges and locks she notices initials carved into the stone. 'So and so loves so and so'. Some of these had been there for decades. 'And I'd know those people, from boating families. So, I could tell you who KW and VW are and what happened between them ... but don't write their names down because that would have been very personal from when they were courting.'

Her observation made me realise how much of the working boat people's lives had been lived in public and on the move. No wonder they'd been a close-knit, even xenophobic community. They needed their secrets to preserve their private lives, which were on view to everyone on the boats threading their way through cities and towns and villages and mooring up along the towpath. And so courting had to be adapted to being on the move, to sweethearts being on different boats passing each other up and down the cut, and rarely mooring close. On that *Narrow Boats* LP, one boater had recalled, resignedly: 'Not much time to talk and meet – we'd be passing and I'd raise the mop off the roof and that meant make a date.' A date might mean a walk along the towpath together before hurrying back to their own boats. In a largely illiterate society notes and letters were no use, but messages might get passed along word of mouth. There was little privacy from family, friends or strangers on the canal.

It was not much different with *Towcester* and *Bideford*. As heritage boats, properly painted, with the long-ago sound of a vintage engine, and one towing the other, people waved or shouted greetings as we passed. A young man working on a boat waved us down. Richard, at the tiller, slowed the engine and steered in beside the moored boat. 'Can I have a couple of cylinders of gas?' 'Sorry, no, they're all empties,' Richard shook his head. 'I'll drop one off when we come back through.' Neither party seemed too bothered by this and, as Jules drifted up on Bideford, it seemed more a chance to stop and talk to a friend. Because of course, with their constant travelling up and down, Jules and Richard knew every serious boater.

Slow travel and talk? In this weather and at this pace I was being seduced by all the positives of working on the canals. Jules had told me about the various 'apprentices' they'd taken on over the years – young, crazy about boats and canals, hard-working. She saw them as another generation to pass on skills. One former apprentice, Ryan, had already got his own boat to work. 'And he plays the fiddle really well,' Jules added. I hoped that he'd arrived to live in the engineboat's cabin already knowing how to play. Narrowboat canals are no place for practice.

We moored up in Apsley for lunch. 'There's a key in your ticket drawer,' Jules told me, 'if you want a shower before we eat.

Jules and Richard locking through their boat and butty. The new apprentice, taking a photo, was not being of much help.

There's a really good one by the marina that we use.' As well as boat-handling skills, a modern working canal person also needs to know the best pubs and cafes and shops and mooring places – and little luxuries like showers. Showered and shaved, I sat in the sun on the back of the boat, chatting across to Jules and Richard on the *Bideford*. We'd fallen into a relaxed pattern of banter and instruction. A leisure boater had strolled over from the marina (I'd noticed a boat with my own name – *Jasper* – beautifully painted on its side panel) to buy a cylinder of gas. Another disappointed customer. But we'd be picking up a fresh batch – twenty or thirty canisters – next morning, along with four tons of coal.

A serious-looking man walking the towpath stopped then turned back to address Richard. 'The wife and I are thinking of getting a barge. To live on. How much does one cost? And you can just tie up anywhere, right?' Richard caught my eye, and gave what was a practised answer to the boating-on-a-whim interrogator. 'Well, boats can cost anything, depending on what it is. Have you ever been on a boat?' The man shook his head. 'Well,' Richard continued, 'hire a boat, because you might find you don't enjoy it. Oh, and you can't really just moor anywhere, so unless you're continuous cruising ...' – the man looked blank – 'moving pretty much all the time, you'll probably need to rent a mooring.' He gestured across at the marina. 'In there could be four thousand a year, and then there's insurance, maintenance ... try hiring first.' The man's face had fallen. He hurried off to catch up with his wife. Richard rolled his eyes.

We moved on in the late afternoon with *Bideford* again on the snubbing line behind *Towcester*. I was steering the engine boat again as we moored under a double-holed bridge (the larger for boats and the smaller to take floodwaters) and then alongside wharfs turned into housing.

On the two boats, a hundred feet apart, Richard and Jules seemed to have a telepathic communication system. 'We're going to breast up again along here,' Richard said. 'So put her into reverse.' *Towcester* slowed to a halt, whilst *Bideford* slid on towards us. Richard was coiling up the tow rope as it slackened. And then, suddenly up at the bows, he was joining front-end to front-end, just as Jules looped a rope over to tie the sterns together. The butty hadn't stopped moving throughout.

Next, they wanted to turn both boats around so that, the following morning, after loading, we would have them pointing in the right direction for the return trip. We were approaching a branch in the canal where excess waters went down a channel and over the weir, whilst the navigation went into a lock. Jules had taken over the tiller on *Towcester* and Richard and I stepped ashore and walked ahead to the lock, windlasses in hand. Richard explained that we'd use the 'draw' of the opening lock to pull the sterns of the two boats round. It was an old skill, based on knowing a waterway, one's boats, and how blocks of water acted. Jules steered the bows of the boats down towards the weir and, as the middle of the boats passed the turn into the lock, we opened the paddles to fill the chamber. The water flowing into the lock sucked the sterns of the boats into the branch. It was far neater than the usual back and forthing – the five- or six-point (or in the hands of a flustered amateur twenty- or thirty-point turns) to get a 70-foot boat turned around in a seventy-five-foot 'winding' hole.

Once we had dropped down through the lock and onto the pound, it was surprisingly easy to stern-haul the two backwards-facing boats a few hundred yards along to our mooring for the night. We tied up in the shadow of another redeveloped wharf and, as we drank a glass of wine on the back counter in the warm evening, watched couples doing the same on their balconies.

As always, our conversation was focused on the waterways. Richard would start on a story: 'This kayak was heading straight towards the boat, and I had to steer hard to avoid it. I shouted at him, "Do you have any idea of how much damage your kayak could do to this boat?" And he said "Er, no ..." And I told him, "Absolutely none at all – but it could have pulped your kayak."' And then they'd get talking about canal lore: 'The big heavy leather belt was part of the costume to carry the windlass, but they'd always have the buckle to the back so it didn't scratch the boat's paintwork.' Or stories of breaking through ice in a hard freeze. Or, a favourite subject, the history of their own boats. *Towcester* had delivered barrels of lime juice to Roses' factory until the 1970s, carrying coal at other times.

Jules talked enthusiastically about the butty, too. She pointed out how the tiller shaft fitted into the top of the rudder – the

Not every boat on the Grand Union was quite as beautiful or traditional as Jules and Richard's *Bideford* and *Towcester*.

'ramshead' – and how that was traditionally decorated with a 'turkshead' (a turban-like weave) of white rope. 'All the old tow ropes were recycled, woven into fenders or mats to protect paintwork or woodwork,' she explained. 'On a boat, everything is done for maximum inconvenience. See here: the cant' – she pointed to the edge of the hull – 'has a strip of ash to protect it, and then there's a piece of painted canvas to protect that, and then a mat over that.' She was smiling at the absurdity.

Keeping a boat as neat and clean as possible despite the coal dust, the filth of the waterways, and the crowded, busy family cabin had been one of the most laudable traditions of the working boat families. 'Ramlin Rose' had dismissed boats and the families that didn't meet those standards as 'Rodney boats'.

Jules and Richard called the plastic cruisers and other non-canal boats 'Noddy boats'. Their sense of pride in doing things properly and keeping up standards was evident.

When we'd been moored up and I had nothing obvious to do, Jules had pointedly put a litre tin of Brasso up on the roof, next to the decorated Buckby water can and the painted mop and boathook handles. She had already explained how in summer, when the cabin stove wasn't used, the chimney became a 'gallery' to hang horse brasses and other brass decorations, while in winter an insulating cylinder was slipped over the chimney pipe. I polished away energetically at the three golden bands and the strap of horse brasses, taken back by the sharp smell of Brasso to childhood hours spent cleaning the bright work on harness and saddlery.

There was more 'brass' set into the wooden threshold of the butty's cabin. Four 1936 pennies, from the year that Bideford had been built. Another tradition kept alive, though they had drawn the line at nailing a tanned horse's tail to the ram's head. As Mal had told me – and Ramlin Rose had reported – a favourite horse's spirit was kept alive through its tail, and even when butties were towed by engine boats many still nailed on a flowing hank of hair.

Next morning we were up early drinking coffee and watching commuters hurrying from their apartments across the water and along the towpath to the train station. Neither Richard nor I had to say anything. Even preparing to hump four tons of coal off a lorry and into the boat, our lives seemed enviable.

Actually I didn't do much humping of coal. The lorry arrived at seven, and the driver – a large, jolly man in shorts and work boot – on the bank, and Richard down in the hold of *Bideford*, had an easy rhythm. They kept a conversation up the whole time – about other delivery companies, characters up and down the canal, and boating. As the assistant – the offsider – I was left to load and unload the gas cylinders. The diesel tank was dipped and then filled, and then a cup of tea all round.

The boats and the crew were full of fuel again and as the lorry pulled back onto the road I cranked the engine and flipped and pushed levers and buttons and – first time – the engine roused itself and fell into a steady trot. Jules had already untied us, and we motored up to the lock, still set for us after we had passed through the evening before. Once on the other side, Richard, on the tiller of *Towcester*, and Jules, on ropes, prepared to drop the butty astern onto the snubbing rope. I stayed on *Bideford*'s helm as the motorboat pulled ahead and then the rope picked her up and she began to move. 'Keep centre, stay in line with *Towcester* because there's not much water,' Jules advised.

At first, being pulled by the engine boat, a hundred feet of tow rope, and seventy feet ahead of *Bideford*, was unsettling. Without an engine on the butty to throw into reverse, there was no way to stop the boat other than drifting to a halt, or somebody jumping ashore with a rope to throw around a bollard. And, laden with coal and fuel, these boats were heavier than most narrowboats set up for leisure cruising, and so had the added momentum of weight. Richard – or whoever was steering *Towcester* – had to anticipate not just the boat he was on but also the boat he was towing. It meant approaching bridges, shallows and locks from the point of view of the butty far behind him. And it required him to adjust speed not just as he passed moored and moving boats, but to take into account my passing the same boats a little later.

But being on the butty, being pulled as if by a horse rather than pushed by a propeller, made for a smoother ride, leaving almost no turbulence as we headed downhill towards Apsley. And it was gloriously peaceful, with *Towcester*'s engine noise reduced to a distant low throbbing clatter. But I also realised what the women talking in *Ramlin* Rose had meant when they lamented the loneliness of a couple working an engine boat and

Keeping up appearances – you can never have too much *Brasso*.

butty. The tow rope and the butty's length combined put 170 feet between Richard and me and Jules. And we were often silent, ourselves, as I concentrated on helming.

Many of the things that Mal Edwards had talked about, or that I'd read or heard from boat people, were making sense now that I had a helm under my hand, and could feel the canal's waters under the hull of the eighty-year-old *Bideford*.

Jules and Richard dropped me off back in Apsley. They were heading north to Stoke Bruerne, where Jules was born and where they kept their live-aboard narrowboat. I visited them there later in the year, to see the Canal Museum, and poke my head

Bill Blewitt and May Hallatt as the Smith family on their traditional, horse-dawn narrowboat in the 1945 film, *Painted Boats*.

into the Bisworth Tunnel, just north of the town. I was curious to see this stretch of the canal, too, having watched a 1945 film called *Painted Boats*, a remarkable attempt to engage with canal culture, made by Ealing Studios director Charles Crichton, and featuring a commentary and poems by Louis MacNeice.

The film is a semi-fictional documentary about two boating families, the Smiths (who have retained their horse) and the mechanised Stoners. Crichton depicts the boat peoples' lives with respect and empathy, highlighting their tough and isolated work, as well as the canals' contribution to Britain's industry and to the war effort (filming took place during the war and there are thinly-veiled references to cargos of munitions). Viewed today (it is posted on YouTube), you wonder at the film-makers' remarkable timing, just before so many features disappeared forever. Crichton filmed on location along the Grand Union between Braunston and Stoke Bruerne, showing fully operational working boats both there and at Stoke-on-Trent and the Limehouse Cut, as well as such canal highlights as the Anderton Boat Lift and the Pontcysyllte Aqueduct.

I felt lucky to have experienced those traditions, even if only as a faint echo from the past.

9
Endurance

'NO! NO! *Not f—ing flapjacks!* I need the savoury ... the *savoury*!'
It was two in the morning, pitch-dark and frosty-cold, on the
Thames towpath at Mill End Lock, just downstream from
Henley's famed rowing waters. Two men in a double kayak had
powered in from the darkness, beams from their head torches
swinging back and forth along the waters. They pulled themselves
onto land, twisted round on their knees, dragged their kayak up
and, lifting it onto their shoulders, trotted wearily around the
lock. That's when their support crew stepped in, pushing food
into the paddlers' open mouths and raising mugs to their lips.
But they'd got it wrong. This was supposed to be a savoury snack
stop – not *f—ing flapjacks*!

'Sorry, really sorry,' one of the crew apologised. 'Here – I've got
coffee here.' He tried holding an insulated mug to the paddler's
mouth, to be met by a renewed outburst of exhausted, frustrated
swearing. 'It's not *f—ing coffee* here ... it's the *iso-drink!*'

The paddlers kept moving, relaunching their blade-thin
racing kayak below the lock gates, and paddled away into the
darkness, their torch beams fading from view. The crew, looking
embarrassedly at their carefully printed instructions for what

food was needed at each point, packed up the boxes of supplies and prepared to walk back to the road and drive on to the next lock. I climbed onto my folding bike, chilled by the early spring night, and set off again after the paddlers.

The Devizes-Westminster Canoe Race is the world's longest non-stop canoe race – and one of the toughest of all endurance challenges. Its alumni include the politician and former army officer Paddy Ashdown, explorer Sir Ranulph Fiennes, rower (and double Olympic gold medallist) James Cracknell, and the first British woman to climb Everest, Rebecca Stephens. But not all the big names make it to the finish. In 2011, world champion kayakers Ben Brown and Ivan Lawler attempted to beat the race record but had to retire after nine hours and fifty-one minutes, defeated by injury, a slow flow on the Thames and a mounting headwind. For the elite double-kayak crews that do complete the race, it means that they have paddled continuously over 125 miles of canal and river – setting out at Devizes on the Kennet and Avon Canal and ending at Westminster Bridge on the Thames.

At dawn that morning – around sixteen hours before – I'd watched as 150 or so kayak teams prepared to set off from Devizes. Rather than a head-to-head race, teams were aiming for the shortest elapsed time. So they based their departure on how long they thought it would take to paddle the 107 miles to Teddington Lock, the start of the tidal Thames. Paddlers had to reach the lock in a small time window, in the early hours of the following morning, to enable the ebbing tide to help them down the final seventeen miles of the river. Military crews in heavy Kleppers, and have-a-go types in a range of solid canoes, were setting off early to be sure of making the Teddington cut-off time. Super-fit racing crews in racing kayaks might not leave until the afternoon, or later still, confident of their ability to power along in time to arrive at the optimum moment.

Deceptively bucolic – an early stretch of the Devizes to Westminster
Canoe Race on the Kennet and Avon Canal.

These elite crews would have in mind the course record, held
since 1979, of fifteen and a half hours. 'But there won't be any
records this year,' I was told, 'the wind's in the wrong direction and the water's too low'. Shallow water means more drag
under the boats, so crews would have to reach down further,
and lift their boats higher, each time they pulled out at the seventy-seven locks. That might sound like a small difference. But
seventy-seven heaves of a kayak make quite a difference.

And there's a fair bit of experience to draw upon. The 'DW
Race', as it's known, was started seventy years ago, by four Scouts
from Devizes, on the Easter weekend of 1948. And the roots of
the race go back even further, to a bet in a Pewsey pub in the
1920s, when, during a transport strike, locals wondered if they
could get a boat down the Avon to the sea in under three days.

The bet was won. The story retained a currency and in 1947 the challenge was repeated – with a boat crew arriving in fifty-one hours. Then, the following year, a prize was offered for any crew that could beat their time.

Canoes, however, were deemed unsuitable for the challenge, which was a frustration for the Devizes Rover Scouts, who liked nothing better than paddling the Kennet and Avon, in home-made double kayaks. So the Scouts came up with an alternative challenge: to follow the Kennet and Avon Canal, then the Kennet river, and finally the Thames to London in under a hundred hours. Four scouts – Pete Brown, Brian Walters, Laurie Jones and Brian Smith – set off, carrying their own supplies and sleeping out along the way. They completed the 125 miles in ninety hours.

It was a creditable time, especially given their basic craft, and it caught the imagination of the local and then national press. The Scouts' finish in front of the Houses of Parliament was watched by thousands – and an endurance race was born.

The start line – then as now – was Couch Lane Bridge, on a wharf of the Kennet and Avon Canal. I turned up there on the morning of Easter Saturday 2017 to watch the first boats prepare to launch the sixty-ninth race. My plan was to follow the race on my bike – an easier option than kayaking – but still not exactly a doddle, cycling 125 miles through the day and night.

As the teams assembled for the start, I was already regret-ting having stayed up late the previous night, playing guitar in the Barge Inn, a few miles down the canal. But a coffee and bacon roll improved things, as I watched the race officials check entrants and support crews have last-minute confabs on meeting points. There was little razzamataz – too many hours of paddling ahead – as a straggle of crews paddled away towards the first checkpoint, with their support, equipped with boxes of food and flasks of drinks, driving away in pursuit.

I got on my fold-up bike and set off after them. The sun was out and it was warming up. As I cycled along the towpath, marginally faster than the boats, I was accompanied by a soundtrack of splashing paddles and early-race throat-clearing and coughing of lungs, even some jolly paddlers' chat. But by Honeystreet Bridge, talk was rare and the paddlers had spread out. I cycled past narrowboats on the move and bridges lined with spectators. I had stood on one myself the previous day, watching as hundreds of paddlers filed beneath me. They were the single kayaks and juniors taking part in an only slightly gentler four-day event, which breaks the 125 miles into four sections, competitors sleeping out in encampments along the way. It was salutary to think that the best of the non-stop racers, leaving a day later, would arrive in Westminster a day or more before this colourful fleet.

Following these elite doubles, I cycled through Bruce Tunnel, one of those classic bits of canal infrastructure, insisted upon by a local landowner, Thomas Bruce, 2nd Earl of Ailesbury, so that a cutting didn't spoil his views. A volunteer marshall was peering into the darkness from a pontoon. Dressed in a shorty wetsuit and with stand-up paddleboard at the ready, he told me that, although the tunnel was only 500 yards long – short enough to see light at the other end – many competitors found it daunting. 'A few of them yesterday preferred to carry their kayaks up over the hill.' Even the tough racing doubles seemed to find the atmosphere intimidating, with nervous chatter and bursts of spirit-lifting song echoing from the gloom as they came through in ones and twos. 'You can switch off your head torches, now,' Andy reminded them as they emerged blinking in the light, and then raced up to Crofton Top Lock.

It was a sunny early afternoon by this point and, spirits revived, I detoured up to Crofton Pumping Station, high above the locks. Built in 1812, just two years after the canal opened, to solve a lack of a reliable water, its Boulton & Watt steam engine is the oldest working pumping engine in the world. 'It's fired up quite often for demonstration days,' I was told by an industrial

Bruce Tunnel – the first landmark of the DW Race.

archaeologist on duty, 'and in recent years it's been hooked back to help modern pumps get more water up – a few years back it was needed to get more water in the canal for the canoe race.' As she spoke, there was a metronomic scrunching sound behind me, followed by a swish and a rattle. A boiler-suited volunteer was driving a square-bladed shovel under a pile of coal and shooting it through the open door into the boiler's firebox.

Not having a support crew of my own, I stopped in the Pumping Station cafe for a cup of tea and a sandwich. Back down at the locks, paddlers were hauling their kayaks and canoes out of the water and running them down to where they could relaunch, their crews trotting alongside, feeding them high-energy foods. I realised with a jolt that it was past three and, what with stopping to talk to people and take photos, I'd gone less than twenty miles, and like the paddlers had a hundred miles of travel ahead.

In Newbury, crews were cooking up hot soups on gas stoves and warming up pasta for their paddlers. Several sat on the edge of the canal, in the last of the evening sun, with swans and ducks gathering round them. But no one had time to waste and soon we were all travelling into the evening chill. I was pedalling rough paths and often it was easier to get off and push. London felt like a very long way.

Around this stage, I found myself recognising boats. I was keeping pace with a fairly evenly matched group of paddlers, while the very fastest were far ahead. Many others were still behind and some had already given up. It was dark when we reached the Thames, just past Reading, where an encampment had sprung up for crews preparing their paddlers with lights, clothing and provisions for the coming seventy miles.

Two of the elite paddlers hoisting their kayak between locks.

Suitably equipped, paddlers set off into the blackness. I followed on the towpath, with my bike light throwing a thin beam beside the river. And it was now obviously a river. Whereas the Kennet and Avon Canal had been dug remarkably true and straight all the way from Devizes to Reading, the Thames had taken hundreds of thousands of years to erode its course. Over the following hours the river looped and curved back and forth. Occasionally I heard the regular splash of paddles from the water and caught the flash of head torches. Everyone was too tired for talking. And then I would reach one of the locks – Sonning, Shiplake, Hurley, Marlow, Bray. It had become important that support crews were waiting at each pull-out point with more food, more drink and extra clothing. It became really important that crews didn't try and post a flapjack into the mouth of anyone expecting a slice of pizza or a sausage roll.

Some paddlers were having real troubles. At Bray I came upon a woman sitting on a lock-side bench, next to a man in his late fifties, the scene lit dramatically by a lamppost. 'I think you should stop, darling ... you've done really well ... it's getting dangerous.' The paddler's younger partner stood by their kayak. I could see what he was thinking. The older man staggered upright. I could see what he was thinking, too. 'No ... give me an energy bar ... let's keep going.' The duo lowered the kayak into the water below the lock and got back in.

The Thames locks were far bigger and longer than the Kennet and Avon Canal ones, and pulling the kayaks out and relaunching was proving ever more of an effort for the paddlers. And on top of that were the current and weirs. And the river was so wide at points, and split by islands, that it was hard for sleep-deprived paddlers to find their way in the dark.

Cycling through Maidenhead, I saw a fox trotting along the riverpath. By now, away from the river with its kayakers and the support crews, there were no people to be seen. It felt a strange thing to be doing, cycling along a riverbank at night, and at one point, stopping on a bridge to wait for paddlers, I fell asleep on my feet, falling forward onto the parapet and jerking awake just before tumbling over. The paddlers were even more tired, of course, but most of the ones who'd got this far would make it to the end, unless they missed the cut off point at Teddington Lock. Then at Staines I saw the man who'd been sitting on the bench at Bray Lock. His wife was walking him very slowly towards a car parked down the towpath in the dark, a blanket wrapped around his shoulders. The younger man followed behind with their paddles.

It was the grey, chill light of dawn when I got to Windsor. I looked for coffee but nothing was open – it was Easter Sunday morning – and I cycled on. The river was misty and filmic as ghostly kayakers passed downstream, locked into their constant rhythm, sixteen hours in. Long before Teddington Lock, where the river became tidal, I could see tired paddlers forced to pick up the pace. If they missed the ebb-tide window, they would be stopped. When I reached Teddington, cycling over the airy footbridge, I met a man looking down at a Klepper pulled up on the bank. 'That's my son. He can't keep going ... exhaustion ... there's always next year.' He didn't sound convinced.

On the bike, I was now on decent surfaces, scooting past London's bridges – Kew, Hammersmith, Putney, Battersea. I'd found a riverside cafe and was energised again. And down on the grey water the canoes and kayaks were flying along on a tide that was doing five knots in places, doubling their speed. On the Albert Embankment, I could see Westminster Bridge ahead, with a large banner spread over its side arch announcing the finish line. There were safety boats in the water and a small crowd up on the bridge, watching the paddlers coming down in ones and twos from Lambeth Bridge. The fastest had completed the 125 miles hours ago, beating me on my bike. But there were still tens of finishers to come.

There was a sudden gasp from the crowd. A bright-red kayak had overturned, within sight of the end. Only yards from the finish. A rescue boat buzzed in. 'Just stand up ... it's shallow,'

The finishing line in sight at Westminster. Note the man standing up in the river, with the Thames at that point no more than canal depth.

a voice shouted. 'Pull your boat over the finish line.' The two paddlers staggered to their feet and waded on, dragging their boat behind them.

Many more finishers arrived under the gaze of Big Ben in the hour that I stayed to watch. A combination of extreme weariness, cold and the stiff wavelets bouncing off the embankment walls was catching many of them unaware, and more of them capsized and finished the race soaked through, pulling their kayaks. Others came in with the regular paddle strokes and easy pace that suggested that they might as happily keep going.

I couldn't. I was too tired to stay until all the competitors had finished and cycled to a friend's house in Battersea, had a cup of tea and collapsed on the sofa.

Over the next month or so, the DW Race began to occupy my imagination. Just how hard was it to paddle that route? I began to regret not having joined in – perhaps not with the elite non-stop kayakers, but at least with the four-day-eventers. So in May I decided to set out and see if I could recreate the original Scouts' bet. Could I kayak from Devizes to Westminster, self-supported, in under a hundred hours?

Actually, I thought, a hundred hours seemed plenty of time. The only critical thing was to hit Teddington Lock at the right time to catch the ebb. I looked up high water at Teddington, did some calculations, and took a bus to Devizes. There I assembled my rather clever Advanced Elements folding-inflatable kayak which I'd been lent to try out on the canals. I packed basic bivvy gear, a bag of food and a few items of clothing, and paddled away under the bridge. It was an idyllic start – a balmy, early summer evening, with coots puttering around in the reeds.

A few miles later I pulled the boat out and made camp. It was approaching dusk and it seemed a good, if odd, plan to use the first of my hundred hours sleeping. So I laid my bag beside a bridge, past Honeystreet. I had been reading recently about the canals during the Second World War and noticed that there were anti-tank bollards still in place at the bridge's end.

I woke at dawn, then fell asleep again until nine. Fourteen hours gone and just five miles under my belt. Ashamed, I forswore breakfast, packed and launched onto the canal. Round the next corner was the angry cob swan I'd heard paddlers talking about during the race; he mantled his wings and hissed as I passed. I paddled steadily through the morning, keeping up a steady three and a half miles an hour, whilst doing calculations in my head: hours, speed, distance ... Teddington Lock (and Westminster) seemed achievable. The locks, though, were a trial. Pulling out of the water at Crofton Top Lock, taking my bags from the boat, and then pulling the kayak onto land took more energy than I'd imagined. It struck me that the real challenge in reaching London in – let's see – another eighty hours, were the seventy seven locks. If each took ten minutes ... that would be ... some six and a half hours spent on getting past locks alone.

As all kayakers must, I followed a mantra – keep paddling, don't think of the distance, look around. And a bit of steel had entered my soul. If I was going to 'win the bet', I couldn't loiter. So, I paddled on in the heat past tempting canalside pubs, ate on the move (thinking of flapjack man), and paddled late into the evening. At one point, by chance, I saw a familiar face on the towpath – Kara, who lived aboard a boat on the Kennet and Avon, and had raised her children on the canal. She called me ashore for a cup of tea. A quick cup of tea.

There was a late stop in Hungerford to get food, and then I paddled until dark. I pulled out the kayak, had a mug of soup and some cheese and fell asleep. At one point I woke to a soft galloping thud along the bank and realised otters were playing only a few yards away. It was easy to get up at dawn, in one of those early mornings where the smell of the air promises a heat-wave. Within an hour of paddling, I was stripped to the waist

Dawn at Honeystreet Bridge – a view from my bivvy bag (before falling asleep again).

and burning, trying to keep my mind in race mode – hydrate, eat, solve problems before they arose. My kayak was tough enough but, with its skin and frame and inflatable sponsons, was vulnerable to a jag of rusty metal or a sharp piece of concrete pulling out at locks.

With *Nicholson's* to hand on the front deck, I could keep an accurate track of how fast I was going, but the kayak wasn't a racing beast, and its most efficient speed was just under four miles an hour, a brisk walking pace. If I put more effort into paddling I was merely wasting energy. At one point I found myself paddling through a mosaic of thousands of dead mayfly. Nearby, I passed one of the canal network's few turf-sided chamber locks; the walls were of earth, like a riverbank, rather than stone, and boats rose and fell between iron stanchions. Cheap to build, these locks proved a false economy, especially on the Kennet and Avon, because of the amount of water they used.

Further on, a flotilla of boats had gathered under the banner of the Boaters' Christian Fellowship – 'Sharing God's Love on the Waterways'. Perhaps it was this, and the heatwave, that made me more and more tempted by the idea of a pint and when I came upon the Rowbarge, on the bank at Woolhampton, I couldn't resist. But the hours were ticking down and I didn't stay long. I had an appointment with Teddington.

Reading came up in the late afternoon. A pack of teenagers had taken over Southcote Lock, splashing around in the evening heat, their tangle of bikes on the towpath. They looked at me through narrowed eyes, but then a girl drying her hair on a T-shirt smiled and asked how far I was going. 'London', I told her and noticed, not for the first time, the look of longing that a kayak stirs in people. The freedom of being able to paddle off for as long and as far as you want.

I reached the end of the canal and joined the Thames at Blake's Lock. Paddling on to the river, I reflected on how boat people –used to the still, confined waters of the canals – feared the Thames and its floods and currents; in *Ramlin Rose*, boatwomen talk about the horrors of being swept along. I had myself been looking forward to riding the river's current, but the banks of the Thames seemed to be all reedbeds, tangles of willow, or mudbanks. There was nowhere to pull out and sleep, until at last I found a small hollow by a fallen tree and scrambled up into a little wood, pulling the kayak behind me. I heated up soup and crawled into my sleeping bag.

Again, I woke before dawn. Making it to Westminster in under a hundred hours was looking very tight, so I packed and launched as the sun rose. I'd got the river to myself. There were islands tangled with trees, woods and rough fields, and then huge mansions with lawns sweeping down to the water, where polished wooden speedboats were moored on pontoons. It was like a mix of *The Great Gatsby* and *Huckleberry Finn*.

Aided by the current, I began making good time. Gulls and terns and cormorant hinted at the Thames connection with the coast and there were swirlings on the surface of the water as sun-seeking fish crashed like submarines under the bow of the kayak. The water smelled soupy in the heat – part compost, part fresh rain. The locks were dauntingly big and on a few occasions I had to stand up in the kayak to reach the bank and pull myself up.

In Marlow I pulled out at the rowing club – a few members looked superciliously from their sculling boats at my kayak – and stuffed myself with an all-day breakfast, glad of the dark shade of the indoors. Heading through Windsor, past swans and badly rowed hire boats, I recalled cycling alongside the non-stop paddlers, and felt how much more relaxed my own rules had made the trip. And then realised my mistake. For if I didn't push hard, I wouldn't make Teddington at ten o'clock next morning and catch the tide. Then I would have no chance of coming in under a hundred hours. It was my own personal target, but it felt real enough.

It was dark when I got to the lock at Staines and set up camp. I'd been paddling pretty much non-stop for seventeen hours.

The swiftest of racing kayaks, powered by two fit, trained people with a ground crew to fuel them, would have got from Devizes to Westminster in that time. Just past four in the morning, I set off again paddling into a glorious dawn. I felt strong and back on schedule, enjoying the entertaining variety of rivercraft – algae-stained plastic cruisers, Dutch barges, steam launches and gin palaces. There were double-storeyed houseboats on pontoons with balconies and decks. River life looked good and I was further cheered by finding two of the locks had canoe ramps – slopes with rollers. I arrived at Teddington a full two hours ahead of the ebbtide.

There, I noticed a boat tied up at the lock gate and, on a run of luck, paddled over to ask if he was going through, hoping I might be able to share the lock with him and save the portage. Yes, indeed he was, he said, but he'd be waiting here for the next five hours until the tide changed. 'What a buffoon,' I thought, explaining carefully that the tide on the other side of the lock was just starting to ebb. He disagreed. 'I've looked it up,' I said, and produced my notebook where I'd written down the high-water times for Teddington. He countered with actual tide tables.

I couldn't believe that I was wrong. But as I dropped the kayak down another canoe roller, I arrived at a thin trickle of water between banks of soft mud. I shook my fists at the skies, and recalled, in my absurd dance of frustration, that it was at Teddington Lock that Monty Python filmed the surreal 'Fish-Slapping Dance'. Cleese and Palin in safari suits and pith helmets, in a sort of Morris dancing routine, the latter skipping up to the former and gently flicking him with a pair of pilchards, before Cleese produces a large trout and slaps Palin across his ear and into the water.

Absurd. Like my whole trip. And maybe that was the thought that kept me going. I still had eight hours in hand, so I'd keep paddling – against the current. And when I launched, there wasn't much current at all – it was only an hour or two after the turning point and the waters were lazily making their way

Canoe ramps with rollers – the most welcome of sights, approaching Teddington Lock and the tidal Thames.

upriver. But over the next few miles it began to pick up speed against me. Navigation buoys canted over with the waters ripping past them. By the time I reached Kew, I realised that parents walking hand in hand with toddlers on the river path were outstripping me. Out in the middle of the channel the buoys were now lying on their sides as the tide rushed in at maybe five or six knots. Soon I'd be going backwards towards Devizes.

I pulled onto land and fitted the trolley onto the kayak, ready to walk off and find transport away from the river. I'd given up. And then came another daft idea. It was only another eight miles to Westminster. I would set off walking, hauling the kayak behind on its trolley.

I couldn't pretend it was fun. The heatwave was still turned up to max. The pull strap I'd fashioned at the bow of the kayak cut into my hand, and my shoulders ached. I got very tired of people telling me that the river was 'just over there'. Then at Putney I noticed that the tide seemed to be going out. It didn't make any sense but I threw in a stick and watched it slowly make its way downstream, towards the sea, towards Westminster. London's river tides are powerful and strange affairs, ebbing and flowing at different times along the length of the Thames. And here, it seemed, the waters had peaked. I relaunched the kayak and scrambled in.

As I began paddling, I was caught on a fabulous rollercoaster ride of choppy current, speeding me down towards Battersea. The river rushed through bridge holes, slapped against the high embankment walls. Chop and wake from big passing boats threw up more waves. I remembered the numbers of kayakers who had capsized in the last miles of the race back at Easter. And the tide was increasing in speed. London was racing past. I paddled to position the boat near the side to ride the torrents of water bullying their way past the pontoons and piers of bridges.

Then, just as I passed under Battersea Bridge, I caught a movement away on the other side of the river. A sea kayak was arrowing towards me. 'Jesus, I knew it had to be someone as stupid as you.' It was Harry Whelan, who, like me, had once sea-kayaked the thousand miles around Ireland. The difference between our circumnavigations was that – until recently – his was the fastest on record, and mine was likely to retain the record for the slowest.

'You've done the Devizes to Westminster route, in that thing?' Harry said in bemusement, as he came alongside and I told him about my own personal hundred-hour challenge – and that I had a couple of hours left.

'Let's go, then,' he said, setting off at a blistering pace, carried along on the rushing waters. With only a few miles left to cover we were opposite the Houses of Parliament and by Westminster bridge in twenty minutes. Harry left me with a cheery wave.

I'd made it from Devizes to Westminster in ninety-eight and a half hours.

10

War and Salvage

ROYAL MILITARY AND STRATFORD-UPON-AVON CANALS

THE DEVIZES TO WESTMINSTER canoe race caught my attention for its strangeness. Endurance events tend to be about extreme environments – ultra-running in the Atacama Desert or Arctic marathons – so it was a surprise to find a major event on Britain's sleepy waterways. But as I delved into canal life and history, I became intrigued by the Kennet and Avon event as an early showing of the shift in use (and perception) of the canals – from a hidden world of commercial boating to leisure.

It turned out, too, that the Kennet and Avon played an important part in the campaign to keep the waterways open and operational. In January 1956, a 22,000-signature petition against its closure was sent to the Queen. To draw attention, it was sent by boat from Bristol, with a cabin cruiser carrying it as far as Bath, from where it was transferred to a canoe paddled by Commander Wray-Bliss for the journey along the canal. His canoe was then carried like a coffin at the head of a procession to the Ministry of Transport in Berkeley Square, accompanied by a Major Edward Falconer giving a solo performance of the 'Kennet and Avon Battle Song'.

A few brave souls had begun to explore the waterways as a form of leisure in the second half of the nineteenth century. In 1869, a book was published with the somewhat exhaustive title, *The Waterway To London; As explored in the 'Wanderer' and 'Ranger' with sail, paddle and oar in a voyage on the Mersey, Severn and Thames and Several Canals*. Though published anonymously, a signed copy suggests its author was Alfred Taylor Schofield, who, with two other young men, and a dog, set off along the Bridgewater Canal to reach London. Their route, as outlined in the title, suggests a lot about waterways transport in the mid-nineteenth century. As much as possible they avoid canals in favour of rivers, attracted by favourable river currents and frustrated by slow canal traffic. On the Bridgewater, where they cross Brindley's aqueduct, they complain 'our patience is now sorely tried; for the next half-hour we meet an endless succession of canal-boats; some with one horse, some with two, others with a trio of donkeys'. On the Ellesmere, near Chester they're sidelined by 'a steamer pulling forty barges'. The trio are initially mistrustful of boatmen, though heading towards Llangollen they load their craft onto a passing boat and report 'that the whole family – father and two sons – are the most obliging, civil, and kind people I have met for some time ... differing considerably in manner from the free and enlightened operatives in Cottonopolis'.

Schofield's account is in some ways a precursor to Jerome K. Jerome's million-selling *Three Men in A Boat* of 1889, a far more whimsical and amusing tale of misadventures along the Thames, again featuring three men and a dog. The two books represent the first hints of an emerging boat tourism on the waterways – it almost feels like exploration – as the canals declined in the face of the railways. Schofield remarks on the lack of boat traffic on the Thames and Severn Canal, which joined Bristol to the Thames, due to 'the immense growth of the American canal weed, the first germ of which was brought into England, only a few years ago.' The arrival of canal weed was another part of

Kayakers on the canals in the mid-nineteenth century, photographed at around the time of Schofield's trip from Bridgewater to London.

the declining canals story; repairs, bank clearance, lock-keeping, water-level maintenance and water weed cutting were neglected on lesser-used and unprofitable waterways. And the weed could become critical. Cyril Herbert Smith's *Through the Kennet and Avon Canal by Motor Boat*, which recounts a journey with his wife (and, inevitably, a dog) in 1928, chronicles mile after mile of thick weed entangling the propeller and reducing progress to bow-hauling. 'There was not a space of a yard square where water was visible,' Smith writes of the stretch above Crofton Top Lock. 'One might have been looking on some derelict field.'

Smith became an early campaigner for the Kennet and Avon, lecturing and writing letters to ensure its survival. But the accounts of all these early waterways travellers were important in the saving of the canals, in their recasting of the waterways and their working families as romantic, rural and bohemian, rather than squalid, industrial and dangerous. I've already mentioned Temple Thurston's purple-prosed – but for Edwardians thrillingly exotic – *The Flower of Gloster*, from 1911, about the joys of narrowboating on the Midland canals. Another bestseller that shaped public attitudes was A. P. Herbert's romantic novel *The Water Gipsies*, published in 1930, in which young Jane Bell leaves poor Bohemian London for a nomadic life on the waterways on the horse-drawn boat of her boatman husband.

Such books introduced the idea that canals were a part of Britain's heritage and something to be proud of, but it was not a view shared by the railway companies, nor the governments of the first half of the twentieth century. There were waterways that continued to pay their way. The Grand Union, the Oxford Canal, some of the canals around Birmingham, and many of the northeast waterways, as well as canals within London, continued to move large amounts of coal around, to carry imported cargoes away from ports, or transport specific cargoes – like chocolate crumb for Bourneville or barrels of lime juice for Roses. But as a succession of canals were closed, or rendered unnavigable by lack of maintenance, or actively dismantled by the railway companies, many industries and factories were forced to build railway sidings to replace the old wharfs and basins.

The salvation of the waterways as a leisure network was slow to take off. In 1907, the first boat rentals were established on the Norfolk Broads – inspired by the growth of yachting as a sport – and as we've seen, there were popular boat trips on the Llangollen Canal. Most of the early enthusiasts for canal preservation, however, looked back to the industrial past, urging that commercial waterways, given investment, had a potential for growth. One proposal was to update Brindley's Great 'X' where key canals joined and united the 'corner' estuaries of England and their ports, connecting the Severn, Humber, Mersey and Thames. In 1943, J.F. Pownall suggested a 'Grand Contour Canal' based on his observation that there was route that ran almost the length of England at the 310-feet contour and went through or close to many important industrial areas. His idea was that a new canal, a hundred-feet wide and seventy-feet deep, could run without locks between Preston and Hertford. It would be big enough to carry 1,350-ton boats, while branch lines would connect to industrial areas, and shipping would be carried up and down in lift locks to give access to the coast. A secondary but important function would have been to distribute water for domestic and industrial use along its length. It was, of course, never built, though the idea was revived as recently as 2012.

Pownall's 'Grand Contour Canal' was proposed during the Second World War, when canals were pressed back into service, to a significant extent as part of the war effort, not least as a safe means of carrying munitions.

Wars and canals had a long history. As noted earlier, some historians argue that Brindley's canals – and their enabling armaments and other goods to be transported – were as important as Nelson and Wellington in defeating Napoleon. In 1798 the Grand Junction Canal had been cleared of traffic for two days so that thirty boats could move troops swiftly and unhindered, and Pickfords offered 400 horses and 28 boats for government use. At the height of the Napoleonic wars, in 1804, work was started on the Royal Military Canal between Seabrook near Folkestone and Cliff End near Hastings. Conceived as a defensive barrier against invasion – the French being considered likely to land on Romney Marsh – this was dug along a zig-zagging course, changing direction every 500 yards so that cannons could be fired along its waters, and with a high embankment to protect a military road.

The Royal Military Canal took five years to complete, by which stage Britain's theatre of war had moved to Spain, with Wellington pursuing the Peninsula War. And the canal, in any

The Royal Military Canal and its raised embankment – very pretty but possibly no great impediment to Napoleon, nor to a Panzer division.

case, wasn't all it was cut out to be, proving not particularly effective even at containing the infamous smugglers of Romney Marsh. William Cobbett, in his *Rural Rides* of 1830, laconically observed that if Napoleon had crossed the Danube and the Rhine, these thirty yards of ditch wouldn't have troubled him.

Still, as Britain's only true military canal, I thought I should see the canal for myself, and on a fine summer's weekend I took the train to Folkestone and set off to walk the twenty-eight miles of the canal. I had a couple of pastoral days' ambling along the towpath. Strollers and dog walkers sauntered along beside the water, dragonflies and kingfishers flashed in and out of the reeds, and a trio of kayakers paddled on clear waters. A heron took off, its legs dangling as it flew, as if wading through the heavy sum-mer air. It all seemed a long way from war. But there were signs of the canals defensive purpose and the fear of invasion – and from long after Napoleon's time. Between the First and Second World Wars, experimental acoustic 'mirrors' had been built at points along Britain's coast and there was still one standing above the canal. It looks like a huge concrete satellite dish, aimed at the Continent, and the idea behind it was that the sound of distant incoming aircraft would be picked up by its parabolic reflector and aerial invasion heard long before being picked up by unaided human ears.

By the time actual German bombing started in the Second World War, radar had been invented and the acoustic mirrors were defunct. But the canal was still seen as a first line of defence – a barrier against the Panzer tanks – if Hitler invaded Britain by way of Romney Marsh. Heavily reinforced wartime pillboxes remain in place at regular intervals. I stopped to admire one on the canal bank below St Rumwold's Church – itself the creation of the Normans, Britain's last successful invaders.

In the Second World War, Britain's canals were collectively seen as a ready-made defence against German invasion – in particular, their tanks. The threat of invasion seemed very real after the British Expeditionary Force was defeated in 1940 and the evacuation from Dunkirk. Intelligence revealed that Hitler had an invasion plan called Operation Sea Lion in place and defences were hastily prepared across the country. Canals were seen as crucial 'stop lines' to slow any invasion. The Kennet and Avon Canal was part of the primary line across the south of England and pillboxes, anti-tank defences and gun placements were hastily thrown up along its length. On many canals, holes were prepared under bridges so they could be blown at short notice. The canals could also create vulnerabilities. German night bombers learnt to

Military hardware remains in place alongside the Royal Military Canal, including this inter-war acoustic mirror for detecting aeroplanes.

follow their glittering tracks to industrial centres like Coventry, so the beams of the locks were painted black with only a white tip (as they still are today), and the mouths of tunnels painted white to allow night-time navigation without lights.

But canals also played a more active role in the war, filling a vital role in moving munitions, coal, ore and food around the country. On the whole, boat families continued to operate their craft, but many men from the waterways joined up to fight, leaving a shortage of labour. In 1941, Frances Marian 'Molly' Traill approached the Ministry of War with the idea of recruiting women to run boats on the Grand Union – much as the so-called 'Land Girls' were working on farms. The Ministry agreed and Traill, with Eily Gayford, began training all-female crews to operate narrowboats and barges. Legend has it that an advert was put in *The Lady* magazine, announcing that 'idle boats' needed crews. The 'Trainees', as they were called, wore badges with 'IW' signifying 'Inland Waterways' – but they became nicknamed (or perhaps self-titled) the 'Idle Women'.

The 'Idle Women' scheme spread to several other waterways, including the Leeds and Liverpool, but it seems that there were never more than around fifty women in total. Their training consisted of two round-trips on the Grand Union, six weeks in total, after which a three-woman crew would be deemed ready to take on their own diesel-powered boat and butty. The scheme attracted capable, independent women, often from comfortable middle-class, urban backgrounds, and the working boat families were apparently sceptical and not generally welcoming. Some trainees lasted only a few days, unable to cope with spartan on-board living – tiny, cold cabins, poor rations (unlike the Land Girls, there were no special food allowances), and long, gruelling and dangerous work. But those who stuck with it invariably came to love the canals – and many of them would become post-war advocates for preserving the waterways.

Margaret Cornish was one such, thriving in her role on the waterways and, after the war, buying a narrowboat to holiday on with her family. Her book, *Troubled Waters*, details the process of attempting to learn all aspects of canal work in a short training period, the triumphs of getting things right, and earning the grudging respect of the professional carriers when they did. She deals with ice on the canals, and even helps a regular boatman, Bill Humphries, get his mule out of the cut when it falls in. The wartime cargoes were varied, with coal and aluminium ingots (for planes) regular loads, as well as steel, cement, sugar, cotton and wool bales, peanuts, raisins, flour and tinned foods. And munitions – including bombs. It could be dangerous work.

In Sheila Stewart's *Ramlin Rose*, the boatwomen discuss the Idle Women in mixed terms: 'Whenever we noticed a fresh scrape of paint on a wall or another brick knocked out of a

A trio of Idle Women at Bulls Bridge on the Grand Union Canal – this was a PR photo shoot in April 1944 to encourage new recruits.

bridge, "Ah!" we'd say, "The Trainees 'ave been at it again! Some of them was 'opeless, couldn't stick the loife ... but some was real game, willin' to learn and stuck it to the finish.'" The traditional boatwomen disapproved of the trainees smoking, their trousers and make-up. But they allowed that they brought some changes for the good – notably, the boat companies started giving two weeks' paid leave to their workers in response to the regular leave that the trainees got.

All this, of course, was the world that Kate Saffin and Heather Wastie had researched, written about and acted on their tours of the Oxford and Grand Union canals. I cast my mind back to travelling on *Morning Mist* and helping with the show at The

Folly at Napton, and I could see how the waterways and boating had drawn in Kate and Heather as they had Margaret Cornish and the other trainees.

With the end of the war –and the canals falling into an accelerated decline – those women who had wanted to continue on the canals found there were no boats or jobs for them. The only Idle Woman I'd heard of who had continued on the waterways was Sonia South, an actor from London, who married a boatman called George Smith.

However, in many ways, the Second World War was a pivotal point in saving Britain's canals. In practical terms, the use of canals in the war effort led to the maintenance of much of the network. But the war also had a psychological impact, creating a nostalgia and reverence for Britain's landscapes and (supposedly) bucolic past – something worth fighting for. British travel and nature books sold well in the war years and were often sent to troops fighting abroad, and one of the most popular was Robert Gibbings' *Sweet Thames Flow Softly*, about boating the length of the Thames in 1938. A rumbustious account, spiced with mildly erotic adventures, nature observations and conversations in riverside pubs, it caught the nation's mood.

In the immediate post-war years, many men and women who had found excitement in travel, and even in battle, weren't at all content to return to the mundanity of their old jobs and the lives expected of them. A few demobbed servicemen bought boats and worked as independent carriers, among them Tom Foxon, who became a noted canal historian (for the Trent and Mersey) and wrote books describing canal life and the difficulties of working boats in these declining years.

Foxon himself, though he would scarcely have imagined it at the time, proved to be something of a trendsetter. The canals were becoming places for escape from the peacetime anticlimax and from the stress of modern working life. As post-war austerity eased, with paid holidays and a burgeoning middle class, leisure became an industry. People started seeing the waterways as a source of adventure and tranquillity, neatly dovetailing with the British passion for old transport and industrial heritage. Others were beginning to experiment with alternative living, and found that they could buy cheap decommissioned barges and narrowboats and live aboard, mainly in London and other big cities but also out on rural canals. The waterways were steadily changing function from industry to lifestyle.

Government was forced to play a part, too. The railways were nationalised in 1948 and, as the rail companies owned many of the canals, so were most waterways. The Ministry of Transport would have happily ditched the responsibility, viewing canals as a needless drain on the exchequer, and in the late 1940s and early 1950s 'Acts of Abandonment' were drafted for many state-owned waterways. But canals couldn't be eradicated with the stroke of a pen. It proved almost as expensive to fill in canals as it had been to dig them, and many of them had other functions beyond transport – as drainage channels, for instance, or as conduits for moving water (like the Llangollen), or as factory waste outlets. Nonetheless, many sections of canals were de-watered, lock gates rotted and weren't replaced, and new motorway, road and rail bridges were built so low over canals that boats couldn't pass below, effectively turning them into culverts. Bit by bit the canal network was being lost, making it easier – even obvious – to make the case for wholesale abandonment.

One of the earliest canals under threat was the Kennet and Avon, which was expensive to keep in water, had complicated flights of locks to maintain and little commercial traffic. Another was the Stratford-upon-Avon Canal, also with numerous locks and two aqueducts. Both were effectively closed through neglect, and there were similar stories across the country.

The canals needed a movement to save them. And at the right moment, two men – Tom Rolt and Robert Aickman – stepped forward. Without this duo, very different in character, and at times almost disastrously at odds with each other, it is doubtful if more than a few individual canals would have survived.

Lionel Thomas Caswall Rolt was an enthusiast for old-style engineering – vintage cars, steam trains, early industry and, naturally, waterways. Before the Second World War, his uncle Kyrle Willans had bought an old horse fly-boat, *Cressy*, fitting it first with a steam engine and then a Ford car engine. Tom Rolt accompanied Willans on early trips and in 1937 bought the boat and eloped with his girlfriend, Angela Orred.

Orred described Rolt as a classic inter-war Bohemian – with 'corduroys and one gold earring' – and their life on *Cressy* followed suit. Rolt converted the boat into a comfortable live-aboard, complete with a bath on a dais to allow the plughole to drain. In *Ramlin Rose* there is mention of a bemused working boatwoman coming across the Rolts as they cruised the water-ways: 'We'd never knowed nothin' like it, a workin' boat being turned all over into a n'ouse. We thought it a terrible waste of 'aulage use and Mr Rolt her Captain, were not quite the ticket. But he was always very civil in passin' and "she" were very pleasant too.'

Rolt was a pacifist and worked in engineering through the war, continuing to live on *Cressy* on the canals. In 1944, he published a lyrical, nostalgic and well-observed book called *Narrow Boat*, about his and Angela's travels before the war. The book sold well and Rolt received an enthusiastic letter from Robert Aickman, also a pacifist, who, with his wife Ray, ran a literary agency. The Aickmans were invited to stay on *Cressy*, which at the time was moored on the Worcester and Birmingham Canal at the top of Tardebigge, Britain's longest flight of locks. It was to be a momentous meeting and, as Aickman later described the trip, 'the best time I have ever spent on the waterways'.

Tom Rolt steering *Cressy* at Hawkesbury Junction, where the Oxford Canal meets the Coventry Canal, 1940s.

I cycled out to the Tardebigge Flight from Birmingham to pay homage, on a drizzly May evening; the heatwave of a few weeks before had gone like a mirage. I pushed my bike up the flat, rise, flat, rise towpath running up past the thirty narrow locks and found a bit of shelter to sleep out, just where the canal ran into the Tardebigge Tunnel. Next morning, with harder rain falling, I made my way to Tardebigge Wharf, still an active boatyard, in whose basin were moored a group of live-aboards converted from old working boats. I asked one man, almost as venerable as his boat, where *Cressy* had been moored, and he pointed me down the canal to a small memorial, with a plaque that reads, 'At this spot in 1946, on board *Cressy*, Tom and Angela Rolt first met Robert Aickman and decided to form the Inland Waterways Assoc.'.

Another plaque below corrects the date to 1945. And it was in May 1945 that the first meeting of the Inland Waterways

Association was held, at Aickman's Bloomsbury flat. Also present among a small group of enthusiasts was the canal historian Charles Hadfield, who, like Aickman, had written admiringly to Rolt. Within a few months the fledgling group had 150 members. However, almost from the start there were significant differences of opinion in how the waterways should be protected. Rolt, despite the Bohemianism, didn't want 'an arty cult' of canals but to protect the traditions and the few remaining commercial carriers. He saw leisure boating as a necessary evil to provide support and funding and was pragmatically inclined to lose canals that were unviable and which gave ammunition to authorities intent on closing down all the canals. Aickman believed that the value of the canals lay in their unity and totality, and argued that not a single canal should be sacrificed. As a non-boater, Aickman, it might be argued, was the more visionary, seeing a wider and more varied use for canals in the leisure age, and indeed over the years he pioneered events that brought in a wider public.

About the time of the IWA's foundation, Aickman began an affair with a young writer, Elizabeth Jane Howard, who at the time was married to the artist and naturalist Peter Scott (son of Scott of the Antarctic). The affair, which continued for some years, doesn't seem to have generated any great rancour between the two men. Scott, having divorced Howard, became an enthusiastic vice-president of the IWA, working closely with Aickman and Rolt; he later bought his own boat, *Beatrice*, to cruise the canals. Howard, the first secretary of the IWA, accompanied Aickman on exploratory boating trips – the two of them usually sleeping in a tent on the towpath – but also became firm friends with his wife Ray. Bohemianism, indeed.

In her autobiography, *Slipstream*, Howard describes Aickman and the other personalities of the IWA with much candour. She found Aickman 'physically unattractive' but nonetheless fell under his spell, dazzled by his knowledge and energy; he would dictate the contents of the IWA newsletter without pause

Inland Waterways Association pioneers Elizabeth Jane Howard and Robert Aickman 'canal-busting' on the Huddersfield Narrow.

or need to look up facts, and was an indefatigable walker. But she also found him paranoid about his friends and 'chronically serious', all too often banging on about what a disappointment the twentieth century was. (Aickman, in Howard's account, often sounds like a dress rehearsal for her later curmudgeonly husband, the novelist Kingsley Amis.)

Howard makes Aickman and Rolt sound like a couple of steampunk fogeys, happy to stop technology in the Victorian era, before mass production and the internal combustion engine. But she admires their intense ambition and visionary zeal, which, despite much personal rivalry, resulted in their saving much of what remained of Britain's waterways. The two actually worked together most effectively during Howard's time, in the late 1940s. In the following decade, tensions and disagreements between the two men grew and almost led to a split in the IWA. The divisions between the two were in theory over how best to save the waterways, but in reality the disputes seem to have been prompted by private jealousies, clashes of will, tangled lives and personal differences – Rolt, touchy but practical, Aickman nervy and flamboyant. Both men were also pursuing literary careers, as was Elizabeth Jane Howard. Rolt is best known for his books on canals (and, later, steam trains), while Aickman had a highly successful career writing 'supernatural' stories.

But, for a time, the IWA was a glamorous campaign group that everyone wanted to be a part of and saving the canal heritage became a national cause. Big personalities that Aickman signed up included the Earl of Portsmouth, who was keen on canal use for agricultural purposes; the landscape artist Algernon Newton RA; and Lord Bingham, who made trips in his own boat *NB Hesperus* with his son, the future disappearing Lord 'Lucky' Lucan. Popular actors like James Robertson Justice also came aboard, while more practical support came from Samuel Barlow, who ran one of the biggest independent canal carrying companies left in Britain.

By the late 1940s, the IWA had become influential enough to send deputations to the British Transport Commission, who were deciding post-war transport policy, and thus the fate of the canals owned by the state. The IWA also began to actively purchase and restore parts of the canal network themselves. In 1947, the Basingstoke Canal, a private waterway, was put up for sale and a canal committee was formed with IWA support, buying it up for £6,000.

Local IWA branches were formed to promote the interests of different waterways. In 1948 alone, these were established for the Midlands, the northeast, the Kennet and Avon and the Fenlands. They were a mixed blessing from the IWA's point of view. They brought in energy, publicity and able volunteers, but also clashing personalities and ambitions; often branches and individual canal committees broke away. The Fenlands, for example, felt itself distinct from the rest of the canal system. It was connected to the canal network only by the River Nene, had seen significant tourist use since Edwardian times, and with its agricultural history had little in common with Britain's 'coal' canals. Its supporters were happy to work alone.

'Canal-busting' trips were an excitement that still united Rolt and Aickman. British Transport had a statutory obligation to allow boats to travel on waterways, in return for paying tolls. The IWA and particularly Rolt pushed this obligation to ensure canals remained in use. For example, when a new bridge was installed at Lapworth on the Stratford-upon-Avon Canal that was too low for boat traffic, the IWA forced the authorities to provide work parties to jack the whole bridge up – several times in 1949 – to allow passage for Rolt's *Cressy* and other boats. That same year Rolt managed to voyage *Cressy* back to where she was built in Trevor, at the head of the Llangollen Canal, which was only in water as a feeder for the local reservoir. As often happened on the failing canal system, the voyage involved scraping over shallows, squeezing into and often being winched out of lock chambers that had bulged inwards over the decades, and risking tunnels that might prove blocked far into their depths. The Rolts had been joined on this journey by the Calvert family in a more practically sized home-made boat pulled by a donkey.

One of the great attractions of becoming a canal-saver in these pioneering days was the challenge of exploring rickety canals – and especially of going underground. I'd felt the pull of this myself when looking at the barred entrance to the fifty miles of underground tunnels in the Worsley Delphs at the start of the Bridgewater Canal, and again as I failed to wangle a lift through the three-mile-long Standedge Tunnel. I had got a frisson from paddling through the Bruce Tunnel on the Kennet and Avon, too. But it was nothing on the daredevil exploits of the canal-saving pioneers. Charles Hadfield entered the flooded subterranean chambers and channels in Worsley, together with the last of the working miners. Photographs show him dressed in a tweed suit, lying flat to squeeze under tunnel roofs that had sagged from eight feet down to nearly water level. Aickman, Rolt and a bunch of die-hards took a hired boat, *Ailsa Craig* ('its engine never failed to fail us'), on a trip up the Huddersfield Narrow and got themselves stuck fast inside the Standedge tunnel. They were able to continue only by removing the rubbing strakes to gain an inch or so of leeway. Another IWA exploratory cruise – all with the practical purpose of proving particular canals were passable and keeping alive a 'right of navigation' – involved a boat in the Harecastle Tunnel having to be freed by ballasting it with two hundred bricks to make it sit low enough in the water.

Rolt's books on the canals and his practical experiences of how the system worked – and might work again – engaged public interest, whilst Aickman's genius was finding powerful allies amongst politicians, celebrities and the wealthy. Some of the MPs Aickman lobbied became such tireless deliverers of the IWA message that parliamentary question time rules were changed to limit the number of questions on a single subject.

There was certainly a battle to be fought. British Transport, the government's agency which owned most of the canals, wanted to get rid of as many as possible, or at least to give up any obligation to keep them navigable. The government was persuaded that the legal right for any craft to use any canal – and for that canal to be kept in a condition to allow such use – was not viable, and the right was terminated. The IWA tactic of 'canal-busting' waterways on the edge of dereliction was thwarted. However, the publicity of such campaigns had created a groundswell of public and parliamentary opinion, forcing the future of Britain's canals onto the national agenda, raising issues of leisure provision, heritage and even the nascent science of ecology and habitat.

The IWA and independent single-canal based associations also worked hard on a practical basis, holding the closing of canals at bay and then helping to restore them. One approach was to take the money it would cost to decommission or 'abandon' a canal – often considerable – and get subscriptions to make up the shortfall required to repair and rebuild it to a navigable standard. The culture of the canals was also rediscovered and promoted. In 1949 the Rolts assembled an exhibition of canal-related arts and crafts – Buckby cans and door panels painted with 'roses and castles' designs – that was put on display at Heal's store in London before touring the country. It was a big success and its aesthetic contrasted strikingly with the British Transport plan to paint all nationalised boats on the canals in a corporate yellow and blue livery.

Rolt fell out badly with Aickman in 1950 and withdrew for a time from IWA events. Not, however, from canal life. The same year saw his marriage to Angela collapse – she ran off to join Billy Smart's circus and married the ringmaster – and he began living with Sonia Smith, the former Idle Woman who had remained working on the waterways. A little ironically, his interests turned more and more to the world of steam trains – the very transport system that had sent the canals into freefall.

Aickman, meantime, drew on his genius for organisation and networking to put on a big canal rally in Market Harborough. This was a major event in the awareness of the waterways. An impressive fleet of boats arrived, and over the six days of the festival 50,000 people attended – a huge number for the time. Highlights included the screening of Charles Crichton's film *Painted Boats*, with a script by poet Louis MacNeice extolling canal traditions, topography and culture. At the festival's formal dinner, Aickman's top table included James Robertson Justice, poet Cecil Day-Lewis and the architect and broadcaster Hugh

Casson. Rolt was not invited but came anyway, on *Cressy*, and ate at another table with his canal boat friends.

The IWA had grown in size and scope but had become riven by in-fighting. In December 1950 a vote was carried to campaign to save all canals, not just the most viable, that led to the resignations of, among others, Tom Rolt, Sonia Smith and Charles Hadfield. The organisation threatened to sink at the most critical period in its battle. At governmental level the cost of keeping the canals operational was being vigorously debated as the Inland Waterways chairman Reginald Hill pointed out that 1,200 miles of British Transport Commission waterways generated ninety-eight per cent

Canal rallies and awareness-building trips on the canals took place throughout the 1950s and 1960s, here on the Kennet and Avon Canal.

of traffic, whilst the remaining 800 miles were in the government's view a drain on public finances, costing £300–400 a mile to maintain each year. In 1955, the Government published a survey that divided waterways into three categories: 336 miles were deemed worthy of development, 1,000 miles were to be 'retained' with minimum maintenance, and nearly 800 miles – including the Huddersfield Narrow and the Llangollen – were doomed to closure. A further 1,000 miles would be demoted to the doomed category if they weren't sufficiently used, and some through-routes, like the Stratford-upon-Avon Canal, were put in two different categories, which would effectively destroy them.

The British Transport Commission were pleased with this 'solution' and obviously expected it to be policy, signalling the end of a unified canal network. But they hadn't reckoned with the IWA and its 2,000 members. Canal-saving took on the allure of a counter culture, anti-establishment protest. In parallel with its political battles, the IWA engaged its members in practical volunteer tasks, opening up derelict and abandoned canals. Anyone with a boat (however basic) or boots could help redis-cover the neglected and abandoned wharfs, basins, tunnels and lock flights – many of which had never had wide public access – and, not least, the old working boats just waiting to be restored.

The renovation work was truly astounding, as was the IWA's ambition to bring the whole network of more than 2,000 miles back into usable condition. Sixty years on, it is amazing to reflect on how they succeeded against all the regulatory barriers, the cost and the technical challenges – all to enable future holidaymakers, or those in retreat from a busy life, to head off for weeks, months or a lifetime of slow travels.

It was the quixotic nature of the challenges that seems to have driven the most enthusiastic of the canal savers. And the IWA was lucky in having at its service a young architect called David

Hutchings. A practical visionary and a genius at enthusing others to get things done, Hutchings had been living on his narrowboat, *Ftatateeta*, when he heard about the IWA and, unbidden, produced posters to drum up support and fly-posted them around the Midlands. With the IWA in some disarray, he stepped in to organise a canal rally in Coventry, joining forces with a dynamic wartime local heroine called Pearl Hyde, the city's Lord Mayor. Then, when Warwickshire County Council applied to effectively close the Stratford-upon-Avon Canal by lowering a bridge, removing a lock and removing the Victorian aqueduct over the road at Wootton Wawen, Hutchings organised a 'disturbance' of boats to gain public support for establishing a trust for the canal.

The IWA itself was rescued from disarray – it had continued to argue over the 'all or nothing' policy – by John Smith from the National Trust, who proposed to Aickman that they could act as a temporary caretaker for some of the canals and help with lobbying MPs. Another influential voice was that of David Bowes-Lyon, the Queen Mother's brother, who proposed that the National Trust should take on all those navigations not wanted by the Transport Commission. There was a synchronicity in pairing the conservation of inland waterways with the National Trust's own Operation Neptune, which had bought up hundreds of miles of coastline to save them from development, though many in the Trust were wary of the vast expense involved.

Meanwhile, the government's Bowes Report (called after its chairman, Leslie Bowes) gave some ground for hope, stipulating a right of appeal when canals were considered for closure, and arguing that the value of canals should be assessed not just in terms of the tolls collected from carrier companies, but also taking account of possible future business opportunities, the canals' importance as drains and flood defences, and the social value of waterways-based recreation and leisure. Perhaps most importantly, the report led to the establishment of a new body, the Inland Waterways Redevelopment Advisory Committee, on which Tom Rolt was persuaded to be a member.

The IWA, meantime, fought constant battles against the closure of short canals, which were being pushed through branch by branch. Some of these individual lines were scarcely worth the effort of defending. But in 1959 the Transport Commission proposed to close the Dudley Tunnel – the second longest tunnel in Britain and an important link in the Midlands canal system – claiming that its roof had fallen in and it was unsafe. In response, Aickman and another IWA committee member set off in a tiny plastic dinghy through the two miles of tunnel, equipped, as a last-minute thought, with a lamp bought from a local bicycle shop. It must have been a nerve-racking trip, with the lamp's

Pearl Hyde (at the prow) on an IWA trip on the Stratford-upon-Avon Canal with campaigners including Robert Aickman (at the stern).

weak beam, and no safety equipment, but the trio established that the tunnel was navigable.

The IWA were still sticking to their commitment to no closures, in order to save the whole canal system, but the Transport Commission would often demand proof of viability in impossibly short timeframes. There were setbacks and successes. A five-year moratorium was placed on the closure of the Kennet and Avon Canal and nearly ten years of restoration of the Lower Avon drew to a conclusion under the driving force of another vital canal saver, C. Douglas Barwell, who, among other sterling qualities, taught himself to dive in order to save the cost of professional underwater inspections.

As the 1960s dawned, the Stratford-upon-Avon Canal became a major focus. The National Trust had been given permission to lease its south section after its abandoned status had been refuted by the discovery of a toll receipt issued to a lone canoeist in 1957. In June 1960, the Trust put David Hutchings in charge of its restoration and – with his wife, three small children and a dog called Creosote – he moved into one of the canal's barrel-roofed lock-keeper's cottages. Hutchings set his volunteers the target of restoring the canal to working condition within three years; his slogan was 'Boats to Stratford before the Russians reach the moon.' At one point the team were making and replacing a lock gate a week, but there were also aqueducts to repair, pounds to puddle and towpaths to clear, and plans to celebrate the canal's reopening on the fourth centenary of Shakespeare's birthday in 1964 were further hampered by the famously hard winter of 1962–63. Britain's big freeze was a tough time for other canals, too, as they iced over and locked in working boats. For many carriers, the weeks of enforced idleness were a final nail in the industry's coffin as they lost contracts and fell into debt. Leisure boating was looking more and more like the only future for the waterways.

Hutchings himself kept his volunteers working through the freeze and when the army work details he had been allocated

David Hutchings (left) working with volunteers on the Stratford-upon-Avon Canal, in the 1970s.

were transferred to clearing roads, he appealed to the Prison Commissioners and was given gangs from Winson Green jail. Against all the odds, the canal was ready just in time for the Shakespeare centenary festival in July. Aickman threw himself into what he liked best, organising events and promoting waterways culture. The canal's reopening was a national news story. There were two hundred canal boats in attendance, including a narrowboat called the *Linda*, on which the Queen Mother was enthroned on the bow. After the ribbons were cut, and the canal officially opened, there were fireworks and Handel's Water Music and a production of *Henry V*.

The reopening of the Stratford-upon-Avon Canal was a decisive moment in the battle to save the waterways as a unified system, with access to all, whether on water or on foot.

The National Trust, however, fearing the huge costs if they became custodians of all the canals, looked to distance themselves from future waterways projects. Aickman was glad of this, concerned that his aim of saving 'all the canals' (though even he was beginning to realise that might not be possible) would end up being reduced to the preservation of a few beauty spots as industrial monuments.

Battles remained to be fought through the 1960s. But in a sense the war had been won. Rolt, Aickman, Hadfield, Hutchings and the hundreds of volunteers on canal restoration projects had created a public consensus that saving the waterways was a good thing. Like Britain's railways (which also needed protection after Beeching's 1965 cuts), they were seen as part of the national heritage – a resource for everyone to use.

Post-war politicians – wary of their budgets in an era of austerity – took a while to cotton on. But, when Barbara Castle became Minister of Transport in Harold Wilson's Labour government, things changed radically, and for the better. Castle was prepared to learn about the canals and was invited by Joe Skinner, from a famous working boat family, on an eight-mile fact-finding cruise on the Oxford Canal. She was won over – the *Daily Mirror* had also taken up the canal cause – and in her 1968 Transport Act set out a strategy that acknowledged the value of Britain's canals and ensured their long-term future. Castle's vision, which gave a sense of purpose to the British Waterways Board (the body set up in 1963 to oversee the canals), was a nationwide leisure network. It would allow the public access to the waterways for boat cruising, fishing and other activities, complementing the national parks she had helped to establish. In this, Castle echoed – a little less lyrically – Robert Aickman's definition of the canals' value 'in varying proportions, for commercial carrying, pleasure-boating, water supply, and angling; also sometimes for land drainage; usually for towpath lovemaking and general amenity-gaping, history study, botany study and bird-watching'.

But there was another factor, without which the canals could not have been saved – and perhaps would not have deserved saving. This was the quality of their original construction. Two

The minister for canals – Barbara Castle inspects a model of a lock with British Waterways chairman John Hawton.

centuries after the earliest canals were built, their fabric was still, for the most part, in repairable and restorable condition. During the golden years, everyone involved had thought that canals were a water machine that was going to be in use forever and, although their engineers and workmen might have saved costs where they could, quality generally trumped expedience. Engineers went to great lengths to get the best of bricks, the right stone, well-founded iron and steel, and good-quality clay for puddling and waterproofing the channels. Accommodation bridges, lock chambers and wharfs were built to high standards so that most had survived in good condition. Swing bridges and lock gates might have needed repairs or replacement but the technology was simple, and committed volunteers and unskilled labour were able to do much of the work, and become skilled in the process.

Rolt and Aickman's pronouncements on the commendable values of earlier times, as opposed to our own disposable culture and infrastructure, were fogeyish, certainly. But in terms of the canals, they were spot on. It is hard to imagine any other major engineering projects that could be salvagable if after sixty-odd years of construction, use, maintenance and development they were then worked for the next century with little maintenance, no real investment and then abandoned for fifty years.

The canals were constructed intelligently. Built when horse power seemed to most minds the power source of the future, they were made to a scale and size appropriate to their time. If this had seemed a disaster when the greater efficiency of the railways challenged and vanquished commercial water carry-ing, then the limited dimensions of the narrow and broad canals alike worked in favour of their next incarnation. Most of Britain's canals were small enough to be worked on by amateurs, cheap enough to keep in water, intimate enough to appeal to hobbyists, simple enough to engender nostalgia.

11

Force Leisure

THE TRANSFORMATION OF THE CANALS from working
waterways to slow ways for leisure – and as an alternative source
of housing – began in a makeshift, ramshackle way. In the 1960s,
the remaining canal carriers were short of work, particularly in
the summer months, when they needed other cargo. One answer
was people. It was a simple matter to clean out the coal dust (as
they had often done for pre-war workers' trips), raise a tarpaulin
on a scaffold of poles, and set out some army-surplus camp beds.
And there it was – a camp-boat – cheap and cheerful, and ready
for a troop of Boy Scouts to set off on their summer expedition.
The camp-boats were appealing to a new hippy-style generation
of grown-ups, too, wanting to do their thing on the cheap, in the
British countryside. The music writer Mark Ellen told me about
hiring a self-drive boat in the early-1970s with a bunch of students and spending a glorious fortnight on the Llangollen Canal,
equipped with sleeping bags and guitars. Their boat didn't even
have old camp beds – just the tarpaulin 'roof'.

There were more luxurious options, of course. Companies
had offered cruises on certain canals since the 1930s, and there

were pioneering narrowboat conversions, too, using old hulls converted to sleeping cabins. But it was in the 1970s and 1980s that the canals switched over wholeheartedly to live-aboards (of which more, later) and to narrowboat holidays and tourism. Aickman's passionate goal of preserving a functional canal network has by and large been achieved, as has Barbara Castle's idea of a linear national park, fulfilling a myriad of roles for bird-watchers, anglers, dog walkers, kayakers, cyclists, industrial archaeologists, poets, pub musicians and artists.

The Crick Boat Show – a canal jamboree held each May at Crick marina on the Grand Union Canal – offers an insight into just how firmly canal leisure and lifestyle has become established. It is ostensibly a trade fair and gathering for narrowboat owners, who can meet suppliers for all their worldly needs, but it is as much as anything a celebration of the canals as a vibrant part of British culture. You don't have to arrive at its marina site by narrowboat (though hundreds do), but pretty much everyone attending enjoys, at least for a few hours, the fantasy of moving onto the canals, to live, or at least to holiday.

Hire companies advertised themselves to the land-based and curious, the gateway to full immersion in the waterways. And for that, there were builders and brokers with flotillas of boats – new and second-hand, converted and heritage, narrowboat and wide-beam. Some companies offered live-aboard craft that, aside from the engine, read more like a house on a modern estate: 'Beta Marine Engine, bow thruster, heating, solid oak flooring, double glazing, and traditional hand painting. Prices from £137,950 incl VAT.' But most of the stalls offered more practical assistance to already committed boaters – satellite dishes and solar panels, bilge pumps, mops, finance, or full-size engines. On-board Wi-Fi was a big concern. The internet and mobile phones have revolutionised canal living, with memories of phone boxes and ten-pence pieces almost as distant as those of working boatmen. A less alluring preoccupation was that bugbear of any boat life – the loo – with companies like LeeSan offering a 'One Stop Pump Shop – The Power from the Behind'.

I stopped with a small but appreciative group squeezed into a small canvas booth to listen to Helen Babbs reading from her book, *Adrift – A Secret Life of London's Waterways*, about her year living aboard a boat in London, observing the wildlife and other boaters and the city around her. And then I called into the Canal & River Trust tent, where volunteers were handing out leaflets and answering questions about every aspect of the waterways, from fishing to buying a boat. The CRT was in many

Basins full of beautifully turned-out heritage narrowboats at Crick.
Boaters in stetsons are not hard to spot either.

ways the end result of Aickman's vision, a single body dedicated to preserving and managing England and Wales' waterways. It was formed in 2012 as a not-for-profit organisation, taking over from the old government quango of British Waterways (itself a 1963 successor to the British Transport Commission).

Even as writer-in-residence for the CRT, and a part of their arts programme, I remained bemused by just how many aspects of canal life the trust had to manage: the issuing of licences for narrowboats, kayaks and the last remaining commercial boats; the maintenance of locks and bridges, towpaths and pounds; the running of marinas and moorings; protecting wildlife, and looking after the interests of fish and anglers. And there were some distinctly modern roles, too, like charging companies to run fibre-optic communications cables under the towpaths.

Strolling on, I stopped to talk to with John Barnard, who painted boats to 'coach finish standard'. He took a boat's outside panels back to bare metal, he explained, 'and then it's ten coats, each one rubbed back to get a proper finish – though I'd do more if the client would pay for them'. He seemed disappointed at the cheapskatery of the modern boater as he brushed a final layer of dark-blue paint on a metal panel and it dried to an enamel sheen. 'In the old days the final coats would be rubbed down with pieces of cuttlefish,' he explained. 'The chalky bit they give to budgies – it's so fine it polishes them as smooth as glass.'

In the same tent, Jon Leeson, a third-generation signwriter, was demonstrating his skills, effortlessly sweeping a fine brush along and around a letter 'A', creating a fluid line with a crisp edge. And, further along, a craftsman was weaving and knotting ropes to make a large, rugged button fender for a boat's bow.

After watching the craftspeople who decorated and dressed 'heritage' boats, I went in search of the boats themselves. Which wasn't hard. There were marina basins full of them, with their sparkling paintwork, candy-striped swan-neck tillers, battalions of decorated Buckby cans and buckets, and boat names and home 'ports' – Cowroast, Tewkesbury, Braunston – painted in flamboyant lettering like a Victorian fairground. There was white decorative rope work all over the boats – rams heads and turk's heads and fancy knots and coils of mooring ropes – and around the black chimneys were polished brass hoops and chains of horse brasses.

I was drawn towards a battered old engine boat called *Aldgate*, with an engineless butty, both with open holds and small cabins. Nick Wolfe, the owner, had been a lorry driver before setting up as a canal carrier, taking whatever bulk cargoes he was offered – timber, gravel or other heavy goods. He told me about moving the whole stock of a chandlery from one canal-side premises to another, then introduced me to Joe Oliver, who was developing a marina further along the canal. That seemed like a good business, I said, thinking that with so many more people wanting to buy boats, it seemed a no-brainer to move cows out of a canalside field, dig it out, flood it and set up a watery meadow with a herd of boats. But apparently it wasn't that easy. Water was – as it had always been – an expensive commodity, and in short supply on the canals, especially up high, where we were, and there had been extended negotiations with the Canal & River Trust to ensure there was no leakage, and to fit stop gates for low-water periods. But things were going ahead now, and Nick would be bringing in the materials needed for hard standings, pontoons and the like.

Moored to a pontoon a little further along was another neat heritage narrowboat brought to Crick by the Dudley Canal & Tunnel Trust. Curious, I climbed down a few steps into the boat's roofed hold to find a dimly lit corridor with a gallery of photos on the Dudley Mines. I knew something of their story already – having read of Aickman's heroic mission with the dinghy and bicycle lamp – but I hadn't realised their extent, nor the long battles by local activists to keep them open. Pauline Farnell, from the Dudley Trust, noted my interest, as I started taking notes. 'You must come up to the tunnels,' she said. 'And if you want to give it a go, we take people right into them in boats, and you can do some legging if you want.'

I needed little more persuading.

After missing my chance to boat through Standedge Tunnel – and frustrated by the barred gateways into the Duke of Bridgewater's mines – I was eager to go underground at Dudley. At the Trust Centre, I put on a white hard hat, shrugged on a life jacket and climbed aboard the *William*, reflecting on the good fortune that had led Rolt and the IWA, and then local activists, to save the Tunnels. Had the British Transport Commission succeeded in closing them in the 1950s, the West Midlands would have lost what is now one of its top tourist attractions.

The history of the Dudley Tunnels begins in 1774, when the local landowner, Lord Ward, realised that he could use a canal to service his limeworks. A first huge shaft – Lord Ward's Tunnel – was completed, then extended to link various basins and mines for limestone and iron ore. And two decades later a further, ambitious tunnel – Dudley Canal No. 1 – was driven right through Castle Hill to the Birmingham Canal, saving boats a day of travelling circuitous waterways to get down to the Stourbridge Canal. Together, they formed Britain's longest canal tunnel, after Standedge, and earned good money for more than a century.

But it was the story of the saving of the Dudley Tunnels that had caught my imagination. After Robert Aickman had proved the authorities wrong in their assertion that the canal was no longer navigable, local activists were inspired to make trips into the tunnels, and in 1962 organised a boat rally at Stourbridge, encouraging participants to use the Dudley Tunnel on their way. The British Transport Commission disabled balance beams and paddles in an attempt to block access to the canal, but the activists fought back, clearing cuts, repairing locks and removing barriers. Unlike the IWA's lobbying at Westminster,

Leggers at work – here, on the 572-yard Barnton Tunnel on the Trent and Mersey Canal.

the battle of the Dudley Tunnels was more akin to the 1932 mass trespass of ramblers on Kinder Scout in the Pennines to force access to the moors and mountains. Proper people power and bloody-mindedness. And they were proud of it. On the wall of the Trust Centre a plaque read: 'Dudley Canal Tunnel: Closed by the Government on behalf of the people, opened by the people on behalf of themselves'.

The efforts of the early activists were continued through the 1960s as more and more people went underground in boats to push through the tunnel or explore the limestone mines. Word got around of these Indiana Jones exploits and soon an old wooden work boat – the *Electra* – was pressed into service to take larger groups in at weekends. The boat was initially legged through the tunnels but as the Tunnels became a tourist attraction an electric motor had been added.

Becky, our guide, took the helm and, as the boat purred through the tunnel entrance, mentioned that on makeshift early boats the electric motors had come from milk floats and the contacts often jammed, leaving it stuck in forward. Our engine was better behaved as we cruised through Lord Ward's Tunnel. There was plenty of light ahead as some of the early lime workings had been opencast, dug out from above as craters. Indeed, within a few hundred yards we'd slid out into Shirts Mill Basin, a bowl of rock open to the sky, with a fringe of trees high above us. 'There's a wagtail's nest over there,' Becky pointed to one side, 'and it's a fabulous habitat for bats ... Daubenton's and Pipistrelles, mainly.'

We purred through another underground corridor and into the light of Castle Mill Basin, before setting off into another long tunnel. Becky's voice echoed off the walls as she eased the boat into the darkness. 'We're only going to cover about five percent of the underground routes, on the trip,' she told us. 'There are more shafts below us but you'd need scuba gear to go into them nowadays.' She slowed the boat to show us limestone stalactites hanging from the roof, and then eased the boat round a sharp bend as the tunnel opened out into a great quarried vault known as the Singing Cavern. Lights behind the buttresses of rock changed from purples to blues to greens as the boat idled mid-water. The miners had named the cavern, Becky explained, because wind blowing through the tunnels would set it moaning like an organ pipe. 'Schoolchildren love it,' she said, though it seemed our adult party was too inhibited to give it a bit of 'Amazing Grace' or 'Bohemian Rhapsody'.

In Victorian times, Becky told us, the chamber had become a tourist attraction with music recitals and boat trips, and in 1849 the geologist Sir Roderick Murchison gave a famous speech here, proposing a new geological period called the Silurian. This was his name for the era when Dudley's limestone was created, fossilising the era's aquatic life – notably the *Calymene blumenbachii*.

Miners chiselled out these trilobites, some 420 million years later, to sell to collectors; they became so widespread and popular that they became known as Dudley Bugs.

Easing back through another tunnel, we passed a tableau of miners working a seam to one side of the canal, some on ladders against the rock face, frozen mid-pickaxe swing or shovel-heft. Becky had bleak statistics on their lives, working by candlelight and then gas lanterns. The mines had been profitable and productive, but for every 2,000 tons mined a miner died directly from drownings, explosions or falls, whilst the limestone dust was a slower danger to health.

We had looped around, in a bewildering labyrinth, to meet the northern end of the Dudley Tunnel. There were neat brick walls alongside us, and the width of the tunnel was little more than that of the boat. 'Does anyone want to have a go at legging?' Becky asked. We needed two people, one either side, and for a moment it seemed I wouldn't find a partner, but then a woman stood up in the gloom and said she'd have a go. A wide plank was laid across the width of the boat and we lay across it, head by head, my legs over one side and hers over the other, feet up against the wall. 'I've done this before, years ago,' said my legging partner, who instinctively led the way as we strained to get the boat moving. But once it had momentum, all we had to do was walk our feet in a sort of shuffling gait, crossing our legs back and forth over each other, pacing along the wall, and to keep the boat moving. It was the old magic of the friction-light canals – the tiniest bit of energy could move the heaviest of boats.

It was a lot of fun. But for the professional leggers of the past, who would take two or more boats at a time through the Dudley Tunnel, it must have been a hard life. It took about two hours to push one boat through the 1.8 miles, maybe another hour if there were two boats, and they were fined if they weren't through in under four hours. In the early twentieth century the leggers were put out of a job when a steam tug boat was introduced, but there was work again when reduced traffic decommissioned the tug. Jack Wheeler, Dudley's last professional legger, retired in 1949 at the age of seventy-six. Apparently, he preferred to leg alone, lying on top of the boats and 'walking' along the tunnel roof, so he could pocket the full fee. As we coasted along, I thought of him legging through the darkness hour after hour, day after day, and the awful working environment when engined craft were introduced alongside horse-boats and the constricted tunnels choked with smoke and particulates.

But at least, before then, the Dudley Tunnel was relatively safe for leggers. As a narrow tunnel, the leggers' bodies stay mostly inboard on the planks, or atop the load, and there is little risk of falling in or getting crushed between boat and wall. Wider tunnels were a different matter, where narrow planks had to be cantilevered out from a boat's hull so that the legger could reach the walls, and it was only too easy to fall off in the dark and drown. At the Tardebigge Tunnel, close by where Rolt and Aickman had met on *Cressy* and started the IWA, nine leggers drowned between 1818 and 1846, including a lad called Solomon Allen, who was just eleven years old.

You don't need to be around Birmingham's waterways for long before someone asks if you know the city has more canals than Venice. Which is quite true: Birmingham has thirty-five miles of canals within its city borders, as opposed to twenty-six miles in Venice (though it has to be said Birmingham also has a population of over a million, as opposed to Venice's peak of 270,000). Nonetheless, the canal lengths are impressive, and all the more so if you take account of the wider metropolitan region. The Birmingham Canal Navigation Society run a two-day marathon challenge whose aim is to cover as many as possible of its 120 miles of canals. The rules include a complex handicapping system for length of boat, number of crew, route taken, adherence to all speed limits and lock protocols – and, very definitely, bonus points for legging or even going through the Dudley Tunnel.

My trip, alas, didn't coincide with the marathon, but I was fired up by canal tunnel tourism. So, after disembarking from the *William*, I cycled off to nearby Bumble Hole, a green oasis built over an old clay mine, in order to pedal through the Netherton Tunnel. The last to be built in the canal age, the Netherton opened in 1858 and, as befitted the most 'modern' tunnel of its time (the future of canals if the future of canals hadn't been the railways), it was wide enough for two narrowboats to pass, had a towpath either side to avoid awkward tangles of tow ropes and horses, and was lit (by gas and later by electricity) throughout its 1.7-mile length. It is still serviceable today, but is in a somewhat

A circle of light at the end of the Netherton Tunnel – after a very long 1.7 miles of canal darkness.

dilapidated state, and, in good Aickman tradition, my only illu-
mination would be a bicycle lamp and the occasional pools of
light that were focused down from 'pepper pot' air vents.

The canal was eerie from the start. A mile and a half of dark
is a long way on a bike and it was slow progress along the rough
and potholed towpath. There was a rail between its edge and
the water but the black liquid seemed to attract the bike and my
imagination began to work overtime. It was hard to do otherwise. One stretch of wall was glazed in sheets of lime, another by
a gauzy curtain of spider webs. And the Netherton, I had read,
has its ghosts. People walking through had seen wet footprints
ahead of them that suddenly disappeared, and there was said
to be a grey lady ghost. There were also real doom stories from
its working days. A policeman had been killed and disposed of
in the underground waters. A boatman had reported seeing a
woman with two small children sitting at the tunnel mouth as
he passed into its depths, and when he returned found a bundle
floating in the canal deep in the blackness – the two small children wrapped in a petticoat and drowned.

All the canal tunnels had their ghost and horror stories for the
working boat people. As did many locks. There were stretches that
no-one wanted to moor along. Wharfs with bad atmospheres.
This wasn't mere superstition – the canals could be dangerous
places. They were an edge-land, good for disposing of weapons,
evidence and even bodies, as witnessed by many episodes of
Peaky Blinders, Birmingham's own version of *The Sopranos*, based
on the city's real-life gangs (its canal sequences were filmed at
Dudley and Ellesmere Port). Canals also drew the depressed and
suicidal, and the unprotected banks put folk only a stumble away
from drowning. Another aggregation of nineteenth-century news
stories pointed the finger at drunkenness and industrial smogs –
one body after another fished out of Birmingham's canals having
left a pub to walk home along a towpath in a pea-souper.

Perhaps it was an aspect of the waterways that had united
Rolt and Aickman, and indeed Elizabeth Jane Howard, in their

unlikely shared interest as they saved the canals. All of them wrote horror and ghost stories. In Aickman's case it became his life after he stepped back from the IWA, as he wrote and edited volumes of psychological thrillers and paranormal stories, many of them influenced by the canals. Given their joint canal-busting trips through darkened tunnels that might well have ended in roof falls or sinkings deep inside hills, Rolt and Aickman could be forgiven for finding a dimension of horror in the waterways.

Tunnels – with their mix of water and darkness – had the worst reputation for ghostly and uneasy feeling and I was getting a bit of that feeling in the depths of the Netherton, its darkness only emphasised by my feeble bike light. Noises – my gears cranking, the dripping of water, heavy breathing – echoed along the brick corridor. The few pools of light from the air vents came so far apart that they emphasised how deep underground I was. So it was a relief to see far ahead a glimmer of light growing bigger as I pedalled on, thinking it was the end. And then I realised it was something or somebody coming towards me. Another cyclist. We stopped in surprise and relief, eager to chat. He turned out to be a large, tough-looking Pole, doing a week's training in Dudley for an electricity company. He'd been using the tunnel for a weatherproof shortcut between his training centre and digs, and I was the first person he'd met.

The true end of the tunnel grew as a proper circle of light; the half-round reflected in the water. There was fresh air, and all the colours of the outside world seemed more vivid. Like a reverse wardrobe portal to Narnia, the tunnel had carried me from the green park of Bumble Hole into industrial Dudley.

Just outside the tunnel entrance there was a lone fisherman. Cradled in a folding chair, he was looking glumly at the water through Polaroid glasses, his long wand of a rod extending nearly halfway across the cut, and a neon-orange float resting depressingly motionless, up towards the far bank. Beside him there was a Thermos and a mug of tea. And next to that a plastic

The trinity of canal parklife – narrowboat, jogger and angler.

pot full of slowly writhing maggots. Like many a canal fisher-man, he was dressed in the browns, leaf-greens and camouflage patterns of a military sniper.

After hundreds of miles of travel on the waterways, angling was one of the canal pursuits that still mystified me. This chap seemed even more morose than most of his fraternity along the banks, but I was so relieved to be out in the light again and amidst human company that I forced him into conversation. 'Chub?' I asked, knowing this was a likely catch from a conversation with one of the volunteers at the Dudley Mines. He brightened slightly. 'Or carp ... maybe bream,' he answered, before stopping any further loose talk by reaching down to pull out a plump ivory-white maggot and stick it between his lips so he could rebait the hook and return to contemplation.

Actually I had begun to puzzle out something of the appeal of coarse fishing along the canals from the few words I'd had with fishermen (I had not seen a single fisherwoman) dotted along the towpaths. One on the Kennet and Avon had talked about the wildlife: 'Voles, I do see them, though they're rare. Kingfishers, I love a kingfisher. I see otters when I'm night fishing, though if I do I may as well go home because they disturb all the fish.' Another, fishing through the night on the Shropshire, had smiled wryly when I met him at dawn (I'd slept out by the next bridge): 'I just like to get away from it all ... from the wife, out of the house, be on me own. No job, so I've got the time, and things to think about.'

In Devon, on the Grand Western Canal, I'd met a more talkative man in his twenties, up from Exeter and dressed like a surfer dude in shorts, sunglasses and a white jungle hat. He'd been happy to point out the ale-coloured rudd in the clear water as they swam with the tiger-striped perch and the beaten brass and pewter bream, the shoals of different species flickering across the gravel and stones or disappearing into veldts of weed and water lilies. And, he explained, alongside the small fish in this aquatic Serengeti, there would be predators – pike laying in ambush ready to explode out. He was casting a wet fly, a pink shrimp, as he talked. He pondered when I asked him where the fish came from in this isolated canal, which even in the recent past had burst its banks and drained dry. 'Well, fish eggs can be brought in on birds' feet or even live fish dropped by herons.' It seemed a haphazard way for fish to have arrived? 'Probably it's been restocked, as well,' he conceded.

As custodians of the waterways, the CRT were responsible for the fish in them. Ed Fox, who had signed me up for the Trust, was a keen fisherman himself and had described how, when cuts had to be drained or a lock dried out for repairs, the first job was for a team to net or stun the fish and transfer them to safety. It was also a chance to see just what was going on under the surface. That was how two giant catfish, each weighing more than forty pounds, had been discovered on the Grand Union Canal. And it was one of the ways that invasive species like Chinese mitten crabs, killer shrimps and zebra mussels could be monitored. The zebra mussels had arrived at English ports on boats docking from Eastern Europe and spread rapidly, blocking lock paddles and sluices. The mitten crabs also moved with vigour and speed and threatened the canals' infrastructure, burrowing deep into banks and causing erosion along towpaths, and in the worst cases opening up breaches that could drain a cut dry and flood local lands. I'd seen signs, too, along the Kennet and Avon, warning about the killer shrimp, which lived up to its name, decimating the larvae of all kinds of insects, slaughtering the fry of fish and ousting the gentler native shrimps.

Killer shrimp were something like a submerged mink. And mink, of course, were another invasive species that had adopted the canals as home, transport, larder and love hotel. Other less concerning invaders included red-eared turtles, which I had seen sunbathing on the Regent's Canal in London, and which were said to have been dumped by children, or their parents, as they outgrew their tanks during the Teenage Mutant Ninja Turtles craze. Dumping, due to an outgrown tank, was the probable explanation, too, for those giant catfish.

It wasn't just the animal world that was threatening the canals. Plants, like the water weed that had afflicted the Severn and Thames Canal in the 1880s, and had choked the Kennet and Avon in the early twentieth century, are still a problem today. On the Llangollen Canal I'd met a contractor who numbered off the botanical bounders muscling native species out of their own homes. Japanese knotweed was his most difficult towpath foe. 'And on the canals there's floating pennywort, and water fern;

both of them can kill a waterway – cover it like a carpet so no light gets down below, and smothers the fish.' And I thought of Kate teaching me always to throw the engine into reverse after going through a patch of weed to – hopefully – unwind the strands and fronds from the propeller before it became so entangled that one had to stop, open the inspection hatch and cut ropes of weed off the blades and shafts. The CRT cited a figure of around £700,000 a year spent on waging battle against plant species alone.

It was a pity, I often thought as I'd walked along the towpaths and seen the measures needed to clear invasive plants and species, that they didn't have a value that allowed them to be harvested rather than just destroyed. Could the huge piles of weed dragged out of the waters and left to rot be used as biofuels? The crayfish and mussels turned into eat-to-save-the-environment dishes on fancy menus? I presumed not, because, if so, someone living on the cut would have been doing just that. Canal dwellers are great foragers. Every live-aboard boat seemed to have raw firewood piled up along its roof, neatly logged, split and, stacked to season, in the case of the tidy-mined. And on the Grand Union I'd come across a narrowboat business called Wildside Preserves – 'a foraged flavour in every jar' – selling jams, chutneys, cordials and vinegars from their 'Jam Butty'.

Of course foraging was open to everyone. I'd picked nettles, sorrel and other plants to add to camp suppers on my travels, as well as blackberries and apples – as boaters must have done for generations. Some canal historians suggest that boat families might even have planted hidden gardens along the towpath hedgerows, so that when they passed they could pull up a few carrots, onions or potatoes. But all the accounts from boatmen, and from the landowners alongside the canals, showed that it was much more common for the horseman or a young lad to jump over into a field and grub up a turnip or a handful of spuds as they passed. (Boaters did, though, typically buy a whole leg of ham at waterside pub-shops and leave it stored in the dry of the inn, dropping in to have a few slices carved off when they passed).

An odd and rather appealing new canal pursuit – mixing foraging with fishing and metal detecting – was 'magnet fishing'. I'd never seen this before a morning walk along the Grand Union, near Stoke Bruerne, where I came upon a man casting a long line with a big round metal plug on the end. Beside him, on the towpath, were a collection of metal objects – screws, car parts, bolts and a ten-foot length of scaffolding. He gave me the rod to try on the pole – which it clamped to and lifted with ease. 'They're neodymium magnets,' he told me. 'You can get bigger ones that will pull five hundred pounds – but this does just about as much as I can lift. It's a nice way to pass the time on a canal – I've found old coins, toys, all sorts. People have pulled in sawn-off shotguns and cartons of bullets, so I've heard.'

People throw all kinds of things into the waterways. Shopping trolleys are the classic image (no problem, my new friend told me, for a decent neodymium magnet). But most debris that finds its way into Britain's canals is plastic – and it needs fishing out. And for that, it needs volunteers.

Luckily, volunteering is something modern canal culture thrives upon. The CRT and many local canal trusts depend on volunteer workers to maintain and repair the network, and on the plastic front they have the support of a remarkable operation called Plastic Patrol. This is the brainchild of a woman called Lizzie Carr, who, after being treated for thyroid cancer, decided to celebrate life by stand-up paddleboarding (SUP-ing) the length of England – four hundred miles of canals and navigations from Godalming in Surrey to Kendal in the Lake District. Along the way she became ever more alarmed by the amount of plastic waste and decided what the canals needed were groups of volunteers – on SUPs, in kayaks and canoes and on foot – to clear it up. So she set up an organisation to do just that.

On a wet summer morning, I joined Lizzie and a small group of newbie paddleboarders on the Walsall Canal. The CRT had provided a small fleet of inflatable Red Paddle Co boards and paddles, along with buoyancy aids, tubs and grab-sticks. 'Anyone paddled before?' Lizzie asked. Seeing an array of shaking heads, she handed out paddles. We followed her demonstration, pulling our paddle blades through imaginary water. 'Right, let's get afloat,' she encouraged. 'Start off kneeling till you feel confident. Only two people I've taken out have fallen off this year.'

We got onto our boards – they were just over ten feet long and surprisingly stable – and set off around the Walsall Canal basin. The water was clear – 'the cleanest it's been for years, maybe ever,' one of the CRT workers assured us – but once we'd passed onto the canal branch there was much to harvest with our pistol-grip tongs. Flotillas of coffee cups, submerged shoals of plastic bags, seams of plastic bottles lodged behind a bank of reeds. There was a strange satisfaction in pulling out other people's rubbish. Two fellow volunteers, Lindsay and Chrissy, had come along for the chance to try SUP-ing but were finding the rubbish-picking just as addictive.

Chrissy said that she'd picked up some coconuts floating in the water. I'd seen a couple, too, as well as drifts of orange flower petals, and had remembered Ed Fox at the CRT telling me that a number of canals near Hindi communities were used for offerings. There had been a problem at one point when these included tea lights, plastics and other stuff that didn't biodegrade and even jammed up lock mechanisms. But it seemed that the communities had accepted the need for ecological offerings and settled on coconuts – symbolising fertility and purity – and flowers. 'Oh, no, I feel awful,' said Chrissy. 'I've taken someone's gift to the gods. I'm going to put them back.'

Lizzie Carr, the founder and director of Plastic Patrol, filling a tub with plastic rubbish on the Walsall Canal.

There seemed to be some kind of lesson in the Hindi adaptation of an important ritual to keep the canal waters clean. I was paddling with Craig, who had been tempted to join when he saw the boards being inflated earlier that morning. 'My girlfriend's expecting twins and the flat's small, so I was out for a fag and an hour's mooch, and thought I'd give this a go.' He stopped to whistle at a mate leaning on the balcony along the undulating façade of the Waves Apartments. They fished together, he explained, recounting a recent battle to land a thirty-pound pike. He was enjoying the novelty of SUP-ing but was just as pleased to be helping to clean up the canal he fished in.

One effect of pulling out so much trash was to make us all think about the chain of disposing rubbish. The canals had once been the conduit for moving tons of manure and night soil out of big cities and into the countryside, but in those times they had also been filthy, polluted and lifeless. Today most canals have never been clearer, but for the scourge of plastic waste. For Lizzie, the trigger moment had been when she saw a coot's nest made of waste plastic.

For me, on my own canal travels, it had been learning that the problem was not so much the obvious pollution but the breakdown of plastics into finer and finer particles, which washed from the canals, rivers, ditches, estuaries and shoreline and into the sea. Scientists were finding microplastics – the almost invisible plastic pieces that might range in size from sand grain to dust mote – in every marine creature, from whales to plankton.

'If we had a deposit scheme on plastic bottles,' one of the volunteers said, 'we'd have earned a decent day's wage'. But for the Plastic Patrol paddlers it seemed that the paddling and the satisfaction of cleaning up the canal was enough of a motive. Johnny, another volunteer, had driven up from Oxford, never having missed a Plastic Patrol. 'It's got to be done,' he explained, as he listed items he'd pulled out on previous trips: 'A car wheel, a shopping trolley, of course, a twenty-five-gallon drum ...' He was like a terrier when he saw rubbish, but we were all doing well, bobbling along the banks and under the trailing willow branches. In an hour we'd filled sixteen bin liners. By the end of the day's session, we had sixty.

As I paddled back with Lizzie, she stopped to talk to a tough-looking fisherman. It had stopped raining and he was in casual clothes, lounging in a plastic chair, takeaway burger box at his feet. Alongside that was a plastic cup of bait, a single-use coffee cup and a beer can. His whole encampment was throwaway. 'We're picking rubbish from the canal. Have you thought about coming out and giving us a hand?' Lizzie stopped to greet him in a friendly way. 'You could have a go at paddleboarding.' He looked at us and shook his head.

Volunteering isn't for all types. But it's another of the openings that canals contribute to the country. It's work that creates friendships and bonds and helps feelings of wellbeing. Lizzie herself said that it was meeting people – as well as the plastic mission – that drew her to give up so much of her time. It was hard not to feel good about the work and the day – despite the rain, despite the stench of some of the bags of rubbish (one so putrid I thought I'd gag). Perhaps, I thought, saying goodbye to Craig and to Johnny, there's a volunteer in all of us, and the rewards of selfless co-operation and community are something hardwired deep into our brains.

Throughout my time on the waterways, I'd been impressed by just how successful the canals and their towpaths are as a shared space. It seems something of a social miracle that such a diverse range of people manage to get on with each other on this long, narrow world. But in the leisure era of canals, everyone seems to be tolerated – dog-walkers, buggy-pushers, joggers, even the cyclists (though not perhaps the Lycra-clad speed merchants racing from A to B with angry belling or, worse, bellowing, to clear their path). And, at least by day, most of Britain's canals feel benign – and more open than at any point in their history. In Victorian times through to the last war, the urban canals were often closed off, and even in rural areas access was discouraged, with towpaths bordered by fierce hedges of blackthorn.

That's not to make light of any dangers. There are canals in London or Manchester or Birmingham where you'd not want to stray after dark, any more than other ill-lit, ropey urban areas. But by day, the car-free canals and towpaths feel like good places for people. Safe for children. Fun for dogs. Places where life is slower and there is time to talk and think. The Canal & River Trust see their own mission in large part as one of 'ways to well-being', preserving the canal network as a benefit for people's health – both physical and mental. They view the canals, once a rigidly commercial enterprise, as 'places to escape', whether you're walking, cycling, boating, volunteering or just having lunch on a bench. The evidence suggests that the benefits to the nation's health, from water and green spaces, and from the 'slow ways' of the canals, are immense.

Not that I was immune from an occasional desire for a bit of speed. Sometimes the towpaths had seemed just a little too slow, and I'd find myself speeding up my pace a bit when walking or whirring my comedy-sized folding bike along for a mile or two. And then, in a fit of madness, I signed up for a half-marathon on the Aylesbury Arm of the Grand Union.

I was motivated enough to have registered, paid my fee, and got myself from London to a park in Aylesbury early on a Sunday morning. I hadn't been motivated enough to actually train, or indeed moderate my progress through a hearty supper the night before. It was a chilly autumn morning as I assembled with some 600 other towpath runners. Most were dressed in clothing that seemed a little too skimpy even for a run and were keeping warm touching their toes and doing tango-dancey stretches.

When signing up, we had all had to declare our likely time for the thirteen and a bit miles, and based on that we'd been sorted into groups and were being started off in waves – fastest first. I'd never run in a big group before, and had always been rather dismissive of mass events, so I was surprised to find how much energy I was picking up from the people around me, and how, as my group of thirty or so people were called forward to start, my adrenaline began to spark up. A bit like a narrowboat engine, I mused, as we followed the markers round a long loop of park and were sifted into a towpath-friendly file by the time we turned onto the canal.

And here was the odd thing. Despite all that testosterone and adrenaline and chilled legs and the sugar rush of energy drinks, the canal still exerted some kind of magic on us all. I suppose, right up the front, there were a few folk pounding for

Two Arms on Two Legs – the Aylesbury half-marathon.

the finishing line (the winning time was 1:17:18), but where I was running the spirit amongst us all could be best described as that contradiction in terms, a 'fun run'. A bit of chatting – to each other and even in passing to a fisherman hoping to hook a pike and seemingly unbothered by hundreds of feet pounding past him. Tens of people had come out to cheer us on even at the remotest bridges.

The canal was diverting, too, especially when we turned off the main towpath to follow the abandoned Wentworth arm back towards Aylesbury. Some lengths of this cut were dry and overgrown like remnants of a Bronze Age fort moat, while others had water, or were in the throes of being walled and puddled and banked by modern volunteer navvies.

I was glad to be with my 'around two hours for the distance' cohort, running hard enough to be breathless, but with puff left for birdwatching, canal history observation and chat. And we were polite. Runners waited to overtake until the towpath was wide enough to make it easy, with apologetic 'Er, just coming through' comments. Then, with only a mile or so to go, we somehow got competitive, pacing each other for the last pull as under the two hours looked possible. A final breathy gallumph along the towpath and then the finish line. Two hours and six minutes – but, even as a sucker for targets, I didn't care. You can't run along a canal and not slow down.

With their industrial and commercial purposes gone, I was left to reflect, the reason for canals had become the canals themselves – these long, thin temples to leisure. Peace, slowing down, politeness – all good things to find and enjoy where one could. But I had been travelling the towpaths too long. I fancied another chance to experience these blocks of water – a lock chamber full, the length of a cut, an outpouring over a sluice – as the engineers and canal builders and boat people had done. It was time for a long canal voyage.

12

Coast to Coast

I'D BEEN TOYING WITH IDEAS for another long kayak trip but this time with the focus further north. My first idea was to set out from London and head to Birmingham and then on to Manchester. But it seemed even more fun to go coast to coast. If I started in Liverpool, I could paddle my way across (and, at times, under) the Pennines to Leeds, and keep going to the east coast. For 127 miles I'd be on the Leeds and Liverpool Canal, the longest in Britain built as a single waterway, burrowed out to connect the country's northern powerhouse of mills and mines. And then another thirty-three miles along the Aire and Calder Navigation would take me to the estuary port of Goole, technically the coast, if not exactly the seaside.

So I loaded my inflatable kayak onto its trolley, swung kit for a fortnight's autumnal wild camping on my back, and set off to Liverpool. From London Euston the train line runs parallel with much of the course of the Grand Union and then the Shropshire Union canals, offering intermittent glimpses of the cut, as well as showing the limits of canal speed. It's just over two hundred miles from London to Liverpool and it takes two hours if you get the right train. Canal traffic would have needed the best part of two weeks.

But that's exactly the pleasure of the slow ways, I reflected, as I trolleyed my kayak to Canal Side Park, where the Leeds and Liverpool Canal joins the Mersey. I was keen to be out of the city before dusk, so I got the kayak inflated as quickly as possible. Strapping on my kit, I was watched over by four boys in school uniform who'd arrived on skateboards. 'Will that thing sink?' one jeered. 'I bet it would. Where are you going, anyways?' Leeds, I told them. 'Will you get there today?' one ventured? 'Ah, come on lads,' I said, 'it's nearly a hundred and fifty miles.' They thought about this; cheek was turning to interest. 'Where will you sleep, then? On the towpath? Sleeping rough, like? That's mad ... You'll get killed ... I wouldn't do that.'

They helped me carry the kayak to the water, where I lowered it down and climbed in, and they looked wistfully on as I paddled off. The kayak had that effect on people. It was the simplicity of it, the ease with which I drifted away with all my kit on board, free to follow the water roads. Far freer than any of the working boaters had ever been with their schedules and loads and gaugings. Freer even than the continuous cruisers and the hirers of narrowboats. Just a bit less comfortable.

Paddling through Liverpool, there was graffiti on walls and bridges, and tens of plastic bottles floating along the banks, but the water was far cleaner than I expected. The canal ran along the backs of houses and across the fronts of abandoned factories, warehouses and wharfs. There were rushes and coots and ducks. Paddling beneath a modern road bridge, I noticed a mural of the Beatles' Yellow Submarine, a mirror image of my yellow kayak.

It was knocking off time – I had left far too late in the day – and the towpath was busy with commuters, joggers and cyclists. One man got off his bike to hail me. 'That's a nice-looking canoe. Where are you heading?' 'Leeds, then Goole, across England,' I said, and he too got that far-away look. 'I'd love to do that, if I

Setting out with the inflatable (an Advanced Elements Airfusion Elite, for the tech-minded) at Liverpool. Not the loveliest stretch of towpath.

had time.' 'Couple of days on a bike,' I encouraged him. 'Just go!' He looked off along the towpath that could carry him across a whole country, as if seeing the possibilities for the first time. 'Jesus, maybe I will ... Maybe I will do just that.'

Within a few hours I was thinking wistfully of the comforts the commuters would be enjoying. It was cold and dark and I was still paddling past derelict industry and housing estates. The boy on the bank had been right; sleeping on the side of the canal along here would be mad. It was only beyond Aintree racecourse, prompting memories of excited commentators on the Grand National ('and as they come round Canal Turn ...'), that I could see the dim outline of a wooded slope above a grass bank. I landed, hauled the canoe up into the trees and, unpacking, discovered I'd forgotten my waterproof bivvy bag. That was going to put pressure on my bushcraft skills over the coming trip.

Next day, the joy of a dawn start on a cold bright morning was mitigated when I came across the first of many, many swing bridges. Boaters curse the Leeds and Liverpool canal for this, as it means they have to go ashore and open and close each one, but the water was low enough for me to limbo under, if I lay to one side, stopping myself from capsizing by hanging off the beams.

I was able to measure my speed and the vigour of my paddling against other towpath users. Bikers shot past me, and runners, too. But if I put a bit of effort into it, I could outpace slow joggers and fast walkers in a gratifyingly short time. I was doing about four miles an hour, so even with short autumn days, and some hundred locks to get past, I calculated I should be on the east coast in about twelve days – paddling at a rather more relaxed pace than my Devizes to London 'race'.

I was into open countryside now and enjoying myself, as city gave way to nature. There were kingfishers – dozens of them – and a sparrowhawk bombed overhead, twisting in mid-flight as it came over a country bridge, dipped down to the canal and then saw me and veered off. A fisherman pulled in his line as I paddled up. I apologised. He didn't mind, he said, as he was packing up; happily, too, as he'd just caught an eight-pound pike.

In the late afternoon, with darkness falling, I landed on the quay of the Farmers Arms, about as close to the waters as you could get and not be called the Navigator, the Jolly Boatman or the Lock and Quay. The Second World War had left its mark here, as on the Kennet and Avon. The Leeds and Liverpool had been a line of defence, a moat strung with tank defences and pill-boxes (I'd seen a few along the bank) and, here, a heavy red-brick block house with bricked-up gun ports built into one corner of the pub overlooking the canal.

The joy of birdwatching on the canal – finding a kingfisher, up close, on the towpath beside you.

I parked the kayak in view of the pub window and headed for the bar wearing my buoyancy aid, cagoule and general fancy dress. The early drinkers had questions. Where was I going? Was that an inflatable kayak? How much did it weigh? There were other questions I was keen to have answers to myself. How long was the trip going to take? Where would I sleep?

The talk went on in the bar as I knocked back pints and fish and chips and read up on the route ahead in my *Nicholson's* canal guide. One of the reasons I'd chosen the Leeds and Liverpool, apart from the satisfaction of doing a coast to coast – a sort of kayaker's Wainwright trip – was that as a canal it illustrated so much of the waterways' history. It was conceived as a way of bringing limestone to industrial areas and moving textiles and other local goods to cities and ports, and there was a wrangle from the start over the best route. Two were surveyed:, one going north on as direct a line as possible, the other more circuitous so as to take in towns to the south. James Brindley was brought in to arbitrate, and plumped for the northern route, with an additional branch down to the Wigan coalfields, and when the Leeds and Liverpool Canal Act was passed in 1770, he was taken on as engineer. But within two years Brindley was dead and his role taken over by John Longbotham, the Clerk of Work, and things did not go well. Lengths along the line were duly constructed, and began to pay a dividend from local produce, but the greater project was beset by problems as the engineers strived to bring the canal up and over the Pennines via an array of aqueducts, flights of locks, bridges and, at Foulridge, a mile-long tunnel. The cost of borrowing money became an issue, too, as did manpower shortages caused by war with France after the French Revolution. At one point, construction was brought to a halt for nearly a decade.

It took until 1816 for the full canal to become operational, but ultimately the delays worked in the canal's favour, as mill towns and other industrial areas grew and the industrialists bid for the canal to alter course and come looping south to pick up their business. The decision to build a broad canal able to carry the wide Yorkshire keel boats used on the navigations at either end also proved a boon, keeping the canal in business long after most waterways were losing their trade to the railways. Indeed, commercial traffic – albeit mainly loads of effluent – were transported along the Leeds and Liverpool into the late 1970s.

My fellow patrons of the Farmers Arms watched with interest but little envy as I relaunched into the night and a fine drizzle. But I found a joy in night paddling with the sky reflected in the water, lightening it just enough to make navigation easy. Hearing played a part, too, as I became attuned to the gurgles and splashes of sluices, a breaching fish, a disturbed duck or an otter's dive. And cold shivering breezes carried smells off the land.

Paddling through the town of Burscough, between the lights and shadows, a group of diners by the window of a canalside restaurant saw me passing and waved madly and raised their glasses. The rain had stopped, so I landed a little further on, made quick camp and laid out to sleep. I woke in the night and in the gloom saw what I thought was a rolled-up pair of socks I'd dropped on the towpath. But then they moved and scuttled away – a hedgehog.

Back on the water, next morning, I felt oddly listless. I was used to kayaking at sea, where periods of effort are relieved by riding a current. Here I began to feel oppressed by the endless trail of flat water, where every yard of progress demanded a stroke, and if you stopped paddling you stopped moving – or, with the constant headwind, actually went backwards. But the birds remained a comforting diversion. You could look far ahead up the ribbon of water and see a raven up high and far ahead, and then turn your head and you might see a kingfisher – malachite green in a sun ray, rather than the usual grey-day azure – only a few feet away.

I was looking forward to following the towpath to Orwell's Wigan Pier – it actually exists, a bleak wharf given a morosely humorous seaside name. The canal skirted the edge of the town, past graffiti, broken glass, old industry, new unit businesses and razor wire, before twenty-one locks slogged their way up into the Pennines. I'd have to pull the kayak on its trolley up the towpath over this two-mile stretch, handicapped by barriers to stop cars and motorbikes ... and kayaks.

I had been warned, too, about bored youths hanging out around here, but the towpathers turned out to be mothers walking schoolchildren home, fishermen, commuting cyclists, and an elderly man who told me he'd had a right good day contemplating the water but now he was off home for his tea. Forced to lift the kayak and my kit over one barrier after another, my muttered curses became the most antisocial thing along the whole Wigan stretch of canal.

I was rewarded for perseverance by supper at the Kirkless Hall Inn, warmed by evening sun and a pint, pie and chips, and comparing notes with two locals, Liam and Anthony, who had just mountain-biked a punishing circuit of towpaths and peaks.

Back on the cut in the moonlight again, the Pennines were a rising bulk ahead of me as the canal hugged contours, with steep banks on the uphill side and sharp drops to valleys below. Off to one side there was the distant sky-glow of some large industry and the muted roar of the M61, but close up it was darkness and peace. I pulled out by bridge 66, set up camp and boiled up a mug of soup, whilst two little owls argued in the trees.

Waking up on the third morning of the trip, I lay under my tarpaulin with an easterly wind blowing gusts of drizzle into my face and didn't feel much like getting up. But then I didn't feel much like lying under a damp tarpaulin either, and once on the water I found that the headwind was barely a head breeze, and in my waterproof cagoule and trousers I was mostly dry. The canal, too, began to cheer me as Pennine scenery took over from urban, and I began to pass odd little narrowboat businesses like the Wool Boat, from which Carol and Colin sold their hand-knitted oiled-wool boaters' ganseys, as well as Technicolor Dream Jumpers. Rather gamely, Colin was wearing one of the latter. 'Well, they are bright, those jumpers,' Carol admitted, 'but it means I don't lose him in Tesco's.'

I stopped for breakfast a few miles along the cut at Botany Bay, a retired mill turned into a busy four-storey retail outlet. The restaurant, naturally, was on the top floor. I left the kayak parked in the garden centre under the manager's watchful eye, alongside large Buddha statutes, pirate flags, dreamcatchers and painted signs reading 'Slow Down, Wine Down'. When I came back down, the wind had turned and was coming from the southwest, the sun was out and the skies were blue, and back in the kayak I was helped along by the changed breeze. Even trolley-hauling past the five locks up Johnson Hillock had its rewards, as it pulled me high up – 350 feet above sea level – to the Top Lock Pub, where canal workers of the past had sated their thirsts after a bout of windlassing boats up through the flight. Hikers, dog-strollers, children-walkers and cyclists mixed around the tables outside with a local fire engine crew who had parked their truck outside to stop for a chat with friends. I joined them before making early camp in the lee of a stone bridge, just past a little hamlet of boats moored along the towpath, one of them decorated from water-line to topsides in vibrant Rasta colours.

There was another early start in cold rain and after a few hours of paddling I was glad to get to the Navigation Inn. It was what in Ireland we'd call an 'early house', and at eleven o'clock in the morning was already serving pints to a bunch of guys. There was a silent TV showing motorbike scrambling and a radio station playing Minnie Riperton and Don McLean. Gouts of rain were coming and going outside and it seemed rather pleasant to sit inside looking out, chatting with hard-looking men who thought the same as me about looking out on the weather.

'You want to watch out for the monster rats up ahead,' one of them warned. 'Pike, too,' added another. 'Have your fingers off if you're not careful.' 'T'bloody sharks are worse,' chimed in some-one else. 'The two-legged sharks, wha', you'll get robbed.'

One of the men, it turned out, had done a bit of canoeing on the canal, and he had a story. He and a mate had been out on the cut, he said, just getting the hang of it, when they'd seen a child's buggy run down the bank and into the water. 'An old granny was screaming "The baby! The baby!" but we couldn't get that bloody canoe to move. There were a bloke on a bicycle and he dived off t'bike right into the water and pulled out the child. You'd think the woman would be have been overjoyed … but, nah, she were still screaming – he hadn't got her handbag out ... and then, bugger it, she bloody jumps in herself to get it.'

It was a good Sunday morning tale and it whiled away the time until the sun came out again. Then I was back paddling and lock portaging and then into Blackburn. 'Careful thought should be given to choosing a mooring site ...' warned *Nicholson's*. I pulled out at a welcoming-looking bar called the Calypso, in a restored wharf with roofed quays. Dave Wilson had created a Caribbean vibe in the lofty wood-beamed space and was reassuring –'Your kayak'll be safe outside the door, people are alright around here' – whilst recommending his curried lamb. There was reggae on the sound system and Dave (with cockatoo, Leo, perched on his shoulder) was a genial host, coming out to sit with me over a beer, talking about the trade that had brought raw cotton up from the docks at Liverpool, and pointing out a 'convicts hole' in the next-door building

No boat is truly complete without a parrot, or at least a cockatoo, modelled here by Dave Wilson in his *Calypso* bar.

that held prisoners waiting to be shipped down the canal to Liverpool for deportation to Australia.

It had been Dave's boat in Rasta livery that I'd passed the night before and he had the sociable air of boaters across the network, north and south alike. One of the things about the single-track routes of the waterways is the sense of community that they build – people meet each other over and over as they pass up and down. And boaters seem to have more than the usual share of eccentrics. Dave told me about a man I'd be sure to meet up ahead – Ben Cummings, who had built a raft, with a shed to live in and an upright piano on the back deck. He was pulling and poling and legging it to London, very slowly.

The drawback of autumn kayaking was how short the days were, and in the early evening I was launching yet again into the dark – and, not for the first time, into persistent drizzle. Ian, a fisherman stomping along the towpath with a Sherpa's weight of rods and kit, stopped to chat. He had been out since that morning, fishing for carp, and showed me a photo on his phone of a pallid white fish, with scales lapped like tiles on a roof, and a startled expression. 'That's a ghost carp ... they're beautiful.' As he talked, he was joined by another fisherman, a young British Asian called Omani, who reckoned he'd be out most of the night. What was the attraction, I asked? 'Well, my father taught me ... and I've no interest in pubs or clubs ... I'm just mad for fishing. Mad for fishing pike.' Ian and Omani traded pike stories for a while – how they can be big enough to take ducklings, and you had a chance of hooking a pike bigger than any caught before. Then Ian headed home and Omani strode off into the night. No, he'd assured me, he wasn't scared on the towpath alone in the dark. He liked it. It was a time for himself, a time to think.

Sipping coffee the next morning, a walker striding past my camp beside a bridge said, 'Oh, it's you again!' 'Again and from when?'

I asked. 'Yesterday. Passed you south of Blackburn in the morning. I didn't stop.' This morning, though, he was up for some talk. He always took his daughter to school on the bus on Mondays and then walked back the fair few miles to Blackburn. He walked a lot, he said. He looked wistfully at my very basic camp, and the kayak, and muttered about wishing he was free to 'head off, keep going'. He shrugged. 'Well, I'll get on then,' he said and leant in to give me an awkward clap on the shoulder.

A few more hours' paddling, along one of the bleakest stretches of cut, I passed a group of young CRT and Prince's Trust volunteers clearing and restoring towpath in the drizzle. They were in anoraks with hoods pulled down. 'We're doing this for people like you,' one called out. 'Making things better on the canal. I hope you're grateful.' They, too, were in bantering mood and my appearance on the water was something different on a slow day. One held up a metal sign reading 'L'POOL 62 MILES' and pointed out the weeds they'd cut back around a restored mile marker. Many of these had been hidden or removed in the Second World War to confuse a potential invasion force. They told me they were burying a small time capsule by the milestone. 'Got something to put in it?' I dug out a damp business card with a photo of the Oxford Canal in the previous autumn's fog, from my boat trip on *Morning Mist*. 'But I'm bad enough at answering my phone nowadays,' I told them, 'so there's not much chance if someone calls my number in fifty years' time.'

A few miles later the green rural world ended in the dark portal of the 599-yard Gannow Tunnel, which carried me into Burnley, a gloomy town but one that has possibly the greatest concentration of canal-heritage sites on the Leeds and Liverpool – factories, mills, basins, wharfs, towpaths, alleys, bridges and confusingly arranged bridges running off bridges.

I was eager to keep an appointment at Finsley Gate Bridge with artist Stephen Turner, who had an on-site residency with his Exbury Egg. The Egg is a 'boat-studio-house' but above all a piece of art, created by Stephen with the help of boat-craftsmen

Stephen Turner's Exbury Egg – one of the highlights on the art trail along the Leeds and Liverpool, celebrating the canal's bicentenary.

on the Beaulieu River in Hampshire. Now on tour, it stood on a decommissioned Burnley wharf – a beautifully patinaed oval of wood resting on the stark stone. I hauled myself up from the canal just in time to catch Stephen, along with Josephine Taylor and her son Steven, the Egg's caretaker-curators in Burnley. We climbed steps through a door hatch and were inside a tiny cabin with berth bed, work desk, storage and curving walls.

'Gosh, it's just like a vardo,' I exclaimed involuntarily, thinking of Gypsy bow-top caravans. To my surprise Josephine knew what I meant. 'I'm Roma Gypsy, our family are horse dealers,' she said, 'and that's what I thought the first time I came in here. I love it. Look at the bed across the end – that's the way it was in the vardo.' We fell to talking about Reading wagons, 'Queenie' stoves and horse fairs at Appleby and Stow, as it got later and darker.

'Borrow this tent, if you want to camp here for the night,' urged Stephen, pulling out a circular bag as the group locked up. 'You'll be behind the gates, so you'll be fine.' It was beginning to rain again and it seemed a welcome idea. First, though, I decided to foray back down the canal and paddled back to the Inn On The Wharf for a meal and a pint. Maybe two pints. But then I met Pete Booth, engineer and brewer at Irwell Works Brewery, and he was too good company, and the Inn too comfortable, for me to turn down more pints and talk. Pete used to run a curry restaurant at festivals. 'We did a deer curry – that was more expensive than the others.' He sank a good draught of beer, and continued. 'And then there was the Tarka Masala, which was like a tikka but a little 'otter.'

It was closing time before I relaunched the kayak and climbed in to paddle the quarter-mile of darkness back to the Egg, and it was a tough scramble to scale the high wharf wall, and pull my kit and the kayak ashore. The tent was one of those tensioned hoop affairs that snaps from a round, flat shape into full tent in a second. It did just that as I pulled it from the bag, catching me neatly under the chin. But as a sort of mini-egg shape I could shelter in, how welcome it was. Through the night the rain got stronger and stronger until it was drumming down like a fire hose.

At dawn it was still pouring with rain, so I lay in the egg-tent and listened to the shipping forecast, which was about bad weather, and then the weather forecast, which was about rain. And then listened to the actual rain some more. It was nearly nine before I launched off along the Burnley Embankment – the 'Straight Mile' as locals call it – running high above the town on causeways and aqueducts to cut across the Calder Valley. One of the wonders of Britain's canals, this had been built – along with the Gannow Tunnel – by Robert Whitworth in the second stage of the Leeds and Liverpool. Whitworth was the go-to man for canal engineering at the end of the eighteenth century, an expert in avoiding locks, where possible, to speed the transport. By this time, navvies must have been an experienced workforce, too, though the tasks remained challenging. The Embankment took five years to construct. At its end, the watershed of the Pennines was only ten miles or so ahead of me. Once crossed, I'd be going downhill (as much as canal water 'goes' anywhere) pretty much all the way to Leeds. And there was a lot of water to go 'down', as rain was still torrenting from the skies.

At Nelson it was even heavier as I 'ahoy'-ed a moored-up converted butty, the *Selina Cooper*, named after a local activist who had improved conditions in the nineteenth-century mills and factories. The boat, like Stephen Turner's Exbury Egg, was part of the canal's Super Slow Way, celebrating the Leeds and Liverpool's bicentenary, and housed a touring arts centre under the direction of Cis O'Boyle and Rachel Anderson. 'Ahoy!' I called and a head – Rachel's – popped out of the waterside door of the narrowboat next door. We chatted about the weather, the bicentennial projects, the women's groups and artists who used the *Selina Cooper* as a meeting and workspace, and much else, until I realised that whilst I was already damp and wearing waterproof gear, Rachel hadn't been damp but was now, from hanging out of her window. I un-'ahoyed' and pushed on.

Kayaking through these rainy days, the silvered and soft-focused canal created a receptive screen to project the past of the canals. I could imagine the horse-boats coming through the mists. The coal boats heading down to Liverpool. The smell of wood smoke from the 'short boats'. These are particular to the Leeds and Liverpool, where the locks are fourteen feet wide but only sixty-two feet long (making the canal off limits today to the fairly common seventy-two-foot-long narrowboats). The size made sense, however, as the squat and beamy boats could carry twice as much weight.

As if on cue, three Asian Goths – two lads and a lass with Amy Winehouse bouffant hair – called out a friendly warning. There was 'a bloody great boat' coming round the bend and I might get sunk. I thought it was light-hearted banter, but then the wide black hull of one of the last running Leeds and Liverpool 'short' boats came into view. I pulled to one side as it thudded round the corner, feeling its force under my kayak.

Three men stood on the back deck in rain-sleeked anoraks, hoods up and drawn tight, one steering with his arm along the heavy tiller. Across the back of the hull, her name, *Kennet*, was picked out in a restrained version of the Leeds and Liverpool boats' traditional decorative 'brightwork' style: gaudy contrasting panel colours, shadings, fleurs-de-lis and the Edwardian-era razzamatazz of the fairground and music hall. Following

A heritage short boat, the *Kennet*, marking the bicentenary of the Leeds and Liverpool Canal.

the *Kennet*, through the day, came a ragbag flotilla of craft, celebrating the bicentenary on a canal-length journey.

Locks, in the years of working boats, had a social function, with blacksmiths often setting up shop alongside, where boat folk could get their horses shod and hear stories and news. And they are still places where people are drawn to pause and, as boaters say, *gongoozle*. The word today means just 'to stand around and watch canal life' – around locks, especially, where you'll sometimes find a pub called 'The Gongoozler'. But the term seems originally to have been used for the crowds at canal openings, often attracted by the offer of free beer from canal companies wanting to make a splash.

There was quite a crowd of gongoozlers at Barrowford Locks, where the *Kennet* flotilla was being locked down with the help of its seasonal lock-keepers, Michael Heathcote and Andy Lowe. Seasonal lock-keeping is one of those perfect jobs if you're good at that kind of thing. A busy season up and down a flight of locks, keeping them working, helping people solve problems, and then the winter off to do what you will – in Andy's case, living and writing in Spain. I was eager to ask the two of them about the Foulridge Tunnel, which was up ahead, and seemed a bit of a grey area for a paddler. The Leeds and Liverpool Canal and the Aire and Calder to Goole has been designated by the CRT as a canoe trail, but it wasn't yet officially open and Foulridge felt like a challenge, given its mile-long length and its alternating one-way system.

'You wouldn't want to meet a boat coming against you, there's no room to pass,' cautioned Andy. 'But you should be fine. Just keep an eye on the lights – it's red to stop and green to enter, and you've a ten-minute window to enter and then twenty minutes to complete the trip before the lights change.'

I was just deciding to put my head torch on and chance my luck when a narrowboat owner who was locking up overheard the conversation and offered to take me and the kayak as deck cargo. So I ended up cruising through the tunnel, a mug of tea in hand, with Bill and Maria and their two dogs. They were good company, sharing their tales of diving for deep wrecks, as well as canal voyages. They liked to travel the canals in autumn and even winter: 'No queues at the locks. No problems finding a mooring for the night.' We talked, too, about a cow called Buttercup, who fell into the canal here in 1912 and swam the whole way through the tunnel, to the beckoning light at the Foulridge end, where she was revived with a hefty shot of rum.

I relaunched at the end of the tunnel and paddled off into Yorkshire and the dusk. I had been finding a magic in the darkness, and the moonlit path of the canal, passing moored boats with their curtained windows glowing with the blue light of televisions. On the water, my own company consisted mainly of owls – little owls and tawny owls – and the swans ghosting along. I had the night to myself and fell into that state of mind where paddling was easy and kept me warm as the temperature dropped. I went on until I saw a grassy niche off the towpath, with a sheltering ivy-wreathed wall, perfect for a night's camp.

An early-morning dog walker recommended a cafe in East Marton for breakfast – 'You'll find it by the next bridge after the double bridge.' Sometimes those kind of directions sound obvious when you hear them, and then later, on the water, you start wondering if the 'double' bridge is two bridges close together, or a bridge with two arches, or a local name for a bridge with nothing 'double' about it at all. But the Double Bridge was exactly as billed – an arched bridge built on top of another arched bridge – and the Abbots Harbour Cafe was indeed close by, up a muddy road. Leaving the kayak in the cafe garden I entered a centuries-old warren of stables and barns, with ancient wooden animal stalls converted for dining. The building, the chatty manager told me, had been a staging post for goods and travellers moving between two local monasteries, in packhorse days, long before the canal. The full English breakfast was of welcome Friar Tuck proportions.

During the few days I'd been paddling – and over the 400-plus feet I'd climbed – autumn had properly arrived. The air was chilly even in the sun. Birches and beeches were turning to yellows, reds and browns. One stretch of remote canal country, beyond East Marton, ran between small woods of pines, birches and oaks. Robins, chaffinches and wrens called and sang in the trees. A troupe of long-tailed tits cavorted through the branches. And there was also the rattle of mistle thrushes – the sound of coming winter.

A proper double bridge at East Marton. You really couldn't miss it.

At Bank Newton there was a rash of locks along a ten-mile stretch, and rather than coming in flights they were spread out, a half-mile apart at times. It made for difficult choices – when I'd pulled out, did I then relaunch to paddle for ten minutes to the next lock, or just walk the kayak on the trailer to the next one, and then put in and paddle to the next or keep walking?

It was also the busiest stretch of the canal I'd come across so far, awash mainly with hire boats, which were keeping another seasonal lock-keeper, Nigel, busy. We chatted. Nigel had begun living and travelling on his own boat, before getting this job with the Canal & River Trust. 'I needed to change jobs – I was a workaholic, stressed out. So I did one of those lifestyle assessments – you know, smoking, drinking, shift work and that – and it said I'd be dead before fifty. This is the perfect job for me. I've lost a stone already.' Cycling and walking between locks did indeed seem an idyllic way to change one's life. And to slow down.

I, on the other hand, had to speed up in order to reach Skipton by late afternoon. The bivvy bag I had forgotten had been sent to the office of Pennine Cruisers for me to pick up – and I was going to take a break from sleeping rough and the cut by going to stay with a friend up on the moor. But, after all the locks, I found I had several miles of Swing Bridge Roulette to play, limbo-ing beneath them, where I could, but all too often having to clamber ashore and carry the boat to the other side.

Coming into Skipton, the Leeds and Liverpool winds in above the town, offering glimpses of the town houses below, seen between converted warehouses and industrial chimneys. There were little suburbs of moored-up narrowboats and a busy junction where Pennine Cruisers had their hire boats, offices and shop. Zoe Clarke greeted me there with my bivvy bag parcel and was happy for me to leave the folded kayak with them. Zoe probably had a bit of sympathy for a fellow paddlers as the previous summer she was in a team who stormed Canadian canoes the whole length of the Leeds and Liverpool – 127 miles, remember – in just four and a half days.

I'd covered a hundred miles in a week and didn't feel a sense of hurry. Skipton was a chance to clean up, wash clothes, sleep in a real bed and walk on the moors. I deflated, folded and packed up the kayak, bundled all my other gear into a bag, put on my dry 'shore' shoes and clean socks and retired to the Boat House for a pint, pleased with my almost instant transformation from kayaker to bloke in a pub. Except I'd got so used to wearing my buoyancy jacket that I'd forgotten to take it off. I still looked like a kayaker, just one without a kayak.

Staying with my artist friend Bridget and her dog, high up on the moors, gave me a new perspective on the canals. They had their own microclimate; often lined by mature trees, they are almost insulated from the surrounding countryside. On the high ground the skies were so much bigger, the weather wilder. Instead of kingfishers, ducks and songbirds, we walked among grouse, buzzards and snipe. I had intended to get back on the water and start paddling eastwards again after a couple of nights, but what with striding through the heather, and good company and roaring fires and excellent food, it was impossible not to stay longer. One more hot bath, another evening in front of the log fire, a last night under a ceiling.

And then back to the kayak and the water, which was bathed in sunshine. Assembling the kayak, as ever, drew onlookers. And indeed, it was a bit like a magic trick, the conversion of a large bag into a fully operational kayak. But setting off, waving to the watchers on the wharf, my confident air was soon punctured. 'You're going the wrong way if you're heading to Leeds,' someone shouted to me. 'Or if you're heading to Liverpool.' Normally on canals there are only two ways to go – and Skipton's branch line had fooled me. So, too, had the *Pearson's Canal Companion* which I'd picked up for an alternative take on the Aire and Calder ahead. I had already absorbed the *Nicholson's*, which likes to call itself the 'Bible of the Waterways', and thought I'd check out the opposition, which self-defines as the 'Shakespeare of the Canals'. The two guides were quite different in style, layout and content and the *Pearson* took a bit of getting used to, with its maps randomly orientated to fit the page. But, however oddly aligned, it still had the essential locks, distances and pubs marked.

Once I had got my bearings and felt confident I was heading for Leeds, I spent an afternoon of what I call 'paddle strolling.' You can't drift on a canal, as there is no current, but you can paddle lazily, barely dipping the blades into the water and without any hauling or pulling or puffing – and that's what I did. Looking into fields, saluting swans, singing to myself. I stopped as I drifted past Ben Cumming's shed-piano-bath raft, which Dave at the Calypso had told me about. In the flesh it was as much performance art as vessel. A raft with a shed and a piano on its deck, and a floating bath towed like a tiny butty behind. It had no engine and Ben had got this far by bow-hauling alone. London was a good year's travel away and Ben, it turned out, was away on shore leave.

Having paddled leisurely through the day, I kept going late into the night, with the waning moon casting a silver path across the water for me to follow. At one point I heard a gurgling behind me and, turning, saw a male swan swimming hard towards me, wings out and mantled to chase off the yellow interloper. I eventually stopped under a tree by one of those handy abandoned bridges that cross from one field to another and provide a shelter from the wind, threw down my bivvy bag, pushed my sleeping bag inside it, and fell asleep.

It was just breaking dawn as I packed and launched. I planned to make Leeds by mid-afternoon, which was around twenty-two miles' paddling. In theory there was plenty of time but I'd been a bit bothered by rumours – possibly inflated and out of date – of teenage gangs lurking with intent on the towpaths of Leeds' westerly outskirts. *Pearson's Canal Companion*, tipped narrowboaters to 'get through bandit country early in the day, before the yobs grow restless', though it did add that their mission was 'not to scare you off'.

It all seemed a bit alarmist as I paddled into the dawn sunrise of birdsong and towards Bingley Five Rise Locks and breakfast at the Lock café. I wolfed down the calories, stopped for a chat with the genial Marcus behind the counter and, full of energy, trundled the kayak along the towpath. Bingley Five Rise is the steepest lock staircase on the whole waterways system, with a gradient of one in five, and it wasn't worth relaunching until after the Three Rise Locks, a further quarter of a mile on, so I stayed on the towpath with the cyclists, joggers and dog-walkers, admiring the feats of watery engineering.

When I finally relaunched, I was soon in a classic Pennine valley, squeezed between high ground in which the rivers, canal, railways and roads competed to take the lowest line, crossing each other on bridges and viaducts and running through culverts and tunnels. And then, after Bingley, the canal soared over the Aire River – the same river that I'd be transferring onto in Leeds – on an aqueduct. Rounding a bend I was met by a very rough mirror image of myself – an inflatable kayak carrying a bearded bloke, though there the resemblance stopped. Koot had a blue craft and was a dapper dresser in jaunty cap, snazzy shirt, neoprene top and tattooed forearms. He was an artist and designer – 'a few album covers back in punk days, The Exploited, things like that' – and was commuting up from Saltaire, a few miles downhill. 'I don't know why more people don't do it,' he mused. 'It's beautiful, this stretch – you'd think it would be full of paddlers, but you're one of the few I've seen.'

Saltaire was one of the jewels of the Victorian industrial age, a vast mill complex built by Titus Salt, along with a 'model town' for its workers. Salt had moved both the mill and workers from Bradford, appalled at the city's pollution, and had endowed his workers' new town with philanthropic zeal – building schools and institutes and parks (and a stern absence of pubs).

Passing below the vast mill complex of Saltaire – with its Venetian bell-tower chimney on the left.

It was with a sense of wonder that I paddled past an ice-cream narrowboat and under emerald-green weeping willows and then into the steep but airy canyon formed by the walls of the two main mill buildings. Salt Mills, in its heyday in the 1850s, employed 3,000 workers on 1,200 looms, and shipped out 30,000 yards of cloth a day – much of it using alpaca wool. Saltaire's textile industry gradually declined, as throughout West Yorkshire, but the mill only ceased operations in 1985, and had been preserved well enough for conversion to leisure use. In my haste, I was missing a gallery of works by local boy David Hockney.

The Leeds and Liverpool itself was largely redundant for mill traffic – from Saltaire and even Bradford – by the 1960s, when the transport authorities recommended closing stretches. But it has always been 'in water' and, at one of its lower ebbs, in 1972, it was the location for a magnificently odd film called *The Black*

Safari, created by the writer Douglas Botting for the BBC's *The World About Us*. Botting followed a group of African travellers who – in a kind of inverted homage to David Livingstone – journey along the Leeds and Liverpool in search of the quaint customs of the natives.

Botting's film of Yorkshire's 'natives' came into my mind as I powered along towards Leeds, putting in fifteen-minute miles to try and arrive before dusk. I knew exactly how fast I was going, timing myself between the mile and half-mile markers, which were positioned like timekeepers on the canal banks. The thing about the canal system is that everything is measurable – except, perhaps, how long it takes to get a kayak through a swing bridge.

I was just approaching one of the lowest swing bridges I'd yet come across – a light footbridge with its underside almost touching the water – when a woman came out from a moored boat, through a complicated gate sealing off the pontoon and its boats, and swung open the bridge so that I could paddle the kayak through. Mariella was from the Netherlands and she and her partner had had their bicycles stolen the day before. 'Three lads ... people saw them sitting and waiting for hours over there, then when no-one was looking they came across the bridge. They had cable cutters and, they cut the bikes off and then ... just ... gone!' She was still angry and upset.

It was the first crime I had come across on my canal travels and it seemed oddly out of keeping as I paddled through a gorgeous stretch of countryside, frequented by happy natives cycling, jogging, strolling and generally enjoying the towpath. Pulling out to pass Newlay Three Rise and Forge Rise locks, I met seasonal lock-keepers AJ and Steve, and asked them about the Leeds locks. They too had heard the 'bandit country' talk, which they felt was daft – and they were at pains to stress that things had greatly improved since the CRT had paved the towpath, restyling it as a cyclists' and joggers' way. Both groups had soon begun using it, followed by dog walkers and anglers, parents with pushchairs and young children. Apparently the old trick was working: by making the environment more pleasant, more valued, the attitudes of those using it improved too. And I was amused that the speeding commuter and racing cyclists who are often seen as the bane of the towpath had been in the vanguard of those making it user-friendly.

Within a mile, just as dusk was falling, I found myself on the towpath on the edge of Leeds, folding and packing the kayak in order to trundle it to an Airbnb. I felt a little foolish that I had feared the day's journey on account of a few offputting rumours. Two women walked towards me along the towpath. They seemed entirely relaxed despite the fading light and stopped, as people so often do, to chat with me about the kayak. It turned out that one of them, Linsey Jones, was an actor who had performed in two canal-themed shows, 'Multi-storey Waters' and 'Seven Bridges', by Stephen Bottoms. Everyone, it seemed, had

'Bandit country' – one of the tranquil stretches of the Leeds and Liverpool, between Saltaire and Leeds.

some canal connections. But when I asked where I should head off for a taxi, I was a little surprised by the matter-of-fact delineations they made about safety on the bank. The next stretch of towpath would be darker and best avoided at night. I should get a taxi at the Kirkstall Bridge Inn, they suggested, and it would be better if I went in and phoned rather than waited on the street. It reminded me of advice other women and men had given about following your instincts on the towpaths at night, where your exit might be blocked by a person approaching or walking behind. Theirs was a tip I was glad to follow.

An hour later, the kayak and I were inside a comfortable house, with a bath running and the guidebooks out, as I contemplated the next day's transfer to the Aire and Calder Navigation and the final forty miles to Goole. Next morning I made my way back to the brewery building where I'd stopped the night before. It was one of those typical urban canal edge-lands, the waters bounded by wasteground, houses behind high fences and abandoned yards. But even here there were cyclists, dog walkers and anglers, and the only abuse I had was a youth spinning past on a BMX singing 'Row, row, row your boat … up your arse'. I chose to take it as cheerful and remarkably tuneful banter.

I pulled out of the water to pass another six locks, and lost time chatting to people interested in where I'd come from. 'Liverpool?' repeated one bloke struggling with the concept. 'Today?' There were live-aboard boats moored up on the outside bank (the one without the towpath), one narrowboat draped from end to end, its full sixty feet, in a 'skin' of wool-knitted panels portraying cheerful maritime scenes, with mermaid dolls, scatters of seashells and shoals of fish. Bonkers. But brilliantly so.

I'd mentally relaxed. Coming into the last mile of the Leeds and Liverpool Canal it felt that, with 127 miles behind me and a mere thirty miles almost dead-straight paddling down the Aire and Calder Navigation ahead, I was almost at the end of the coast to coast. But I'd overlooked the difference between a canal and a navigation. One is a tame, man-made, 'shallow-enough-to-stand-up-in' water road. The other is a wild river brought under partial control by the application of big locks, heavy banks and weirs. It is quite a distinction, and as I looked down over No. 1 River Lock, the junction between canal and river, I realised the degree of my ignorance. The Aire and Calder was a big working waterway joining industries, past and present, to the sea. And here, where it reached into the city, it ran below high walls. There was no obvious place to put the kayak in, and no obvious place to get out if things went wrong. The waters looked dark and oily.

I considered my options. One was to stop and to consider the trip a success – I'd paddled the length of the Leeds and Liverpool, after all. I rather foolishly dismissed this. Perhaps, I pondered, I could pull the kayak on its trolley through however many housing estates and industrial areas to find access to an easier stretch of the water to launch. That seemed unappealing. Then I saw a niche in the wall, with steps leading down to a point a mere four or so feet above the water – a water taxi pick-up point.

I gave it a go. Hoisting the emptied kayak onto my shoulder I manoeuvred it past barriers, down the stairs, and lowered it into the water using its mooring rope. I then let myself down to stand precariously in the cockpit, keeping balance with one hand in a crack between the massive stone blocks whilst lifting down the heavy bag, the trailer and my kit and lashing them onto the deck.

It was a precarious operation, and things seemed only a little better when I was sitting in the kayak, paddling eastwards down the river. The whole scale of my watery world had changed. Buildings towered above me on either side and I passed under huge bridges. Wharf buildings soared into the air, sized for big boats and big cargoes. And the locks, too, were suddenly on a giant's scale. The first one came after less than a mile. More feats

A long way down. Stage one: drop the kayak in. Stage two: get the bag strapped. Stage three – get in – still to come ...

of balance and strength were needed to pull myself up onto the side, and then lie on my stomach to reach down at full stretch to drag the gear up and lift the kayak clear. There was a dispiriting trundle past the immense lock and another heart-sinking moment when I saw how big the drop was at the far end. Once again lowering the kayak down, I was apprehensive that I might tear or puncture its skin.

The city bustle had dropped away and been replaced by big industry. The river passed under John Smeaton's viaduct, carrying the A61 over my head, and the connection with the canal engineer bucked me up a bit. There were a few narrowboats moored along a quay. They too were dwarfed by the scale of their surroundings, but I reasoned that if they could moor and land safely, then so surely could I.

It was almost dark now and the river had widened out. Rather than the usual canal choice between going the 'right' way and the 'wrong' way, there were now waters leading off in all directions. I was dazzled by distant gantries of lights where massive flood defences were being worked on. Huge empty basins formed deadends. A push-tug and a barge of waste passed to one side, far across the waters. The river and the navigation had split, separated by a narrow strip of land. More possibilities for confusion as I checked I was on the calmer, tamer, of the two. A bit of serious navigation was needed.

The next lock felt easier to climb up on to and trolley the kayak past. I was beginning to get used to them. And when I relaunched I found that the urban and the industrial chaos had dropped away and I was on a wide river with steep overgrown banks. Seen in my head-torch light, and felt through my paddle, it was like paddling on one of Europe's big rivers – the Rhone, say, or the Danube. I'd kayaked both in the past and the thought made me feel more at home, even relaxed. And also tired. I passed a homely row of live-aboard boats moored against a long staith, their curtained portholes and windows glowing with light. A mile or so beyond was an abandoned, overgrown quay, just a concrete edge and a few bollards amongst the willows. I pulled out and set up camp on a patch of grass trampled flat by anglers. Bivvy bag down beside the kayak, spirit stove lit to heat up supper, a quarter-bottle of wine opened to sip as I ate, wrapped in my down sleeping bag. Then sleep.

I woke to find the waters shrouded in thick fog, the scene like an autumnal Seine painted by Manet. Then there was the sound of oars as a rowing eight appeared from the club upstream, all eight women and the cox wearing party hats. By the time I'd made coffee and was ready to launch, the rowers had passed by again, the sun had seen off the fog and the day was heating up. The kayak drove along nicely, helped by my first proper current of the trip. All was well with the world. It was a joy to glide below the rushing cars and trucks roaring over the huge M1 bridge.

It seemed odd, though, to be paddling between banks devoid of villages, cafes and pubs. These were big waters, prone to catastrophic floods, and everything was set back well inland. If I wanted breakfast I would have to make quite a detour, and I was keen to keep going. But I did need to buy food for the coming days, so when I spotted a small basin with boatsheds I pulled ashore. Brothers Shane and Dave of Supreme Marine were can-do, what's-the-problem kind of guys. Of course I could leave the kayak and my bags up on the side of the dock whilst I went shopping, picking up energy-rich foods and an inner tube for the trolley, which had picked up a puncture.

Back at Supreme Marine, Dave and Shane made mugs of tea and took me into their emporium of masculinity – a workshop with a full-size pool table, numerous fishing rods, and a squadron of downhill bikes. These were serious machines with heavy shock absorbers and top-of-the-range gear sets. Both brothers were experienced down-hill bikers, and had adrenalin-fuelled stories of 50-mile-an-hour off-road descents down big mountains and horrifying crashes.

I didn't get much further that night – just another hour of paddling on the long, twisting stretch of river that old boatmen used to call 'Five Mile Pond'. Pulling out at the huge Bulhome Lock, I found two Polish fishermen packing up. The younger one was talkative. He'd caught three pike. He gestured towards the dark, deep, swirling waters where the River Aire rejoined the navigation and the current moved heavily under trees and steep banks and measured the fish out with his hands. A foot and a half for the biggest. Did he eat them, I wondered? He looked at me as if I was a halfwit. No, of course he didn't – didn't I know that you could get ready-prepared fish cheaply in Aldi? Who'd want to stink up the house gutting fresh fish?

This river stretch had wild, overgrown, steep banks, with plastic debris high in the trees showing how high up floodwaters reached. The water had a rich, composty, riverine smell. I ended up camping on an area of plant-covered dried mud under a steep wooded bank. I had a bed of rushes, mint and nettles; soft and aromatic, but stingy if I misplaced a hand or bare foot.

I had to wade knee-deep into the water the next morning to launch the kayak. It was cold but the sun was out again. Ducks lifted off the surface of the water ahead as I passed and fish plunged down, leaving swirling ripples. I thought of the anglers' stories of twenty-five-pound pike they'd pulled out of the Leeds and Liverpool Canal waters. There was the current to help me and a following westerly wind and, turning at one point, I saw a narrowboat chugging slowly along behind me. Within a mile it had caught me up on a wide bend in the river, just as another narrowboat with a plastic cruiser hitched to its side came up from the other direction. For a moment the three of us formed what constitutes rush-hour traffic in the slow lane of the navigation. I drifted a while, pushed along by the breeze.

Ahead I began to see signs of big industry – another Meccano set construction on a scale with the Anderton Lift. *Pearson's* identified it as the coal-fired Ferrybridge Power Station. It had closed the year before – a relic of another redundant industry. I drifted into a huge channel under its tower where tug boats once delivered 'pans' of coal – three pans in a set, filled with around 500 tons of coal from Yorkshire mines. Each pan was picked up by the huge rusting machinery still soaring over my head to be tipped into the maw of a hopper. For its last years in commission, however, the power station got all its coal by train. Boats had carried coal down to Goole, often chained together, leading them to be known as 'Tom Pudding' boats, as in a train they resembled a string of black puddings.

I stopped at the Canal & River Trust's maintenance yard at Heck Bridge, where CRT engineers Keith and Mick were preparing their boat and crane arm for a foray upstream to work on the

Ferrybridge power station – a recent addition to Britain's industrial ruins, once the recipient of tug-hauled coal from the Yorkshire mines.

lock gates in Leeds. 'Everything's sinking round here,' Mick told me, referring to the landscape – and, indeed, the waterways – slowly subsiding into subterranean voids created by centuries of coal mining. It was an obvious metaphor, too. At one end of the yard were heaps of rubbish that the CRT had pulled out of the waterway – traffic cones, a bed frame, fridges, numerous bicycles and inevitably tens of shopping trolleys. I'd seen very few of them in the waters for the past 140 miles and had begun to wonder if they'd become an endangered species. It seemed not.

Pollington Lock was the last of my trip, and I could have reached Goole that evening if I'd pushed on. But, as so often with a good journey, the end suddenly seemed to be coming too soon, and

I slowed down to absorb the wildlife and canal history around me. There on the right, running parallel to the channel of the navigation, was the Dutch River, a dead-straight dyke dug in the reign of King Charles I to drain the southern marshlands. Drax was in view to the northwest, another coal-fired power station, though pinning its hopes of staying viable by part-converting to biofuels. There were businesses dedicated to growing and baling those biofuels and ranks of wind turbines. Nesting boxes on poles were meant to encourage barn owls but seemed to have boosted the numbers of kestrels too, with several at a time hovering in the westerly breeze, dropping down in steps – drop, hover, drop, hover – zoning in on a mouse or vole before the final deadly dive.

The dead-straight channel and dead-flat land gave me a view towards distant Goole. And towards a disconcerting sight. A large boat, with full navigation lights, was powering out of the late-afternoon gloom and down our shared corridor of water at a fair lick. It was a commercial boat, the *Exol Pride*, a two-hundred-foot 'lubricant barge' working between Hull and Rotherham on the River Don. I pulled to the side, and as the skipper saw me he powered down. There was still a big wake, giving me the first seriously moving water with waves that I'd faced on the trip. The inflatable was in its element, though, the bow lifting over the first wave like a swan and easily riding the messy chop as fast-moving waters bounced off the bank.

People enjoy a jolly eccentric on the canals and I got a warm welcome as I walked into the Black Horse at Rawcliffe Bridge in waterproofs, buoyancy aid and soaked hat and gloves, as if making landfall after some trying sea trip. It was the first actual waterside pub I'd passed since leaving the Leeds and Liverpool. Sharon behind the counter pulled me a John Smith and gave me the bad news – the kitchen wasn't open. But then the good news – there was an order going out to a takeaway and I could add whatever I wanted. I ordered another pint whilst we waited and got talking to the landlord, Phil, a wiry small man with a dapper pork-pie hat. He and Sharon were running the adjoining marina

The only waterside pub on the Aire and Calder – the very welcoming and community-minded Black Horse.

and a small caravan park 'as people need somewhere cheap to stay if they're working round here'. The handful of men drinking with me were doing just that. The pub provided their community, a home away from home.

'Sleep on the lawn out there under the tree,' Phil told me. 'There's shelter and you'll be safe.' He gave me a bit of paper with a code on it. 'That's for the shower and toilet block so you can have a wash and a Tom Tit in the morning.'

I set off for Goole next morning shaved and washed, paddling between the huge blue storage tanks of a sharp-smelling chemical works, and a marina full of elderly narrowboats, old work boats being turned into homes and plastic cruisers fighting mould – that cycle that all boats are prey to, decaying from neglect if not actively being kept up by hard work.

As I paddled to the estuary, a flock of several hundred field-fares swept overhead, in for the winter. They are often seen as harbingers of colder weather, coming in to Britain as temperatures drop further north in Scandinavia. The last miles went quickly, and as I came into the outskirts of Goole I saw a group of kayakers on the bank – youngsters getting their introduction to paddling, dressed in wetsuits and buoyancy aids, launching from the grassy bank. I stopped to talk to the organisers for a while, pleased that others were using the waters, and then pushed onto the Yorkshire Waterways Museum, on the edge of Goole Port, which opened onto the tidal Ouse – and so the sea. It was time to change into my shore clothes and turn the kayak, my live-off-board home for the past twelve days, back into a piece of luggage. With 160 miles of paddling behind me, I was a land-lubber again.

13

Live-Aboards

REGENT'S CANAL, RIVER LEA
AND MACCLESFIELD NARROW

AS I TRAVELLED THE CUT I began to absorb the life and culture and infrastructure of the waterways. I noted the subtle differences between locks on distinct canals, the wharfside buildings, the different kinds of bridges. I'd even become proficient in identifying the different kinds of boats: the heritage narrow boats (two words) and modern-built narrowboats (one word); the Dutch barges and smaller Dutch *tjalks* found on the wider waterways; old horseboats with retro-fitted engines, butties with tacked on cabins, flats and keels and trows; and actual barges (a twice-width boat that could ply the lower Grand Union, the Thames and other broad canals and navigations).

I had also become adept at recognising the different tribes of live-aboarders. Since the 1960s, when the old commercial canal transport had begun to be sold off, all sorts of people had taken to living on the waterways and often, it seemed to me, their boat names defined their demographic. Forty- and fifty-somethings revealed themselves with names drawn from songs or albums from their formative years – *Piper at the Gates of Dawn, Purple Haze, Tea for the Tillerman* (good, that one), *Free Bird* – or with references to Middle Earth and Narnia. Others declared their sense of humour, generally with a pun, the best taking a moment or two to register or needing to be said aloud: *Norfolk Enchants*, *Ship Happens* and, a favourite, *Unsinkable II*. Nature and particularly birds were popular themes. There were veritable flocks of *Kingfisher*, *Grebe* and *Little Owl*, and occasional flights into Latin, such as *Pica Pica* (the scientific name for the magpie), painted in smart black-and-white livery on one narrow boat. There was many a *Willow Wren*, too, though they came under the category of canal history, from the eponymous carrier company. Another popular thread was a celebration of a new life begun or an old life escaped: *Break Away* (also a musical reference – so a high-scorer in Boat Name Bingo), *Dunravin'* (spotted, inevitably, on the Kennet and Avon), even a *Twit to Woo*.

Since I'd taken to the canals, people – friends, strangers in bars, everyone – wanted to know when I was going to get a boat and solve my housing, office and transport problems. My enthusiasm waxed and waned. Sometimes living aboard seemed a sublime life option; at others it looked like shackling oneself to a sinking asset and all the demands of an aged and needy relative. I had thought of a name, of course – I offer you *Bailed Out* – but I wasn't sure what waterways tribe I might align myself with. Was I the right age or temperament to retire to a floating marina suburb? Free and easy enough to become a New Age voyager in an encampment of random craft bought cheap and bodged into comfort? Interested and knowledgeable enough to run a heritage boat from the 1930s, with an original tiny cabin?

I got my eye in on live-aboard life walking the twenty miles down the Macclesfield Narrow Canal from Marple to Bosley Locks. Leaving Marple in the evening, passing the roving bridges, called 'snake' bridges locally, I'd written in my notebook that the smell of wood smoke from live-aboards had brought the canal alive. Seeing boaters coming onto deck from their cabins through the narrow back doors, I'd scribbled that they had a 'practised shoulder-shrugging shimmy' as they came up the steps and out through the narrow doors. One boat was called *Xanthippe*. Intrigued, I'd look up its meaning and found it was the name of Socrates' wife, who'd been an ancient byword for nagging and shrewishness.

It was bad manners, I knew, to glance in through boat windows but it was hard to resist curiosity. Often they were like those dioramas of 1950s life found in small museums. The formica worktops and gas hobs of a caravan-ish interior. The practical foodstuffs of an earlier time. Tinned milk, Heinz beans, Marmite, cornflakes – all easy to store. Usually cans of beer or bottles of wine. Plain mugs, Tupperware, tins of Vim. Products and smells I remembered from childhood boating holidays, on the coast in my case, but with the same underlying smells of diesel and bilge water, rust and grease.

It was almost dusk when I'd stopped to talk to Melanie and Ron, narrowboaters who were walking their dog along the tow-path. They were opinionated about the upkeep of the canals. 'They shouldn't have done away with the lengthmen,' they told me, when I said I was a writer for the CRT. 'They'd see a tiny hole in the bank, they'd see a bit of water below in the field, put two and two together and they'd do something about it before it was a real problem, before there was breach.' But they conceded that managing the modern waterways – a complex and delicate machine – with so many people using the canals for different purposes was challenging. The chat made me realise how knowledgeable live-aboarders become in many ways de facto lengthmen, getting to know a stretch of waterway well, seeing changes and often being the first to notice a problem and call the CRT.

Walking along the next day, deep in the country, I passed a live-aboard encampment on the other side to the towpath. Beside one boat were toolsheds and a collection of vintage tractors, on one of which an overalled bearded man was working. 'That's a strange combination,' I called across to him, 'boats and tractors'.

There was a long pause from the man; then, 'I suppose it is.' But the pause had been long enough for me to think again, that it wasn't at all an odd pairing. For people whose boat is their house, the allotments, flower gardens, shacks, old machinery and cars alongside their moorings are just part of their estate, and an overflow from their boat roofs. A necessary extension of their realm from the narrow confines of a traditional boat, which in proportion to length are barely two-dimensional, a thick line drawn between the distant points of front and stern.

I had rather broken one of the unspoken rules of waterways life, which is to act as if the boats – *homes* – moored in remote stretches of countryside with their windows at knee height – aren't there. The long thin world of the canals, with their towpaths offering rights of way for any dog-walker, hiker, cyclist or nosy-parker, can be an awkward shared space, creating, at worst, loneliness without privacy. But, although most boaters kept their bankside windows curtained, and looked out on the waterside at the mallards, coots and grebes, a distinct minority seemed to make it intentionally hard to pass without staring, creating mini-galleries or exhibitions in their windows.

On the Kennet and Avon I had been given pause by a stunning and cheery display of all things Marmite in a cabin window – jars of all sizes, and tins, mugs, promotional tat and advertising signs. And I'd got used to boats decorated to any number of themes: pirate boats, with skull and crossbone flags, dark Goth caverns, Buddhist temples with dreamcatchers and mandalas. And surely it would be rudeness to pass without inspection a lovingly restored heritage boat with its traditional paintwork, decorated Buckby cans, brass-swagged chimney pipes, Blanco-ed white top cloth 'strings' and blackened hull.

And some boats were businesses which actively wanted to attract the attention and custom of passers-by. I never ceased to be amazed at the diversity of these boats, which seemed the exact opposite of Britain's ever more standardised high streets. Of course, they enjoyed advantages over fixed retail spaces,

No net curtains for this provocative narrowboat window.

particularly suited to a craft workshop or artist's studio: no business rates, a footfall of walkers and tourists and boaters as a customer base, and, if one stretch of the cut didn't work out, the option to move on and try another, or tie up at one of the summer boat rallies and festivals.

In my own travels I'd given custom to numerous cafe and ice-cream and cake boats. But I'd also come across potters, a blacksmith, an on-board hairdresser, a tarot card reader and a hand-knitter of tough, oiled-wool boatmen's jumpers. Then, of course, there were the traditional boat crafts, best done aboard. Mal had been making his button and other styles of fenders, and I saw more fender-makers' boats along different canals. Signwriting was another popular craft and, with all those names needed, on some 35,000 canal boats, there was a good trade for the experienced conjuror of bright script, flourishes and motifs.

One of the most niche and yet satisfying boat businesses was a couple travelling on the *NB Lois Jane*, aka the 'Pen Maker's Boat', on which they did exactly that. The pens they made incorporated a proper canal dweller's zeal for both heritage and recycling: the barrels of the pens, often lathe-turned from pieces of discarded wood salvaged from heritage boats being restored, married to parts fashioned from gun metal, rhodium or silver.

Narrowboat and other live-aboard craft are so established across Britain's canal network that it seems hard to imagine a time when they didn't exist – and when all canal boats were commercial craft. As mentioned earlier, Sheila Stewart's *Ramlin Rose* has the boatwomen remark on the strangeness of Tom Rolt converting his narrowboat, *Cressy*, into a comfortable live-aboard boat, wasting all its carrying space. That was in 1937, and it was not until after the war that others began to follow his example.

Rolt and his wife Angela were not the first outsiders to live on the canals – London had its Bohemian houseboat-dwellers from the 1920s – but they were the first to do so as cruisers, and were influential pioneers, inspiring a generation of roving live-aboarders and weekend explorers. Rolt's books painted a pleasing picture of travel over the hundreds of miles of waterways, living a life free of constraint, dressing like an opera costumier's idea of boat people and consorting with the colourful canal folk themselves. It was an exciting prospect in the post-war years, even if elective live-aboarders had very little in common with the working families pounding up and down the same stretches of canal at the beck and call of carrying companies, and living in cabins little bigger than the *Cressy*'s bathroom. Not that it was easy for the newcomers. The still-busy waterways could be difficult to navigate, whilst neglected canals often had little or no water, broken locks and dangerous tunnels, bridges and aqueducts. It was an adventurous and unconventional life to choose in the 1940s or 1950s.

It was, however, cheap. The post-war collapse of commercial canal transport meant that there were plenty of craft available, for those who knew where to look: narrowboats, butties, fly boats, Dutch barges and the rest. These decommissioned boats could be acquired for a song and were not hard to adapt into living quarters. The remaining boatyards were glad of such work, and plenty of live-aboarders, then as now, were more than capable of creating a comfortable houseboat themselves.

Untold narrowboat luxury – the bathroom (and *bath*) on Tom and Angela Rolt's *Cressy*, converted in 1937.

For the best part of a half-century – from the 1950s on – the canals provided cheap and relatively easy options for the growing bands of boat-dwellers. Volunteers had brought more and more waterways back into commission, and with relatively few boats on the cut, outside the summer holiday rental season, boaters could moor up pretty much anywhere – and often for as long as they liked. The redevelopment of city wharfs, basins and towpaths was yet to get going in earnest and you could park your narrowboat for nothing in the heart of Birmingham, Manchester or London. Nothing, that is, except the cost of maintenance, fuel, repairs and the constant live-aboard tasks of emptying toilet tanks and filling up with water.

Living aboard in the early days might have been cheap but, if you were short of cash, it was rarely comfortable year-round. In Yorkshire I'd met an artist called Lucy who lived on a boat on the Oxford Canal for two years in the 1970s whilst studying painting. She listed the downsides of life on the waterways: rats coming in from the land, having to empty the Elsan toilet in the local boatyard, her anxieties when cycling home along the dark towpath, and above all the cold and damp. 'The beds were always soaking, we'd have frost on the inside of the walls, milk would freeze and explode out of its carton. The boat was lit by gas and we had to cart the cylinders for miles. I wouldn't do it again.' Pressed for the upsides, though, Lucy became nostalgic: 'The reflection of the water dancing on the ceiling, and swans and their cygnets tapping on the windows to be fed. Oh, and endless parties. And a winter when there was a big freeze and we took gas lights, a battery record player and mulled wine and skated in the moonlight.'

Living on the waterways now is a different story. Modern live-aboarding has been made comfortable, if you can afford it, by better new boats and complete restorations, effective insulation, efficient heating, solar power and good battery storage, WiFi and mobile phones, on-board showers, electric bilge pumps, virtually silent generators, and a plethora of handy twelve-volt appliances. Most boaters are inveterate buyers of gadgets to make tiny house living easier. And since Lucy's time in Oxford, on-board toilets have improved, with modern cassette toilets and even 'proper' loos with tanks (though these need pumping out at regular intervals, otherwise you risk them becoming over-filled, pressurised and exploding – not a good scenario). Evangelists wax lyrical over eco-friendly composting loos that reduce waste to the minimum, though they seem to require knowledge and attention through all the stages of fermentation worthy of that of a winemaker producing a grand cru.

In the countryside, on less popular canals, I met people still living a cheap, come-and-go, moor-where-you-like way of life (possibly one that still involved coping with rats, indoor ice and bucket toilets, too). But there are far fewer opportunities to drop off the grid since the popularity of canal boating has increased. In a pub on the Kennet and Avon, I was told, conspiratorially, by a boater that two contestants on the 'run-and-hide' TV game show *Hunted* had escaped CCTV detection, surveillance and suspicion by taking to the towpaths to get from England to Wales. But the idea of canals as hideaways was roundly poo-poo-ed by his mate, who pointed out that you could hardly disappear if you were taking a seventy-foot boat onto a network of single-track waterways.

And many of those waterways are becoming ever more crowded. Around 37,000 boats are currently registered on the 2,000 miles of waters managed by the Canal & River Trust, more boats than at the height of commercial canal use. Around 11,000 of these are full-time live-aboard boats, half of these with a permanent mooring, and the other half designating themselves as 'continuous cruisers' – meaning that they have to keep on the move through the year, under the terms of their licence. Continuous cruising is by modern standards a cheap

Eco-design on the Kennet and Avon, with an insulated grass roof.

way to live, though a licence costs several hundred pounds a year (paid to the CRT for the maintenance of the canals and towpaths), and insurance could add another thousand or more. The continuous cruiser's pattern of movement has to satisfy the criteria of 'bona fide navigation', which is defined as at least twenty miles in one direction every year, and no mooring in one place for more than two weeks.

Live-aboarders who have been on the canals for decades – for a couple of generations in some cases – and who have built lives around mooring freely within a small compass whilst they sent children to schools or took local jobs, are often resentful of these regulations, which were once scarcely enforced. It's understandable. Permanent moorings are expensive, even in the numerous marinas dug out along the canals to provide homes for the growing numbers of retirees and downsizers, and in the locations where people most want to live afloat they have become almost impossibly rare.

In the Barge Inn, on the Kennet and Avon, a waterway which had long been a haven for groups of independent-minded boaters, I listened to a musician singing, with heartfelt conviction, 'There's a C-R-T in "Charity" but there's no Charity in the CRT.' And indeed I knew people on the canal who had found the regulations tough. I had called in earlier that afternoon on a friend called Kara, who was moored nearby, and over mugs of strong tea by the stove she had told me about bringing up three children as a live-aboard 'continuous cruiser', having to get her youngest son to school when she had to move a minimum of at least twenty miles in one direction each year, and move at least a short distance every fortnight.

So, I wondered, what was modern boat life like for kids? Mostly, it seems, they think it's cool. Children adapt easily enough to the normal that surrounds them. Kara's youngest son, Urthe, thought it kept him fit and also tuned in to the environment, though it could be boring when they were moored away from any other kids to meet up with. And the continuous cruising life hadn't put off her eldest son, Joe, from getting his own boat, which he had moored at the back of Kara's and which provided a home between his travels.

Most live-aboarders in the country were as much boaters as householders, but in cities things could be different. In the 1960s and 1970s the comparative cheapness of decommissioned work boats, and the freedom to moor up in central locations, had created a new fleet of urban houseboaters, whose first and some-times only consideration was affordable accommodation, and to whom the waterways' workings were of passing interest. Instead, living on a boat was for many a bohemian adventure.

A. P. Herbert's novel *The Water Gipsies* described raffish life in houseboats on the Thames in central London in the 1920s. Fifty years later, Penelope Fitzgerald's Booker prize-winning novel,

Offshore, depicted a group of drifters, drawn from the author's experiences living on houseboats in Battersea Reach. In between these two books, the war had left a legacy of motor torpedo boats (MTBs) and landing craft, while the decline of canal and river traffic meant that Thames Sailing Barges, carrier boats and engineless lighters were decommissioned and available for a song to anyone prepared to take them on. So, in ramshackle fashion, floating villages of live-aboarders sprang up on pockets of the Thames, as well as along the capital's own extensive canals,

The Regent's Canal, especially where it joined the Grand Union at Maida Vale – the area known as Little Venice – was prime 'bohos on boats' territory. A young Richard Branson bought a houseboat called the *Alberta* when he arrived in London in 1971, and continued to live on houseboats until 1984, well after he had made his first millions and had his first child. Even after that, he had his Virgin office on a houseboat. It was a useful locale for the infancy of Virgin Records – funkily apt for the original hippy label and, even when Gong and Henry Cow had given way to Culture Club and Phil Collins, still a neat delineator with conventional companies like EMI.

Branson's barge actually played a significant role in the Virgin story. Branson was famously uninterested in music but became convinced of the genius of the teenage Mike Oldfield and his instrumental concept album, *Tubular Bells*. The challenge was that each track on the album lasted a full side – 22 minutes – which made promotion tricky. So Branson invited John Peel onto his barge for lunch, during which he played the entire album to the captive DJ. Peel, fortunately, loved the record and played both sides on his next Radio 1 show. *Tubular Bells* went on to sell 15 million copies, launching the Virgin empire.

Branson may have moved on (as one former employee told me, 'he's got Necker now – and a Caribbean island is like a houseboat

for a very rich man') but Little Venice remains a prime mooring area for London live-aboarders.

On a sunny winter's day, I met with Nancy Campbell, the CRT's poet laureate, to cycle the Regent's Canal and take a look at how its live-aboarders and culture had developed. We started at the Waterside Cafe, a converted boat moored nearby one of the canal's longest-running businesses, a trip-boat called the *Jason*, a hundred-year-old boat that has been carrying passengers along the Regent's Canal for more than sixty years. A few more boat lengths along the towpath was another London canal institution, the Puppet Barge.

I'd been there before, to see a performance of Wendy Cope's *The River Girl*, a dreamy message-play in which the eponymous girl (a river sprite) loves and then leaves a self-pitying poet due to his flirting, drinking and chauvinism. It was the latest in a line of puppet plays, for adults as well as kids, that had been put on since the early-1980s in what had once been the cargo hold of the *May Brent*. Juliet Rogers and Gren Middleton had been offered the decommissioned Thames lighter – seventy-two-feet long, no engine, a massive rudder – for free by a boatyard, as long as they paid them to do its conversion work.

I met up after the show with their son-in-law Rob, who told me about the theatre's early touring trips – once up the Grand Union as far as Tring, where the lock walls had bowed, making it impossible to continue, and for twenty-five summers along the Thames as far as Abingdon. But for the past decade the theatre has alternated between Little Venice and a summer season in Richmond (where they also have a Norfolk reed cutters' boat as accommodation for the puppeteers). The show that I had watched featured Rob's son Stan, the boat's third generation of marionette master, who has – of course – his own live-aboard narrow boat nearby.

The Puppet Theatre may be a venue rather than a home, but its problems and attractions are those shared by all live-aboarders. For the audience the atmosphere of the boat is key to the

Gren Middleton and Juliet Rogers in the 1980s, outside their Puppet Theatre Barge on the Regent's Canal.

experience. 'Half the battle is won when people come aboard and they're on the water,' Rob told me. 'The real drawbacks of having a boat on the canal are the shit tank and getting water.' The theatre's most important relationship, he said firmly, was with the pump-out boat: 'He works really hard and turns up at all times of day and night – I know the sound of his engine from way down the canal.'

Continuing along the towpath with Nancy, I felt much as I had walking down the Macclesfield. That the boats, in all their variety and decoration, from heritage authentic to student squat, through hydro-space-age, folksy, Mad-Max-meets-Waterworld, and Scandinavian clean-line – made sense of the canal and brought it alive. But there were also more unsettling signs of canal living: a cheap pop-up tent squished behind the trees in a tiny corner of wasteland in the angle of a bridge; and occupied, but near-derelict boats. I'd seen this on every canal. Boats that had become the last resort of someone unable to look after them or themselves. Sometimes I'd seen a wheelchair outside, on a muddy, rutted towpath. The dream of live-aboard life can too easily turn into a nightmare of loneliness, discomfort and illness, and organisations like the Waterways Chaplaincy and Thames Reach, and the CRT's own welfare officer, make efforts to identify and help vulnerable canal dwellers, who through age, infirmity or plain bad luck find it hard to stay afloat.

Such images are in startling contrast to the prime real estate overlooking the canal around the edge of Regent's Park, created in the early 1800s by the architect John Nash. His plans included landscaping the park, as well as building a cluster of grand villas, and the canal was pressed into service as a water feature. It was, however, placed in a deep cutting, so as to keep its noise, smells and boat crews away from the noble residences, and boats were forbidden to moor up – then, or now. In the era of working water traffic, of course, there would have been little reason, as barges and lighters moving around the city would have had live-ashore crews, whilst provincial narrowboats would have been moving on to Paddington Basin, or to the docks at Limehouse, to pick up or drop off their cargoes.

Nancy and I finished our towpath trip along the Regent's Canal in the Narrowboat pub, where I'd first met Ed Fox to discuss this book. Now, a year later, Nancy and I talked about the live-aboard communities we'd passed, and how they had helped to transform areas of London, turning them from edgy and sometimes dangerous areas into highly desirable pockets of real estate. Camden Lock was the most obvious case in point – once a semi-derelict part of the city, where boats had played a part alongside the canalside market in creating what had become one of London's top tourist attractions. Paddington Basin, where the Regent's Canal meets the Grand Union, was a more recent and equally dramatic example, a huge redevelopment of housing, offices and shops where the canal was integral to its appeal, adding tens of millions of pounds to its value.

The same thing had happened around the canal at King's Cross, where a London Canal Museum was itself a new tourist attraction, housed in a former ice warehouse. This had been built in the 1860s for Carlo Gatti's ice-cream business when ice – 3,500 tons of it a year –was shipped in from Norway and barged in along the canal from Limehouse. Then the business of ice storage stopped overnight, in 1897, when it was discovered that ice could be made artificially.

Boats had been moored everywhere along our cycle route and on this bright day they had looked especially seductive. Would you live on the canal, I asked Nancy? She was thoughtful. We had talked about the realities and costs and the on-water competition for moorings as we had pedalled the towpath. 'I've always dreamt of living on a boat,' she replied, 'though in London it's getting beyond a poet's means. But if I had the money, I'd buy a houseboat and set up a trust so writers could live aboard for a year, rent free, to give them time to write. That would have been a dream for me, when I was struggling in London in my twenties.'

Poetic trusts notwithstanding, many hundreds of Londoners have turned to the canal for housing in the post-millennium years. While in earlier decades London boat living was as much about a sense of community – about bohemian and then alternative lifestyles – it is now the loss of affordable housing that is the chief driver. The CRT estimates that there are more than 3,000 live-aboard boats on London's canals – and just 2,000 moorings. For those who can afford it, the answer is a permanent mooring –which can cost upwards of £5,000 a year – often twice that – and even then are not easy to find. For those who can't afford a mooring, there is a system of musical chairs in place, as live-aboarders struggle to keep to the terms of 'continuous cruising' licences, moving every fortnight – or more often from popular moorings. It's hard to know how this could be run better or differently, as the CRT's focus is on keeping moorings in the capital available for cruising traffic. And they do offer discounted winter moorings, with the right to moor in one place from November to March. But they are not, as they are at pains to point out on their website, a housing association.

Not that this is much comfort to those attempting to live and work in London when changing moorings means they find their commute to work made more awkward, or end up doing time on some of the edgier stretches of the network.

To find out the reality of modern boat living in London I met up with Sarah who, with her partner Kate, had made the move onto the water in the hope of saving money for a deposit on a flat. A friend had told them about a boat for sale 'and it snow-balled from there', Sarah explained. 'We eventually settled on a sixty-six-foot narrowboat, built in the 1970s. We had a survey done on it, but to be honest what sold it for us was the Rayburn, with its back boiler and radiators.'

As saving money was the main object, Sarah and Kate decided to chance it as continuous cruisers, despite both having regular jobs. They had survived their first winter, though it hadn't been easy. 'Especially when Kate had to work in Bristol for a month, so I had to look after the boat on my own and call on friends or family to help move the boat between moorings. And the Ray-burn wasn't all it could have been. I'd come in from work and stoke it up, and then it would smoke and I'd have to open all the windows. And if I'm alone, well, the engine and the batteries, if they go wrong, I'm lost. Kate did the diesel engine course while I did a two-day introduction to helming.'

What had saved them was the sense of community. There always seemed to be someone to ask advice, to show them what to do or to help with practical problems. But it had been a steep learning curve. The first time they had moved had shaped their

Narrowboats on both sides of the Regent's Canal, coming out of Maida Vale. Most of these are lucky enough to have permanent moorings.

route over the whole summer. 'We started at Stonebridge, where we bought the boat. And then on our first move there was a strong wind that spun us round and I panicked and turned off the engine and we started drifting.' They'd been rescued by a boater who jumped aboard to sort things out, but by then they were pointing the wrong way. 'We wanted to go into London but we couldn't face turning again, so we just went the way we were pointing, up the Lea Valley.'

'Actually, that turned out okay.' Sarah listed off the advantages of a country rather than city mooring, and some of the places that they'd stayed: 'Roydon was lovely – fields of sunflowers, only a few boats, sunbathing on the roof. It was hard to believe we were close to London.'

When they had cruised so far up the Lea River that they had to start commuting into London by train instead of bike, they turned around and headed back into London. 'We had wanted to stop in Little Venice but there wasn't a mooring and we had to keep going, and going ... and we ended up where we're moored now, in Alperton. It feels like an edge-land, a bit on the fringes of society, so I've changed my work times to cycle home in the light.' The boat's security, too, is a worry. 'We've seen a couple of boats sunk. And there was a really stormy night – that was horrible, being on board in bad weather. You can feel very vulnerable. But there is a community with the boaters. Some of them have been great. When we were moving recently, we had to double-moor, and the other boat owner was a woman, who was just great. She lived on her own and talking to her helped to normalise our situation. Oh, and she was better at explaining the technical stuff.'

The urban waterways might have all their different tribes, and the online groups for live-aboarders sometimes sputter into spats, but boaters do support each other. A spate of break-ins along one stretch of canal, a boat taking on water and sinking, an oil spill on the Lea River that stopped all boat movement for days – and people rally round to offer pumps, to meet for clean-ups and to rescue oil soaked birds or keep watch on each other's boats.

This sense of solidarity is important – not only for the boaters, but for the communities they moor alongside. You could make a strong case that live-aboarders (like towpath cyclists and joggers) have made many stretches of canal safer and friendlier just by their presence, reducing antisocial behaviour and changing the social dynamics of a neighbourhood for the better. Pubs and other businesses, too, especially along rural canals, are often kept viable year-round by wintering live-aboarders.

Boaters can also bring a dose of culture and festive spirit, too. On a summer afternoon, at Mile End Park, just up the Regent's Canal from Limehouse Basin, I set off to visit the *Village Butty*, which was moored up for a community fete. The *Butty*'s crew – Alice, Ian and James – take their boat around London's waterways, providing what they call a 'floating village hall' as a focus for events – music gigs, comedy nights, poetry readings, apple fairs and the like. At Mile End Park, a watery caravan of live-aboarders and narrowboat businesses had settled around them, whilst an audience were picnicking on the towpath, or taking part in workshops devoted to such arts as spoon-playing, body percussion and step-dancing. I gave those a miss, but spent a happy couple of hours flicking through vinyl on the *Record Deck* and browsing other narrowboat-shops devoted to vintage clothes, spices and herbs, sustaining myself with a slow baked brisket in a wrap from the *Onion Barge* (another one) and a 'dark and stormy' rum from the *Village Butty*'s own bar.

There was low-key music through the afternoon and then as dusk fell the Butty really came alive. Alice got her lap steel guitar out and was joined by multiple guitarists and a fiddler in full flight. I'd taken along my pouch of harmonicas and joined in from time to time. It was one of those uplifting groups – a core of people who had played together before to give ballast, and some blow-ins to bring new songs and energy – which tempted people into song, on stage and among the towpath audience. Across the water, the balconies of the new-development flats and apartments were full of people enjoying the carnival atmosphere and listening through the dark. A Polish couple on bikes stopped on their way back from the pub (it was that late) and squatted on log stools to sing along. A woman began to tap dance.

Somehow it got too late to leave, so when the music eventually wound down, I wrapped myself in a few blankets and slept the night on the *Butty* floor. The last thing I heard, before falling asleep, was Ian saying someone would be dropping off a dog called Spartacus. In the morning I awoke to find a shaggy

The long, thin stage of the *Village Butty*, around pub closing time. Spartacus was yet to appear.

dog beside me, along with a box of biscuits. All perfectly normal for narrowboat life. I passed Spartacus on to Alice, when she appeared, and set off home along the towpath, musing on the community of boaters and how they seemed to rub along, despite a myriad of backgrounds, financial situations, boat knowledge and indeed boats, not to mention the regular turnover of neighbours created by continuous cruising.

Sarah had mentioned that having to work out your new mooring neighbourhood was both a plus and a downside of continuous cruising – the excitement and challenge of familiarising oneself with a new part of London, and the hard work and anxiety of never feeling settled. But she, and pretty much every live-aboarder and boater, had talked of the sense of togetherness on the canals. That people living on the water helped each other – sometimes grudgingly, sometimes with an acid comment, or patronisingly, but that would have been the same in any village in the past. It was one of a trinity of powerful draws: the sense of community, the feeling of being close to nature even if moored in the middle of London, and the elemental joy of being able to move on, taking your home with you.

I was almost convinced myself, and had found myself almost casually looking at boats on online sites, and noting conditions, length, engine, price, fittings – though of course I'd strip out any boat and do it up myself. On the Aylesbury half-marathon I'd paused at around seven miles to jot down the telephone number in the window of a neat little Springer for sale, though I never made the call. I'd think of all I'd learnt about the downsides – and the narrowboat I'd seen swept away on the Thames in winter floods and pinned for a week against a bridge's uprights before it was salvaged as a wreck. And I thought of Richard of Jules' Fuels being approached by the man keen to move himself and his wife onto a boat without any knowledge, and Richard telling him to hire first.

It seemed time to take charge of a boat. A hire boat. With a bunch of friends and some instruments. A dog, too, perhaps.

14

Carry On Up the Canal

STRATFORD-UPON-AVON CANAL

THERE NEVER WAS A *Carry On Up the Canal* film. The waterways, rich in innuendo and punning possibilities, might have suited Sid James and Hattie Jacques. But the closest the film world got to a canal farce was a 1964 film called *The Bargee*, starring Ronnie Barker and Harry H. Corbett as two boatmen – cousins Ronnie and Hemel – working a canal boat and its butty along the Grand Union Canal. The rogueish duo are under notice of redundancy and are depicted scratching a living, delivering a consignment of lemon peel from Brentford to Boxmoor. The carry-ons, meantime, are provided by Hemel's complicated love life, climbing out of windows to escape vengeful fathers of girls with whom he has liaisons at every canal junction.

I conceived my own *Carry On* trip as a rather less libertine affair – though not, perhaps, without misadventures. Almost from the moment that Kate showed me the ropes, I had been pitching the idea of a narrowboat jaunt to a bunch of pals. We had originally intended to set off in May, to make the most of warm summer evenings on the canal, playing music and drinking wine into the night, and then the date slipped to September. But somehow I could never quite herd all the cats

The Bargeee – a film every narrowboat rental trip can aspire to.

into place, and it was December when I discovered everyone was free for a few days. So I jumped into action, called an obliging rental company called Anglo-Welsh, and arranged to pick up a narrowboat at Wootton Wawen. From there, we could set off for a long weekend's idling to Stratford-upon-Avon, along the south section of the Stratford-upon-Avon Canal.

I was rather pleased with my choice. The South Stratford offered an alluring range of canal architecture – two splendid aqueducts, barrel-shaped lock cottages, interesting bridges and some well-reviewed pubs – not to mention the home of the bard as a journey's end. It had an interesting literary history, too, as a key waterway in Temple Thurston's book *Flower of Gloster*, and as an early and significant battleground for the IWA in their bid to save the canals. What more could anyone want?

I pointed all this out to my pals – Mal, Dave, Helen, Clare, Sophie, Mark and Nat – a motley crew of teachers, musicians and writers – in an enthusiastic collective email. The replies were oddly wary. 'Remind me – why are we doing this in December?' 'Do canals close if there's ice?' 'Who's bringing the whisky?' 'I suppose the dog will keep us warm.'

Ah yes – the dog. No canal trip is complete without a dog, and we were to be blessed by the presence of Wooster, a large English Setter. 'He loves water,' his owner reassured us.

It was the Stratford-upon-Avon Canal that had first fired Robert Aickman's passion when he had walked up the towpath from Stratford-upon-Avon in 1938, saddened by its dereliction. After the war, he had chosen it to go 'canal busting', along with Tom Rolt, forcing British Waterways to raise a contentious bridge to allow them passage. And it was here, too, that David Hutchings, the unsung hero of the restoration movement, had brought his organisational genius and energy to bear, replacing lock gates, clearing pounds and dredging cuts to reopen the canal in 1964, just in time for the four hundredth anniversary of Shakespeare's birth.

It seemed an auspicious backdrop to our trip and so I shared these notes in a final, pre-departure email, along with what I felt were genuinely encouraging factors – that winter was a great time to go narrowboating, as we'd get the canals almost to ourselves, with no tedious queueing at locks, and lots of choice in where to moor up for the night. The only negative thing (and I put this in bold in the message) is that the days are short and we will need to *get to the boatyard before lunch* in order to be shown the ropes and get to our first mooring in the light.

Of course, everyone said. And I'm sure intentions were good. But with a herd of cats (and musicians, especially, I've found), things are never entirely straightforward. This certainly applied to my two fellow band members. Dave the guitarist's car had a breakdown. And Mal the bassist turned up with his full-sized double bass ('I meant to bring the small one, Jasper – I wasn't thinking straight.') Now, narrowboats are perfect for guitars, saxophones, even a drum kit. But a double bass is a challenge. Even Alistair and David, the Anglo-Welsh guys who were showing us how to grease the bearing and use the pump loo, looked bemused. But eventually we lofted the bass over the length of the boat and then angled it through into the front cabin. And we were away. Well, seven of us, anyway. Sophie would be taking a train next morning to Stratford-upon-Avon and would hike up the towpath until she came upon us. One of the advantages of a canal's simple geography.

The boat that Anglo-Welsh had assigned to us – 'a big one, you'll be comfortable' – was, perhaps with some irony, called *Summer*. And with Mal's double bass on board, we only had Wooster to worry about. I've seen dogs that have been deeply suspicious of canal life. But Wooster was made of sterner stuff, leaping happily from the pontoon onto the boat's counter, sticking his nose into the back cabin, tumble-jumping down the steps and then galloping along sixty feet of corridor to reappear on the small deck at the front end. And then doing it again in reverse.

'It's not a crazy time to go cruising, is it?' I had asked Alistair before leaving. He assured me that it wasn't. In fact, he said, they had lots of winter bookings. 'Christmas and New Year are always popular and it can be lovely – frosty fields, breaking a thin layer of ice in the morning.' Alistair and David both lived on boats themselves. 'We had both started living on boats when we came to work here. Jacob over there' –Alistair gestured at another yard worker – 'has just started here and he'll probably get a boat by the end of the year.'

Alistair had listened to my plans, as I described our three-day trip. 'You've actually got more like two days of boating, what with leaving late today, and having to get back before dusk on Monday,' he cautioned. 'It's no great distance down to Stratford,

The crew on *Summer* – with a dog to carry messages from bow to stern.

but keep in mind there's an eleven-lock-flight beyond Wilmcote, and then no winding hole to turn in until you're almost in town.' I was beginning to worry that I'd been over ambitious. I'd done the maths by adding the number of locks – thirteen – to the number of miles – six and a bit – and then dividing the sum by three to come up with the number of hours needed, and then doubled it for the total time required for a return trip. Sixteen hours actually on the move, with no hold-ups. With the reduced daylight, it was tight. And we had to find Sophie somewhere along the towpath the next day.

Boat holidays are meant to be relaxing. And simple. And indeed a narrowboat is in most respects straightforward. David and Alistair had shown us everything we needed to know about the functions of boat and house: how to pump the bilge and check the oil and the backup battery. But when he got to the driving side of things, it was not overly challenging – 'Forward for forward, back for reverse, and just keep going.'

And after that it was just the technicalities of the contract. Responsibility for negligent damage. Tick. No moving during the hours of darkness. Tick. Only mooring at designated spots. Tick. The designated skippers to be responsible for the boat at all times, and to oversee other steerers. Tick. There was a lot of that kind of stuff. It all seemed stressful, if fair enough, as essentially we were going to be moving a largeish house down a watery hill to Stratford-upon-Avon and back again.

Once on the move I felt happier. There was still plenty of light. Perhaps I'd allowed myself to get a bit over-exercised by the paperwork, the packing, the press-ganging of *Summer*'s crew. The sun was out and things felt good. In fact, everything was pretty much turning out as I'd promised. The trees were stark but beautiful in the clear light, the air fresh and chill. There were birds in the hedgerows picking at hawthorn and ivy berries. A couple walking their dog along the towpath waved as we passed them. I imagined them envious of our gentle progress along the waters. We were in a canal story written by Tom Rolt and illustrated by John Nash. And we had the whole canal to ourselves, bar the odd coot or duck. I leant my arm confidently along the tiller, and bobbed forward to nudge up the throttle until we bubbled along, nicely leaving barely a wake behind us. At the front, Wooster was looking enraptured at the passing waters, a 'figurehound' at the prow with his nose raised into the wind.

The canal seemed oddly narrower than I recalled from steering *Morning Mist* along the Oxford Canal. I had read about the Stratford having been built to budget – as tight as possible – to save excavating time, to save on building materials and then, when in use, to save on the water needed to lock boats up and down. And as Mal took over the tiller, I looked up my *Nicholson's* canal guide and told him that the Earlswood reservoir, at the top of the canal, held exactly 14,000 lock-fulls of water – a remarkable computation of water as units of commerce.

Coming around a corner we saw an example of the Stratford's 'shave to save' approach – one of the its unique 'split-cantilever' bridges. These feature two brick piers with just a boat's width of water between them, and, above, not quite meeting in the middle, cast-iron cantilevered platforms. A cunning design, it allowed the horse to walk over the bridge and on down the other side of the canal whilst the towrope was dropped through the gap. It was a simple solution to the problem of how to get a horse from one side of a canal to the other without having to unhitch the rope. But it offered a challenge to a novice helmsman, who had only a few minutes before taken control of a sixty-six-foot narrowboat.

The bow seemed to fill a larger space than there was under the bridge. 'Slow down,' I suggested to Mal, 'but not too much', as he attempted to hold a dead straight line, while the group at the front shouted their own inaudible instructions ('Left a bit ... no, right ... that's it ... straight!') The boat arrowed – very, very slowly – through the hole, and with just the tiniest of bumps up against the bricks. *Summer* was through. The bow posse applauded while Mal and I tried to look nonchalant.

This stretch of the canal turned out to be something of an assault course for steerers. Two more bridges came in quick succession; a bit of a bonk against one, clean through on the next. Then we chugged down a length of cutting dug through high ground and, south of bridge 56, we were into Odd Lock.

I immediately began to display all the annoying characteristics of the worried skipper of an inexperienced crew, rushing around shouting baffling instructions – *Draw the paddles, Push on the balance beam, Drop the centre rope round the bollard.* It's a truism that when you barely know what you're doing, doing it yourself seems far easier than explaining it. I thought ruefully of how relaxed Kate, Jules and Richard had been letting me drive into the lock chambers and breast-up and moor. I might have been as laid back if we'd been handling horses or kayaks or something I knew about. But here I was keen to do everything 'right.' Steer to the bank, into neutral, jump off the back, pick up the centre rope, loop it round a bollard, work *Summer* to a standstill.

The crew were all ashore now, admiring the lock, chatting happily and watching the actions of their frenzied skipper – dashing over to push open the single gate at the uphill end of the chamber, sprinting back to the boat, jumping back on board to grab the tiller, jumping off again to undo the centre rope, then back on board again, nudging *Summer* into the lock.

Perhaps I could delegate just a little. 'Can someone push the gate closed?' Six people and a dog moved towards the beam. I delegated some more, handing out windlasses to Clare and Mal. 'Don't drop them in,' I ordered patronisingly. 'You'll need to wind up the paddles and let the water out ... go really slow at first.' Clare crossed over to the other side – there were two gates at the lower end of the chamber – and soon there was the rattling chunkling of the paddles being wound up. The water and the boat on it began to sink into the chamber whilst I fussed her back and forth by a few inches either way. I didn't want to nudge the gates with her fore-end but I was horrified at the idea of hanging her stern up on the cill. It was a not uncommon accident and it could tip a boat over in the lock, so that it filled with water – in seconds – and sank.

None of this happened. The water dropped until it was at the same level as the pound below. The crew heaved at the beams and the gates opened and the boat rumbled its way out. 'Drop the paddles,' I shouted back, and then added, imagining Kate at my shoulder, '*Slowly*'.

The light, I noticed, had gone a darker grey. It was colder too. I checked my watch. We still had an hour of light. Or did we? I inched up the throttle a bit, increasing our pace to that of a brisk walk. But then immediately throttled back as I saw stretching ahead of us the Edstone Aqueduct, at 475 feet, the longest in England, and so light and flimsy-seeming that it felt higher and more precarious than the Pontcysyllte. It was just a long thin metal channel of water, with the towpath dropping down into a sunken waterless channel beside it, so that from the stern I could look down on the crown of Dave's head as he walked beside the boat, inches away from the hull. And thirty feet below Dave and *Summer* was a rushing stream and the tracks of a railway line. In the days of steam trains, the engines used to pull up under the aqueduct to fill their boilers from a pipe. So simple, though apparently more than once fish got sucked down the pipe and blocked the hose into the engine.

The Stratford-upon-Avon was one of the canals that Temple Thurston claimed to have boated in *The Flower of Gloster*, the first canal bestseller. But many feel that Thurston didn't do anything like the trip he wrote up and instead came and went by train. One clue is that in his account there is no mention at all of the Edstone Aqueduct – which, once you've crossed it, seems like Marco Polo not mentioning tea.

The Edstone Aqueduct – a wonder of the Stratford-upon-Avon Canal.

I was looking at *Nicholson's* again. In the hope that the map might show, what ... a shortcut? A miraculous reduction in miles? The dusk was coming in fast. And then quite suddenly darkness fell. Dark clouds and a fine drizzle had closed off what light there was like a blind pulled down. I remembered Alistair at the yard pointing out the switch for the headlight. I snicked it on, hoping for a powerful beam to illuminate the waters ahead. Nothing. 'Is that light working,' I bellowed at the distant fore-end. 'What?' came the reply. 'The light?! There should be a light – the headlight!' I was sounding tense. 'No! Nothing. But there's a bridge ahead. Can you see it?'

The bow suddenly seemed a long way off and the bridge was just a darker wall against the dark sky with a slightly darker hole in its face. I throttled right back and tried to guide the boat through. Nat had whipped out her phone and was playing the torch along the side of the bridge's eye as I peered down the hull. The boat passed through with barely a touch.

I didn't relax. Another glance at *Nicholson's* by torchlight. Wilmcote was a mile off. There was another bridge. I was getting tetchy. 'Turn that bloody light off,' I snapped at someone in the cabin. Wooster had decided to come and lie between my legs on the footplate above the warm, throbbing engine. This wasn't helpful, either, as I moved back and forth across the stern to look first down one side and then the other. The crew were moving around the boat trying to find something useful to do, or more likely to stay out of the way of their easy-going pal on the tiller who'd suddenly turned into a ranting Captain Ahab.

In my head was a busy conflict of horrors and common sense. There was the contract I'd signed making me responsible for the boat, its contents and the safety of everyone on board. I remembered the list of clauses, several of which were voiding the insurance at this very moment. But then there was the rational thought that we were on a canal going very slowly, that in fact we could wade ashore if there was some kind of 'Wreck of the Calabar'-type disaster. Or we could just pull over and moor right where we were. Was that the right thing to do? Or push on to Wilmcote and the proper moorings – and the pub. Floating into my head came the episode in *Swallows and Amazons* when the four children preparing to sail off and camp on Wild Cat Island are awaiting permission from their father, stationed abroad; the telegram that arrives reads 'BETTER DROWNED THAN DUFFERS IF NOT DUFFERS WON'T DROWN'. It was a rather old-style parenting 'yes' to their adventure.

Avoiding not being a duffer had been a factor in more than a few of my past boating escapades. Back in the 1980s, Dave and I had kayaked the length of the Danube – nearly 2,000 miles, most of it behind the (then) Iron Curtain. We'd had a few hair-raising experiences, especially night paddling when huge rafts of barges pushed along by speeding tugs would come out of nowhere, and seem to fill the quarter-mile river from side to side. Dave was commendably relaxed then and again now; he'd disappeared down into the galley to make tea for everyone. He was a one-man Women's Institute.

'It's snowing,' a voice floated back from the bow. What? It was only raining at the stern. 'The bloody boat's so long it's got two climates,' I muttered to Helen, trying for a bit of humour. But I wasn't feeling it. I knew that crews had worked fly and express boats through the nights and in far worse weather than this. But they had known what they were doing. I didn't. I had been absorbing canal lore and experience for a little over a year, but not much of it on a boat. I was determined to keep to the schedule we'd planned, however modest, and make Wilmcote that evening. Were these signs of culpable dufferdom?

On the other hand, the tiller under my hand and the slow thrubbling of the engine felt familiar, and those several hundred miles paddling the kayak late into the night had given me a sense of the waters and how they worked. And there was just enough light to see the edge of the bank and steer. I began to think I was in control. At which point there was a scraping noise and the boat wobbled slightly. We'd run aground.

I knocked the engine out of gear and then ran reverse. There was a bubbling and surging at the stern. Flashing my torch over the side I could see that the water was clear rather than churning up mud or sand. I gave another burst of reverse – full throttle this time. *Summer* began to move backwards. Not straight back, but off at an angle. Steering a sixty-foot boat in reverse is pretty much like backing a car and trailer – it's possible, it's a skill one can learn, but until one does, it tends to go wrong.

We were off the bottom but now angled across the canal. I pulled the pole off the roof and, like Don Quixote taking on a windmill, pushed it over the side into the side and leant against it to push the stern back out and straighten up the boat in mid-channel. The torch had picked up the waterline on the bank – it seemed low. And we had scraped up onto a shallow spot on the inside of a curve.

I was sweating now despite the cold rain. And the crew were subdued, too, sensing this wasn't quite the jolly they had signed up for in London.

'Bridge, BRIDGE!' A shout from the front end. My lowlight vision was sharper now. And I could see the brickwork, and the bow of the boat slipping past it. Perhaps just a bit askew. In her own torchlight I saw Nat stretching out her hand to fend the boat off in case it bumped. 'NO! NO! Get your hand in! DON'T PUT ANYTHING OUTSIDE THE BOAT!' I remembered Jules shouting the same thing at me when I carelessly put out a hand to fend off the *Towcester* from *Bideford*. A boat might move slowly, but its weight and the almost frictionless glide through the water combined to turn it into a powerful jackhammer. Crushings are serious accidents that can turn a holiday into a tragedy.

The crew were beginning to stir themselves. Somebody had found a strongish torch. Another attempt had been made to get the searchlight up front to work, though to no avail. Wooster had been lured out from under my feet and was down in the cabin. Mark was studying *Nicholson's* by a shielded light. 'We've gone under the last bridge before the bridge at Wilmcote, so we're very nearly there. Where did Alistair say the moorings were? Before or after the bridge?'

Right on cue, a voice came down on the drizzly breeze from the bow. 'Boats! There's a line of boats. They're tied up.' 'Shine a light on them,' I bellowed, and the torch flickered along a tidy, traditional-style narrowboat. Then there was a gap. I wondered if I could moor there. But I'd already chugged *Summer* past and we were passing another boat moored to our left. Ahead, the cut had opened out and the dark raincloud lifted. I could see things more clearly – there was the bridge at Wilmcote. We'd made it.

But the fates had one more spanner to throw. Mal had jumped ashore as I came into the bank ready to moor. 'Bad news, Jasp ... there are signs saying no mooring because of repairs and it's all dug up and there's netting fencing it all off...' I swore under my breath. And then over my breath. We'd have to reverse up the canal in the dark to get back to the gap between the two boats we'd passed a few minutes before. And having felt the boat slewing and veering in the short distance I'd needed to back her off the sandbank, I didn't give much for my chances of using the engine to get *Summer* back.

'Comrades,' I cried, in my best rally-the-troops voice, 'we're going to have to stern-haul the boat.' Was that the right word, I wondered? But I was remembering how easily Richard and I had moved the fully laden coal butty backwards on the Grand Union, and how much control we'd had. I threw the stern mooring rope ashore to Mal, Dave and Mark. Wooster romped along as they began to pull. I had the rudder pushed hard over, to keep the boat away from the bank, and the engine ticking over in case it was needed. I'd also pulled the bargepole along the roof so it was handy if we needed to push *Summer* further out from the bank. 'I wouldn't touch anything with that,' Dave called out.

Morale and humour were returning. Helen and Clare were lighting the way with torches, and Nat had gone ahead to talk with the owner of the boat we'd have to pass to get back to a mooring place. He was up on deck and I could hear him and Nat talking urgently, as the stern of *Summer* approached his boat's bow. 'He's only just done it up and he's worried you're going to prang into it,' Nat reported back. I was feeling a lot more confident now. 'No worries ... we'll just slip by. A couple of you hop aboard to give me a hand. What's your name? Sam? Sam, don't worry, we won't touch you.'

'She's just been filmed for a telly show,' Sam was explaining, wringing his hands in anxiety. '*Amazing Spaces*. It'll be on telly in a few months.' I sympathised with his anxiety – it was his home, his pride and joy, the boat that he'd poured hours of work into. But he needn't have anguished. *Summer* had already slid past and astern of him, I threw the rope back to my tow-horses and a few minutes later we were up against the visitors' mooring and tied *Summer* up for the night.

I felt as if I'd been steering a coaster across gale-whipped seas. A slightly over-the-top reaction to a bit of canal boating, I realised. Especially when I looked at my watch and saw it was only half past five. All that adventure before pub opening time.

By six we were installed in the Mary Arden Inn, before a roaring fire, with pints of beer and a menu of hearty food. Wooster, exhausted by the novelty of being a boat dog, was slumped under the table across most of our feet. We were all in an expansive mood, now that we'd proved ourselves not to be duffers.

'It's not bad, is it this cruising life ...' I looked around the warm pub with its timbers and brasses and chatting locals, 'and winter boating is good, isn't it? We had the cut to ourselves, a bit of variety in the weather ... what more could one want?'

'Five hours more light, perhaps?' mused Mark.

'Ah, well, good you mentioned that,' I was back being the experienced skipper laying plans. 'Tomorrow, we're going to have to start early. First light. Breakfast on the move. We've got twelve locks to go to Stratford and there's no winding hole, no place to turn the boat, until we get to the edge of town. So once we've started, we can't turn back even if we want to.'

'And then on Monday we have to come back the whole way? Somebody, Nat I think, was looking for clarification. 'Right back to Wootton Wawen, in fact?'

'Well, yes. So we really will have to start early on Monday.'

Even I was beginning to sound a little doubtful about the potential pleasure in working twenty-six locks just to go and come back. But on paper – adding locks and miles together and dividing by three – it all seemed possible. Plans for the day after next, the return trip, were left in the air as fish and chips and meaty pies arrived. And the new day's plans remained undiscussed when we strolled back, through what had turned into a cold, clear starry night, to our boat.

In the cabin we lit the stove. We'd got used to the shape of *Summer* and to conducting conversation as if sitting in a tube train, knee to knee, with voices crossing from one end to the other. But there was room enough for Mal to get his bass out and, by dint of sitting almost supine, plunk out loping lines whilst Dave and I played along on guitars. The heat was building up. There was the plock of a cork being pulled from a bottle of Malbec, and the clinking of glasses. We sang late into the night. No canal songs, of course. But folk songs and singalongs and Gothic Americana and cod-jazz.

It was late when, with everyone else gone to their berths, I threaded my way down to the end of the boat and into the back cabin. I'd closed up the stove and made sure it was out. I'd flipped over the electrics so we didn't drain the batteries overnight. I'd checked the automatic bilge pump was on. I was as close to a homeowner, with its delights and anxieties, as I'd ever been. Before turning in, I opened the back doors and climbed up into the night air. Far off a tawny owl hooted and another kiwittted in response. I climbed back down and closed the doors behind me. And as I did so I noticed that, on the electrics panel by the steps, one switch was flicked up. Closer inspection with my torch showed it to be the headlight main control that somebody climbing up on deck, or perhaps Wooster in one of his joyful bounds to join us on the back counter, had flicked off. I switched it on and the canal and Sam's TV boat were perfectly lit.

It was a little past 'first light' when we began getting up. Not quite the start we needed to get down to Stratford-upon-Avon. I checked the bilges for water, and dipped the oil on the engine before starting it up, leaving it ticking away to top the batteries up whilst Mal, as befitted an Irishman, was preparing a full fry breakfast with the efficiency of a short-order chef. Dave had buckets of coffee going around. The crew seemed cheery.

'How do!' The woman from the narrowboat moored behind us had walked along the towpath. 'Are you going downhill towards Stratford? You are? Well, you might want to walk on a bit and have a look at the flight – one of the pounds between the locks is very low on water. We walked up from Stratford last night and it looked very low then.' She headed back to her boat.

Mark, Nat, Wooster and I set off to investigate. I wasn't too concerned. The water had been a bit low the night before when we scraped on the bottom – and we'd got through. A bit low probably wasn't going to stop us. It was a pleasant walk. The sun was out and we passed other dog walkers, Wooster giving a curt nod to some of them and a fulsome greeting to others, based on some unfathomable code of canine sociability.

As we walked, I began giving Nat and Mark a potted history of the Stratford-upon-Avon Canal and its role in the saving of the canals. Robert Aickman as a young man visiting Wilmcote, birthplace of Shakespeare's mother, Mary Arden, and striding along the towpath from Stratford-upon-Avon to find whole sections without water. How this had led to the founding of the IWA and the saving of the Stratford-upon-Avon Canal – in fact, to the saving of the waterways.

Walking the towpath alongside the locks and pounds, we could appreciate the work that must have gone into its restoration. We imagined the lock gates rotten and broken, the walls of the chambers bowed and buckled and the pounds full of rubbish and weeds. The weeks and months of work with shovels and buckets and wheelbarrows. But then our imaginations didn't have to do any work. For, below the lowest of the flight of three locks, we could see the worst thing that can befall a canal.

There was no water.

The long pound had just a trickle running down its muddy length. A child's scooter was revealed in the mud, along with wandering lines where freshwater mussels had dragged themselves from the drying ooze. We looked at each other. This was a problem that wasn't going to get solved in an hour. Or probably in a day. It would need CRT engineers to come out and assess where the water had gone and then let down water from the reaches above through several locks to fill the pound again.

'Well, that's the end of going to Stratford,' I pronounced, rather stating the obvious. We walked back up to Wilmcote to deliver the news. 'We'll have to turn around – thank God there's that winding hole only a few hundred yards behind us. We'll have to go back to Wootton Wawen and up the other way to Preston Bagot. We'll not go far this weekend, after all.'

But if I expected the crew to be disappointed, I couldn't have been more wrong.

Dave swung down to the galley, 'Coffee, everyone? We're not exactly in a hurry.' Mark was on the bank with *Nicholson's* and his phone, reporting that there was a pub, the Crabmill, open for lunch at Preston Bagot. 'It looks rather good, and they do a Sunday carvery all afternoon, so there's no rush.' I was phoning Sophie, who was on a train to Stratford, intending to walk up the towpath and meet us as we came down the locks. 'Change of plan,' I said. 'Can you get off at Wootton Wawen instead and then walk down the towpath and meet us as we come back up? Don't hurry. We'll be a while yet, so you've plenty of time.'

Half an hour later, still only mid-morning, we'd stern-hauled *Summer* back to the winding hole, in warm winter sun. I brought the rope onboard, knocked the engine into forward and drove the front end into the arc of water. It was just wider across than *Summer* was long, and turning was a case of juggling the throttle and tiller and playing forward and reverse off each other to swing the boat round in a series of in and outs, back and forths.

'I think that was a ten-pint turn,' Dave shouted from the bank as I got the boat around. A ten-point turn? 'No, a ten-pint turn – the kind of turn you'd do in a car after ten pints.'

We were getting jolly. Me most of all. After the past year of waterways travels, after a thousand slow miles on foot and by kayak, on the folding bike and on horse-speed boats, I had finally learnt that slowing things down was what the canals did best. That the biggest change that had come over the waterways was in the efficiency-driven, timetable-imposing water machine of the working boaters becoming the slow lane of the leisure boaters and strollers of the twenty-first century. I might have forgotten that with my insistence on getting the boat down the flights of locks to Stratford-upon-Avon and back. But fate had intervened and handed us back the day with almost no goal to aim for except lunch, and having a good time.

With no itinerary to beat, no 'locks and miles and divide by three' tyranny to get maximum distance, with no worries about fading light, we could enjoy just being on the water. I wondered if the old working boaters had ever felt this peace and tranquillity or if they were always too harried by work, money, cargoes and other pressures. From the recollections of the folk who had worked on the canals, it seemed to me that they had felt something special in the pace of the boats and of following the water roads through remote corners of the English countryside. That it had been some compensation for all the hardships. I thought of the women interviewed for *Ramlin Rose* and how often they talked about the quiet of being on a horse-drawn boat as opposed to the engined boats, or the long, high pounds on the Oxford and the Grand Union where the countryside ribboned past.

Our trip had become less expedition and more jaunt. We all took turns at the tiller, showing our personalities as clearly as a Rorschach test. Nat concentrating intently and steering precisely, elated when she inched the boat safely through a bridge. Mark, the only one of us who didn't drive a car, helming like a Cap'n Sparrow swashbuckling the high seas. Mal taking the tiller as if being handed control of a bit of heavy plant machinery – 'My god, isn't it crazy that any aul eejit can hire one of these, and the engineering marvels of all those historic locks and aqueducts could be demolished by one drunken boatman?'

We had picked up Sophie soon after starting from Wilmcote, spotting her standing on an accommodation bridge. 'Ahoy! I've brought cakes! Hang on, I'll get down to the bank and hop aboard.' Sophie had done several boat trips in the past, and over tea recounted a tale of her first narrowboat experience. 'The friends I was with didn't know anything about boats, and they got up early one morning and thought they'd set off while I was still in bed. I woke up to this almighty crash. They'd got confused by the tiller and the throttle and steered straight across the canal into a marina of moored boats. Then they turned off the engine and we were stuck with all these boaters coming on deck in their pyjamas, swearing and shouting.' It hadn't affected her confidence, though, and she and Dave – who had admitted late in the game to having done a bit of narrowboating in the past – swapped the helm between them, taking on the bridges like showjumpers and keeping a score of their faults.

The horse-speed tempo of the canals had won out. 'It's only three miles to the Crabmill,' Sophie announced, 'we should be there in an hour.' It was a thrillingly slow proposition.

Glossary

ACCOMMODATION BRIDGE Bridge connecting farms, fields and villages separated by the cutting of a canal.

ARM A branch running off from a main canal line.

BALANCE BEAM Wooden (usually) beam pushed against to open or close a lock gate, its length and bulk balancing out the weight of the gate, thus making it easier to move.

BARGE Not a synonym for a NARROWBOAT (qv) but a wider cargo vessel sometimes powered by sails and, according to type, working on wide canals, navigations, estuaries and the coast.

BOBBINS Wooden rollers – usually brightly coloured – strung along the rope traces where they run against a horse's sides, designed to stop rubbing and galling when pulling off-centre.

BOW-HAULING Moving a boat with a gang of men on a tow rope. 'Bow' rhymes with 'low' and refers to the loop in the rope not to the front of the boat.

BREASTED UP Two boats – especially an engine boat and BUTTY BOAT (qv) – fastened side by side where the canal or locks are wide enough to move that way.

BRITISH WATERWAYS From 1962 until 2012, when the CANAL & RIVER TRUST (qv) was founded, BW looked after most of Britain's inland waterways.

BUCKBY CAN Water can, usually carried on the cabin roof and often decorated in ROSES AND CASTLE (qv) style. Though made in many different locations, the 'cans' made in Buckby on the Grand Union Canal became the general descriptor for all water cans.

BUTTY BOAT An unpowered boat pulled by an engined (or horse) boat. This doubled the load that could be carried and a second cabin offered room for large families. Butties have larger rudders than engine boats.

CANAL & RIVER TRUST (CRT) Charity established in 2012 as a successor to BRITISH WATERWAYS (qv), taking on the guardianship of over 2,000 miles of waterways in England and Wales. Scottish navigations remain under the control of a public corporation, Scottish Canals.

CILL/SILL Stone or mortar ledge which the bottom of a lock gate rests on when closed.

CONTOUR CANAL A channel cut to follow a line at the same height across a landscape for all or most of its course. Though going a longer distance, savings were made by not building tunnels, aqueducts or locks. Many contour canals, such as the Oxford Canal, were later straightened to speed up traffic.

CUT The popular name for a canal or artificial navigation – from the time of the NAVVIES (*qv*) who literally cut into the land. Used by boatmen in the sense of being 'on the cut'.

DOWNHILL/UPHILL Canal waters fall away from their highest point – the SUMMIT POUND (*qv*) – descending, through locks where necessary, to join with lower canals, rivers or the sea. Boaters think of geography in terms of canals running up and down rather than north, south, east or west. Thus Manchester is 'down' from Birmingham.

FLASH LOCK An opening in a weir across a river that can be opened up by removing timber baulks to allow a boat to be surfed through with the flow or hauled up against it between different water levels.

FLY BOAT Originally a horse-drawn express boat worked around the clock for rapid transportation. The term became used for passenger and cargo boats pulled at speed by relays of horses, having right of way over other canal traffic. Some engined boats also travelled around the clock, when they were described as 'working fly'.

FORE-END The front of the boat, as opposed to the more nautical 'bow'.

GAUGING Tolls were levied on the weight as well as the type of cargo. Some boats were marked on their hulls to show how much they sank down in the water under different weights, or an official would use a gauging stick to measure the difference between the GUNWALE (*qv*) and the water level to calculate the displacement weight.

GONGOOZLE To loiter whilst observing canal life and particularly those operations like mooring and working through locks that might go wrong and lead to mild drama and comedy. Thus a GONGOOZLER – one who gongoozles – as well as a popular name for canalside pubs and cafes.

GUNWALE The top edge of a boat's hull. On a narrowboat, it's where the cabin joins the hull, leaving a narrow ledge as a walkway along the boat.

HELM Often pronounced as 'ellum' by traditional boaters. On canal craft it is the combined tiller arm and rudder, and correctly only applied to a butty's steering gear.

HOBBLER A casual worker employed to help work a boat through a flight of locks. 'Hobbling' can be used in the sense of LOCK WHEELING (*qv*).

INCLINED PLANE A mechanised system of lifting boats up slopes between different water levels, either in water-filled tanks – caissons – or on cradles. This is faster, and uses almost no water when compared to locking through the equivalent heights, but it is complicated and expensive.

INSIDE/OUTSIDE Orientation on canals is not described in terms of left and right but in relation to the towpath, which can be on either the left or the right. The inside is the side of the water closest to the towpath, while the outside is that closest to the other bank.

LEGGING A way of propelling an engineless boat through tunnels, with crew or professional 'leggers' walking their feet along the sides or roof whilst lying down.

LENGTHMAN An employee of a canal company who maintained a particular length of waterway and its towpath, cutting back vegetation and watching for potential breaches.

LOCK Chamber with gates at both ends between two stretches of water running at different heights. By opening PADDLES (qv) water can be let in from the higher level to raise the water and any boat inside the chamber 'uphill', or water let out through the bottom gate paddles to lower boats 'downhill'. In this form correctly called a POUND LOCK.

LOCK WHEELER A crew member going ahead to set a lock and work the boat through. From

the beginning of the twentieth century, bicycles – the 'wheel' - made this an easier task and gave a new name (LOCKWHEELING) to an old job.

NARROWBOAT A traditional-type boat, designed for narrow canals, and so seven feet or less in width and around seventy feet or less in length. Originally these craft were called 'narrow boats', but modern usage has it as one word.

NAVVY/NAVVIES The canals' construction workers. The term comes from 'navigations', the original name for the canals that they built. Also used of their successors on the railways (where many of the nineteenth-century canal navvies found work).

NUMBER ONE A boat owned and worked by an independent boatman, rather than a company.

PADDLE The hatch closing a sluice opening which can be 'drawn' to let water in or out of a lock. Paddles are fitted into lock gates, or as 'ground paddles' in the bank, letting water through culverts.

POUND The stretch of water between two locks.

ROSES AND CASTLES Style of decoration used on boats and their doors, fold-up tables and Buckby cans. They usually feature a central 'landscape' – invariably a stylised castle surrounded by flowers and patterns, often including playing-card suits.

SHAFT A long pole for moving a boat by pushing off the bottom or bank. Called a QUANT on the Broads.

SHORT BOAT Boats twice as wide as but shorter than a narrow boat, carrying up to fifty tons, which were sized to fit the short, wide locks of the Leeds and Liverpool Canal.

STARVATIONER Simple, narrow and long boats with exposed ribs – hence the name – used to bring coal out of the Duke of Bridgewater's mines at Worsley. An early form of narrowboat and very influential in the development of the narrow canals.

STERN The back end of a boat, pronounced 'starn' by many working boatmen.

SUMMIT LEVEL The highest pound on a canal, the water and locks going downhill at either of its ends. Canal builders had to ensure that there was a source of water sufficient to keep the summit level, and thus the whole canal, full.

SWINGLETREE A heavy wooden bar that is held behind a horse's hindquarters to attach the tow rope to, taking the strain from the traces that run from the horse's collar.

TILLER The handle attached to the rudder post, which is pushed over to one side or the other to steer.

TOWPATH Correctly 'towing path', a defining feature of a true canal.

TURNOVER BRIDGE A bridge that allows a horse to cross over a canal when the towpath changes sides, without having to remove the tow rope from the boat. The horse goes up a ramp, over the bridge and down a ramp on the other side that then goes back under the bridge on the new towpath. Also called CROSSOVER, ROVING, CHANGELING or SNAKE BRIDGES.

WHARF Canalside area for loading or unloading cargoes, often lined by warehouses, cranes and factories.

WIDE BOAT A boat usually twice the width of a narrowboat that can be used on wide waterways. A size that was used, for instance, from London along the Grand Union Canal as far as the original canal and its locks had been widened.

WINDING HOLE A wide semicircle cut into in a canal's bank allowing room for a full-length boat to be turned around. Pronounced like the 'wind' that early engineless boats utilised to push them around.

WINDLASS The cranked handle with a socket that fits onto the spindle of a lock's winding gear for raising the sluice paddles. Traditionally carried tucked into the back of a heavy leather belt.

Further reading

BOOKS

Helen Babbs, *Adrift: A Secret Life of London's Waterways* (Icon, 2016). A year as a continuous cruising live-aboarder on London's canals, observed with a keen eye for wildlife and canal-life realities.

David Bolton, *Race Against Time: How Britain's Waterways Were Saved* (Methuen, 1990). A history of Britain's 'most successful environmental campaign'.

Margaret Cornish, *Troubled Waters* (M & M Baldwin, 1994). The best of several accounts written by women trainees who ran working boats during the war.

Euan Corrie, *Tales from the Old Inland Waterways* (David & Charles, 2005). Fascinating interviews with working boaters, revealing detailed memories of routes, cargoes, bringing up children, courting and boat life.

Eric de Maré, *The Canals of England* (1950, Sutton reprint 1987). An early leisure boater, and a talented writer and photographer, de Maré melds history, landscape and canal characters.

Stuart Fisher, *Canals of Britain: A Comprehensive Guide* (Adlard Coles Nautical, 2015). A complete guide to nearly every canal in the British Isles with mile-by-mile description of history, landscape, buildings and wildlife. Boaters will need to pair it with a *Nicholson* or *Pearson* guide. Walkers and cyclists might do better with the e-book.

David Garden and Neil Parkhouse, *A Guide to the Anderton Boatlift* (Black Dwarf, 2013). A fine account of the lift, covering its construction, use, abandonment and restoration.

Derek Gittings, *A Short History of Dudley Canal Tunnel* (Dudley Canal & Tunnel Trust, 2016). Fine history of the Dudley's underground canals and how they were reopened by adventurous visionaries.

Charles Hadfield and Joseph Boughey, *Hadfield's British Canals: The Inland Waterways of Britain and Ireland* (1950; Budding Books revised edition, 1998). The classic history of British canals by the pioneering and still unrivalled historian of the waterways.

Charles Hadfield, *The Canal Age* (Pan Books, 1971) Another fruit of Hadfield's scholarship, covering the golden age from 1760 to 1850, in Europe and North America.

A. P. Herbert, *The Water Gipsies* (1930, Penguin, 1973). This stirring novel of life amongst the poor and bohemian is set on live-aboard boats on the Thames, with one hope of betterment offered by the boats heading off from the river and away on the canals.

Cyril Herbert Smith, *Through the Kennet and Avon Canal by Motor Boat in 1928* (1929, Shepperton Swan, 1990). A period piece journey by boat along the Kennet and Avon, then already close to being abandoned.

Elizabeth Jane Howard, *Slipstream: A Memoir* (Pan, 2003). Howard writes about her relationship with Robert Aickman during early Inland Waterways Association days, their 'canal-busting' trips and IWA feuds.

Liz McIvor, *Canals: The Making of a Nation* (BBC Books, 2015). This book to accompany the BBC TV canal history series is good on themes such as navvies, financing, family life amongst boat people and big waterways projects.

Nicholson's Guides to the Waterways, *7 regional titles* (Harper Collins). In print and regularly updated for over forty years, the *Nicholson* guides cover most of the canals and waterways with detailed information for boaters, cyclists and walkers. The *Nicholson Inland Waterways Map of Great Britain* is also invaluable – a fold-out map showing canals, rivers and navigations, detailing their type (narrow or wide), locks and direction (uphill/downhill).

Pearson's Canal Companions, *9 regional titles* (Wayzgoose). A rival series covering most of the canals and navigations. They are different in style from *Nicholson's* guides with more of the author's first-person experience and opinion.

L T C Rolt, *Narrow Boat* (1944, History Press, 2014). This charming account of the 400-mile voyage made in *Cressy* around the Midlands was the inspiration for the founding of the Inland Waterways Association.

Sheila Stewart, *Ramlin Rose: The Boatwoman's Story* (Oxford University Press, 1993). Using recorded oral histories of boat-women who had been born on and worked horse-drawn boats, mainly on the Oxford Canal, Stewart creates a composite character who, though fictitious, brings authentic experiences and stories alive.

E. Temple Thurston, *Flower of Gloster* (1911, David & Charles, 1984). Thurston's pre-war journeys on the canals – the Oxford, Stratford-upon-Avon and others – are romanticised and frankly unreliable. But this is an interesting account of pre-war canals. Best read in the 1984 edition with notes and images compiled by David Viner.

Michael E. Ware, *Canals and Waterways: History in Camera* (Shire, 1987). Though slim, this book's fabulous archive photography covering every aspect of the canals, the boats and those who lived and worked on them, and in-depth captions makes for a compelling read.

FILMS/DOCUMENTARIES

Painted Boats, *directed by Charles Crichton* (1945). Filmed in the last years of the war, mostly on the Grand Union between Braunston and Stoke Bruerne, with a storyline based on the relationship between two families' working boats, one with a horse and the other using an engine. While the slow-burn romance between Mary Smith and Ted Stoner, provides the narrative the film itself ranges far wider, with a script written and narrated by Louis MacNeice in the style of Auden's 'Night Mail', and a cast of both actors and working boat people. A fascinating view of the end of the canal age. There's no DVD available, but the full film is posted on YouTube.

The Bargee, *directed by Duncan Wood* (1964, DVD). This Ealing-comedy-style film caught the tail-end of working narrowboats, manned here by two cousins played by Harry H. Corbett (with 'a bird in every lock') and Ronnie Barker. There are parts, too, for Eric Sykes and Derek Nimmo, and the script is by Galton and Simpson of *Hancock's Half Hour* fame. It's lightweight farce but there is a genuine story here about the decline of a way of life on the canals, with 'the bargees' given notice by British Waterways that all working boats are to be withdrawn.

Canals: The Making of a Nation, *presented by Liz McIvor* (BBC DVD, 2015). Liz McIvor's casually informative six-part series on the making, financing, working and legacy of the canals features stunning aerial photography, well-chosen interviewees and plenty of waterways landscape to enjoy.

MUSIC

Mal Edwards, *Songs from the Cut* (Canal Productions, 2001). Songs written from experience of working in many canal jobs and with many of the old boaters across the waterways of England and Wales.

Narrow Boats (BBC LP, 1969; Argo 1975). Interviews with the many of the last working boat people, some of whose memories stretch back to events from the end of the nineteenth century. Though it is hard to identify individual voices, characters include famous boatmen Charlie Atkins, Rose and Joe Skinner and Herbert Tooley. Several early traditional and more recent canal songs are included along with the stories. Never reissued on CD, but the LP comes up on eBay from time to time.

WEBSITES

Canal & River Trust
www.canalrivertrust.org.uk
The CRT governs most of the canals in England and Wales and provide information on just about every aspect of waterways, including events, news, and practical details on moorings, facilities and licensing. They also have an extensive online photo archive.

Canal Glossary
www.sites.google.com/site/ canalglossary/home
A 652-term glossary of canal boating terms, with many lost, archaic and traditional words.

Canal Junction
www.canaljunction.com
Information on canal holidays, canals and news as well as an interesting heritage section.

Jim Shead
www.jim-shead.com
Shead is a canal writer and photographer who has posted extensive research on individual canals, boats, traditions and more on his website. Well worth a browse.

Songs of the Inland Waterways
www.waterwaysongs.co.uk
An extensive collection of canal- and waterways-associated songs, many from the modern folk tradition, with some older songs and curiosities like music hall and canal opening celebration verses.

Towpath Talk
www.towpathtalk.co.uk
Online and print magazine for all waterways users.

Waterways World
www.waterwaysworld.com
A long-established magazine with wide-ranging contents on inland waterways subjects.

Many **individual canal trusts and societies** also have their own websites and Facebook pages, covering restoration projects, history, routes and events, often in impressive detail.

Thanks

The *Water Ways* project began as the vision of Ed Fox of the Canal & River Trust who recruited me as their first writer-in-residence. He, and his colleague Joe Coggins were sources of knowledge, contacts and ideas from start to end.

At Profile Books, Andrew Franklin has been wonderfully supportive of the book (and has even reported back from the towpaths), whilst my editor, Mark Ellingham, has steered the writing with a firm hand on the tiller, a steady feel for the throttle and some timely work with the shaft when the craft seemed to have run aground. Nat Jansz also offered welcome insight into, suggestions for and contributions to a number of chapters.

The final manuscript was transformed by the expert ministrations of designer Henry Iles, proofreader Nikky Twyman and indexer Bill Johncocks.

Many, many people along the waterways were generous with their time, their knowledge, and often their boats. They're mentioned in the book but additional and sincere thanks to the following: Kate Saffin and Heather Wastie (*www.alarumtheatre.co.uk*); Jules Cook and Richard Traves of Jules Fuels (*www.julesfuels.co.uk*); the Brind and Poxon families of the Tiverton Canal Company (*www. tivertoncanal.co.uk/horse-drawn-barge*); Alice, Ian and James of The Village Butty (*www.facebook.com/ thevillagebutty*); Kara on the Kennet and Avon; Mal Edwards MBE of the *NB Becky*; Ali Nadal; Nancy Campbell, the Canal Poet Laureate 2018 (*www.nancycampbell.co.uk*); Jim McKeown at the Ellesmere Canal Museum; Nathaniel Mann and the Dead Rat Orchestra (*www.deadratorchestra.co.uk*); Rob Humphreys of the Puppet Theatre Barge (*www.puppetbarge.com*); and Jason Gathorne-Hardy for an inspiring residency at White House Farm, Suffolk.

Anglo Welsh Waterway Holidays (*www.anglowelsh.co.uk*) generously set me at the helm of *Summer* for the winter trip down the Stratford-upon-Avon Canal. Many thanks to the company's Robert Lawrence, Roxy Ellis, Alistair King, Dave Stringfellow, Jacob East and Matt Stearn.

Nick Pipe at Advanced Elements (*www.advancedelementskayaks.co.uk*) kindly provided the AirFusion Elite kayak which, combining portability with performance, proved a perfect craft for the multi-day trips on canals, navigations and rivers described in the book.

My ragtag of kit for walking and cycling, and for bivvying on trips, was chosen for lightness and simplicity; some of the best equipment came from Alpkit (*www. alpkit.com*) and Millican (*www. homeofmillican.com*).

Over a year of slow travels I press-ganged many friends into exploring different canals and navigations on foot, by boat and with bicycles. And many of those same friends offered accommodation, company and feedback when writing *Water Ways*. Heartfelt thanks to Mark Ellingham, Nat Jansz, Miles and Wooster in London; Hassan and Emir at Dominique's cafe; Isobel Barnes in Devon; David Flower in London; Sophie Campbell in London; Mal and Helen O'Neill in Oxfordshire; the Nicholsons in West Cork; the Campbells in Oxford; Bridget Tempest in Yorkshire; David Korowicz and Jonathan Korowicz in Dublin; and to my mother, sister and nephew, Betty Winn, Minta Winn and Rupert Barnard.

Photo credits

Photos in the book are copyright of the following sources. Every effort has been made to contact copyright holders but if any have been missed, please contact the publishers so information can be corrected on future editions.

Alamy: p.104.

Sophie Campbell: p.345.

Canal & River Trust: pp. 56, 61, 79, 85, 89, 120, 123, 131, 158, 164, 176, 180, 183, 234, 236, 238, 242, 249, 252, 254, 256, 264, 281, 325.

Polly Alderton/Dead Rat Orchestra: 168.

Mal Edwards MBE: p.187.

Natania Jansz: p.350.

Getty Images: pp.50, 59, 70, 148.

Gren Middleton & Juliet Rogers: p.332.

Paul T. Smith/Alarum Theatre: p29.

WikiCommons: pp.87, 91, 101, 110, 112, 139, 164.

Jasper Winn: pp.13, 20, 25, 37, 61, 63, 66, 75, 94, 96, 109, 117, 119, 137, 151, 161, 193, 196, 201, 204, 207, 212, 214, 216, 219, 222, 226, 234, 236, 260, 268, 271, 277, 285, 287, 292, 295, 298, 301, 306, 308, 311, 315, 317, 323, 328, 336, 339.

Thanks to David Cornforth of Exeter Memories for providing the image of the Exeter Porte (p.45) and to Peter Darley and Malcolm Tucker of Camden Railway Heritage Trust for the painting of the Pickfords Shed on the Regent's Canal (p.144).

Index

Note: *Entries in italic* with no extra information are boat names; *page references in italic* are illustrations.

A

access restrictions 145–6, 279
accidents 83, 179, 266, 291, 349, 353
    see also drownings; running aground; sinkings
accommodation bridges 21, 257, 360
acoustic mirrors 235, *236*
Acts of Parliament
    Acts of Abandonment 240
    authorising canal construction 57, 76, 142–3, 160, 288
    Canal Boats Act (1877) 179
    Transport Act (1968) 255
Adrift – A Secret Life of London's Waterways, by Helen Babbs 260
agricultural revolution 107–8
Aickman, Ray (wife of Robert) 241, 243
Aickman, Robert *244, 252*
    canal-busting trips 246–7, 252–3
    and the Dudley Canal 262–3
    establishment of the IWA 240–3
    literary career 245, 269–70
    National Trust and 251, 255
    publicity and recruitment skills 243, 245, 247–8, 254
    relationship with Howard 243–4
    relationship with the Rolts 240–2, 244, 246, 248
    and the Stratford-upon-Avon Canal 347, 357
    vision for the restored waterways 243, 255, 259–61
Ailesbury, Thomas Bruce, Earl of 214
Aire, River 305
Aire and Calder Canal and Navigation 165
    kayaking 309–18
Alarum Theatre 13–14, 27–8
Alberta 330
Alde Spring Festival 107
Aldgate 262
Amis, Kingsley 244
Anderson, Rachel 297
Anderton boat lift 160–2, *161*
anglers 46, 68, 270–2, *271*, 293

apprentices 189, 193, 200
Apsley 190, 200, 206–7
aqueducts
    Barton Aqueduct *50,* 56–8, *59,* 65, 69, *70,* 165
    Barton Swing Aqueduct 65, *66,* 165, 186
    Chirk Aqueduct 149
    Edstone Aqueduct 349, *350*
    modeled in cheese 57
    see also Pontcysyllte
Ardrossan Canal 127
arts and crafts, canal-related 152, 248, 323
Ashby-de-la-Zouch canal 34
Astbury, John 146
Atkins, Charlie 175, 185
Aylesbury half-marathon 280–2, *281*

B

Babbs, Helen 260
'backer' horses 126
'bandit country,' Leeds 305, 307, *308*
Bank Newton locks 302
The Barge Inn 213, 328
The Bargee (film) 341, *342*
barges
    narrowboats distinguished from 11–12, 111, 319
    Spritsail and Thames 108, 330
Barnard, John 261
Barnton Tunnel *264*
barriers
    between canals 142
    towpath 111–13, 289
Barrowford Locks 299
Barton Aqueduct *50,* 56–8, *59,* 65, 69, *70,* 165
Barton Swing Aqueduct 65, *66,* 165, 186
Barwell, C Douglas 253
Basingstoke Canal 245
Batty, Captain Robert *139*
BBC *Narrow Boats* recordings 116, 132, 174–5, 178, 200
BBC *The World about Us* 307
Beatrice 243
Becky 184, 192

371

M

U